The Struggle for the Organization of Europe

To Annejet and Aleid

The Struggle for the Organization of Europe

The Foundations of the European Union

Robert H. Lieshout
Professor of International Relations,
University of Nijmegen, the Netherlands

Edward Elgar
Cheltenham, UK • Northampton, MA, USA

First published in the Netherlands as *De organisatie van de West-Europese samenwerking. Een voortdurende strijd om de macht*
© Uitgeverij Coutinho, Bussum 1997

English translation Hans Hoekman, for the University Language Centre, Nijmegen, the Netherlands

Published by
Edward Elgar Publishing Limited
Glensanda House
Montpellier Parade
Cheltenham
Glos GL50 1UA
UK

Edward Elgar Publishing, Inc.
6 Market Street
Northampton
Massachusetts 01060
USA

A catalogue record for this book
is available from the British Library

Library of Congress Cataloguing in Publication Data
Lieshout, R. H.
    [Organisatie van de West-Europese samenwerking. English]
    The struggle for the organization of Europe : the foundations of
    the European Union / Robert H. Lieshout
    Includes index.
    1. European federation—History. I. Title.
JN15.L5813 1999
341.242'09—dc21   99–13612
                                                            CIP

ISBN 1 85898 975 2

Printed and bound in Great Britain by Bookcraft (Bath) Ltd.

Contents

Foreword

Many analyses of European Economic and Monetary Union and the introduction of the Euro focus almost exclusively on the economic costs which these will entail and the benefits they will bring. It is often almost entirely forgotten that the introduction of the Euro is only one step, albeit a very important one, in the process of European integration. This process started immediately after the Second World War and has now been under way for almost half a century. European integration is not just an economic event; it is also driven by political motives. Indeed, this fact must be acknowledged if one is to understand what is happening in the process of European integration and why.

The book which you have in front of you has been written precisely from this perspective. The author even argues that political factors have had and continue to have the upper hand in many areas of European co-operation. According to the underlying theme of this book, the European institutions have been designed to permit a peaceful power struggle between France and Germany.

Since Europe is about more than just economics – however important this may be – it is useful that analyses like this one, focusing on the political aspect of European integration, are being written. They deserve to be read.

W.F. Duisenberg
President of the European Central Bank

The discussion began on the subject of European integration. Mr. Spaak stated that the word 'integration' was foreign to European usage, and that he liked to conceive of it as the 'organization' of Europe.

Minutes of a conversation between Paul-Henri Spaak and Dean Acheson, 19 January 1950 (Department of State 1977, p. 613).

Preface

It would not be wrong to regard *The Struggle for the Organization of Europe* as an exercise in historical international political economy. After all, the book is about the interaction between politics and economics in the international system throughout a certain historical period. At the same time, I am convinced that most of the international political economists who study the past would not easily recognize it as such. This can be attributed to the fact that, in almost all the publications of the practitioners of historical political economy, the leading part is played by economic forces, whereas in this book this role is reserved for political ones. The image of the relationship between economics and politics that is usually conveyed by their work corresponds closely to the classical Marxist interpretation of the relationship between the 'base' and the superstructure (although nowadays this Marxist jargon has been almost completely abandoned). It is the image of almost unstoppable economic developments which politics must follow whether it wants to or not. In *The Struggle for the Organization of Europe* I sketch a completely different picture. A picture of political considerations having primacy, leaving the economy no choice but to acquiesce in them.

Institutions like the European Coal and Steel Community and the European Economic Community were not created because they were regarded as important instruments for increasing the level of welfare in the member states. At most this was a welcome side effect. Nor were they established because important economic actors in the countries concerned actively lobbied for their establishment. On the contrary, as Willis already showed more than thirty years ago (cf. Willis [1965] 1968), these actors strongly objected to both communities. Their interests were, however, subordinated to the supremely political interest of constructing institutional frameworks that would enable France and the Federal Republic to settle their conflicts peacefully in the future.

The completion of this book would undoubtedly have taken much longer if my Dutch publisher, Dick Coutinho, had not told me at the beginning of 1997 that the time had come to finish the manuscript, in view of 'all this commotion about the Euro'. I am very grateful to him for this decisive intervention. Also, many thanks are due to Ige F. Dekker, my former colleague in the Department of Public Administration at the University of Twente. My discussion of the position of the Federal Republic in international law (see Chapter 3, Section 4) is based on texts written by Dekker for the benefit of our former joint course on 'Political and Judicial Aspects of Western European Cooperation'. Should this section contain any observations that may be offensive from the standpoint of international law, this is entirely due to my limited capability to do full justice to his views on this field.

I thank Aad Correljé, Auke van Dijk, Harry Garretsen, Wil Hout, Mirjam Kars, Grahame Lock, Marc van Ooijen, Bob Reinalda, Anna van der Vleuten and Anton Weenink for the dedication and critical spirit with which they read all or part of the penultimate version of the manuscript. I am grateful to Henk de Wit and Erna Veneman for helping me with my search for source material and articles.

I dedicate this book to my daughters Annejet and Aleid, as a token of my gratitude, for always bearing their cross with remarkable cheer. It was fate that gave them a father who stubbornly continues to practise science in a way that does not really correspond to the current academic standards. Instead of flying around the world to maintain international networks, he merely sits at home night after night and weekend after weekend, struggling with sentences that eventually always must be rewritten anyway. I sincerely hope this dedication will compensate for all the small bars of exotic hotel soap they did not get, only because their father refused to be a modern man of science!

Robert H. Lieshout
Malden

1. Introduction

1. A Continuous Struggle for Power

Most citizens of the member states of the European Union do not have a clear view on 'Europe' and the European integration process. It may be said that these two concepts are mainly seen in relation to three matters. First of all, 'Europe' has something to do with economic questions: the internal market, agricultural policy and introduction of the Euro. Next, 'Europe' is associated with a mania for organization, due to the constant flow of directives from Brussels and the decisions of the European Court of Justice which repeatedly encroach deeply on the everyday practice of the individual nations. And finally, there is also the connection with Brussels as the future capital of Europe and the European Commission as the future European government. This image of 'Europe' corresponds quite well with that envisioned by Jacques Delors, the former president of the European Commission. In July 1988, he stated before the European Parliament that 'within the next ten years, 80% of the economic legislation and the majority of the social and tax legislation will be regulated by Brussels'. In any case, it is the image which was conveyed to Margaret Thatcher, the former British Prime Minister, who reacted furiously to Delors' statement in her Bruges speech in September 1988: 'we have not successfully rolled back the frontiers of the State in Britain only to see them reimposed at a European level with a European superstate exercising a new dominance from Brussels' (Van Ooijen *et al.* 1996, p. 243).

The aim of this book is to prove that this view on 'Europe' – however plausible it may seem at first – completely ignores what 'Europe' is all about. By analysing the organization of Western European cooperation in the period 1947–1957, I hope to make it clear that the European adventure should primarily be regarded as a political adventure. When studying the initial phase of European cooperation, one soon realizes that the foundation for the unique European institutional construction was laid by the successful attempts of French and West German – and, in the beginning, certainly also American – politicians, civil servants and military officials to bring about a reconciliation between France and the Federal Republic of Germany. 'Europe' provided the institutional context in which the continuous struggle for power between

1

France and Germany could at last be fought using peaceful means. If war, as Clausewitz maintains, is 'a true political instrument, a continuation of political intercourse, carried on with other means' (Clausewitz [1976] 1989, p. 87), then 'Europe' is also a true political instrument, a continuation of political intercourse between France and Germany, in this case, however, carried on with institutional means (cf. Lieshout 1996).[1]

In this section a brief outline will be given of what was central to the development towards increasing Western European cooperation in the period 1947–1957. In my opinion, everything revolved around the normalization *and* the Western European powers' acceptance of the solution to the 'German problem', which was found, more or less by accident, in the aftermath of World War II.

The 'German problem' had its origins in the Prussian victory in the Franco-Prussian war of 1870–1871. In the following decades, it gradually became clear that the balance of power in Europe had shifted so much in favour of Germany that the European countries, including Great Britain, were no longer able to hold the German power in check by a balancing policy. After Germany's total defeat in World War II and its subsequent unconditional capitulation, the solution to this problem was eventually found in dividing Germany up. This solution was the by-product of the rivalry that, soon after the German defeat, arose between the two great powers which came out of World War II victorious and which controlled the European continent at the time, i.e. the United States and the Soviet Union (cf. DePorte [1978] 1986). In February 1945, at the Yalta Conference, the Big Three (United States, Soviet Union and Great Britain) decided that Germany, after its unconditional surrender, should be treated as a unity and agreed to keep different parts of it occupied until a final peace settlement could be reached. At the instigation of Great Britain, France was also allocated an occupation zone. The Big Three confirmed these agreements at the Potsdam Conference in August 1945. At this conference they also agreed to the Russian annexation of the area around Königsberg (Kaliningrad) in East Prussia and, in anticipation of a final peace agreement, they reconciled themselves for the time being to the fact that the Soviet Union had handed over part of its occupation zone, the so-called *Ostgebiete* ('Eastern Territories'), to Poland.

The division of Germany became clearly perceptible for the first time in 1947–1948. In the summer of 1947 the Soviet Union refused to take part in the elaboration of the plan for the economic recovery of Europe as launched by George Marshall, the American Secretary of State. One of the major consequences of this refusal was the economic division of Germany. The western occupation zones would benefit from American support, whereas the

Russian zone would not. A second significant moment for the division of Germany was the establishment of the Brussels Treaty Organization (BTO) by France, Great Britain and the Benelux countries in March 1948, partly in response to the Communist take-over of Czechoslovakia in February 1948. It was clear to the signatories of the Brussels Treaty that they could withstand possible Soviet aggression only if the western occupation zones in Germany would also contribute in some way to the defence of Europe in the foreseeable future. The division became final in 1949, when, at the instigation of the three occupying powers, the three western occupation zones merged into the Federal Republic of Germany (FRG), and the Soviet Union reacted by transforming its zone into the German Democratic Republic (GDR).

As far as the Western European powers and the Federal Republic were concerned, the acceptance and normalization of the division of Germany was primarily the result of the policy pursued by the United States, which, after some hesitation, was supported by Great Britain. The United States held the view that Western Europe itself should make a credible (i.e. the greatest possible) contribution to averting the Soviet threat. According to the United States, two methods were particularly suitable for this purpose: firstly, the economic recovery of Western Europe through the establishment of a free Western European internal market, and, secondly, West German participation in the Western European economy and the defence of Western Europe. The United States was of the opinion that the Soviet Union's advance could be stopped only if the Federal Republic made a substantial contribution. Not only did this mean that West Germany had to participate in the defence of Western Europe, but, in particular, that it had to function as the driving force of the so desperately needed economic recovery of Western Europe, as 'the recovery of Germany and that of Europe were two aspects of one problem' (Wall 1991, p. 79). At the same time the United States realized that such a policy could succeed only if the neighbouring Western European countries were offered a guarantee against renewed German dominance. This led to the American policy of 'double containment': 'the containment of the Soviet Union at arm's length, and of West Germany with an embrace' (Hanrieder 1989, p. 6).

The French views on Germany's role in the recovery of Western Europe were initially quite the opposite of those of the United States. France's greatest frustration was that it was no longer one of the actors in world politics, but rather one of the theatres in which these issues were fought out. In the French view, the Americans would do better to focus their policy on establishing a French dominance in Western Europe and, as a logical consequence, on keeping Germany weak and permanently subordinated to France. Around 1950, however, there was a growing awareness that the

French situation was so desperate that for France to be able to keep ahead of the West German recovery and to play a dominant role in Western Europe was out of the question. In this same period it was realized that 'Europe' could become the instrument that might secure France's position *vis-à-vis* the Federal Republic. The launch of the Schuman Plan can be seen as the first step towards the organization of Europe.

2. The Primacy of Politics

At first sight it may seem as if the chapters that form the core of this book (Chapters 5–8) mainly deal with economic issues and questions of peace and security. However, also in this case, first impressions can be deceptive. The political character of the organization of Western European cooperation persuaded the leading actors ultimately to judge these economic and military matters on their political merits. Emotions may have run high during the talks on the form and scope of the West German contribution to the defence of Western Europe (see Chapters 5 and 7), negotiations on the decartelization and deconcentration of the West German industrial conglomerates may have been long (see Chapter 6), and discussions on the harmonization of overtime pay may have been acrimonious (see Chapter 8), yet when all was said and done, they were merely 'technical' issues, which, according to the actors involved, were subordinate to the realization of certain political objectives.

Of the leading actors, the German politician Adenauer had developed this 'political' view on the Western European integration process most clearly. According to Hanrieder, the Chancellor was 'at bottom not very much interested in either economic or security issues. He appreciated their intrinsic importance but consistently subsumed them to political priorities' (Hanrieder 1989, p. 246). But this was also the view of the technocrat Monnet and the economist Zijlstra, who was appointed Minister of Economic Affairs in the Netherlands shortly after the establishment of the European Coal and Steel Community. Monnet explained in his autobiography that he, in the light of the 'essentially political' character of the French plan for a European army, had had no need at all for military experts in drawing up the plan (Monnet 1978, p. 345),[2] while Zijlstra stated in his memoirs with regard to the ECSC that 'one could speak of a primacy of politics over economics' (Zijlstra 1992, p. 53). After all, 'from the perspective of economic logic, this community was an absurdity'. In his opinion, what really mattered was that with the establishment of the ECSC 'a fundamentally political stand was taken, which would set the course for further developments' (Zijlstra 1992, p. 55).

This undoubtedly raises the question of what is meant by the 'political'. In this context, Easton's much used description of politics as 'those interactions through which values are authoritatively allocated for a society' (Easton 1965, p. 21) leaves much to be desired. In Easton's view, the authoritative allocation of values that forms part of the normal routine of daily life would also be part of political activity, whereas, in reality, this latter is all about the formulation of solutions to problems for which there are no adequate rules or routines (cf. Miller [1962] 1965, pp. 13–14). Succinct as it may be, Lasswell's famous typification of politics as 'who gets what, when, how' is not satisfying either from this point of view (cf. Lasswell 1936). Kuypers' definition of politics as 'shaping the future of society as a whole or exerting influence on this process' (Kuypers 1973, p. 164) is much more adequate in this respect, although Kuypers, like Easton, erroneously confines politics to attempts to shape 'society as a whole'. Political processes play a role at all levels – from the level of personal relationships such as friendship and love to the more abstract level of relations between states – which also implies that the 'political' is not equivalent to 'politics'. An adequate description of the 'political' will in any case have to do justice to the following three aspects. First of all, the 'political' has something to do with the ability to recognize problems that are the result of the logic of the *status quo*, i.e. the logic underlying established rules and patterns of behaviour. In addition, it includes the ability to formulate new rules and patterns of behaviour that will make it possible to break away from this logic. Finally, the 'political' involves the art of convincing those who have power and influence that it is also in their interest to accept these new rules and patterns of behaviour.[3]

3. Outline of the Book

In the following chapter, entitled 'The States System', I explain the theoretical body of thought that I used as a guideline for studying the organization of Western European cooperation during the period 1947–1957. Particular attention is paid to the question of how cooperation can be achieved in a system, such as the states system, which lacks an agency that can force the members in that system to abide by the rules and fulfil the promises made. This chapter has been included primarily to show that the history of the organization of the cooperation between the Western European states, although evidently unique in the history of the states system, is not a subject in need of special theoretical explanation. It can be understood with the concepts provided by regular international relations theory, especially in the form of 'institutional realism', as I have called it. Readers not interested in the structure and quality of the 'web of imaginative construction' (Collingwood

[1946] 1957, p. 242) that enabled me to 'catch' the historical material presented in Chapters 3–8 may wish to skip this chapter. The 'historical' chapters are perfectly comprehensible without needing to first make a study of their theoretical background.

This may be the right place to emphasize that a theoretical framework does *not* enable a researcher to explain or predict why an event takes place at a given moment: for example the Schuman Plan, which was launched at 6 p.m. on 9 May in 1950. The same goes for the exact content of the plan, its actual phrasing and its punctuation. Such an achievement does not fall within the realm of any theory that tries to explain how the world works. Even Newton's theory of gravitation, perhaps the most successful empirical theory ever developed, cannot explain or predict the moment that a leaf will fall from a tree or the trajectory of its fall. This is only possible if all kinds of idiosyncratic circumstances – which defy all theory – are taken into account. What I try to express in Chapter 2 are the ideas about the way the states system functions that have guided me in my attempt to shed some light on the organization of Western European cooperation in the period 1947–1957.

In Chapter 3, 'The German Problem', I discuss briefly the origins of this problem, its development since 1871 and the solution that was eventually found and formulated between 1945 and 1948. In this chapter I also explain the views on Germany's position in Europe held by the powers that feature prominently in this book – i.e. the United States, France and the Federal Republic – and those of the powers that played a secondary role, i.e. Great Britain and the Soviet Union. In addition, some attention will be paid to Germany's position under international law.

The fourth chapter, entitled 'The Might of the Dollar: from Marshall Plan to OEEC', describes how the United States held out the prospect of an economic aid programme on an unprecedented scale in order to entice the Western European powers to take the first steps towards European unity. The United States hoped to achieve this by demanding from the Western European powers that they decide in mutual consultation on what should take priority in the reconstruction of Western Europe and also agree to the establishment of a 'permanent organization' that would supervise the implementation of this programme. This American attempt failed because the Western European powers, with Great Britain and France taking the lead, did not want to have anything to do with American ambitions concerning a united Europe.

In the fifth chapter, 'From Treaty to Organization: the Creation of NATO', I sketch the ways in which the United States unintentionally and unknowingly became entangled in the defence of Western Europe by responding to Western European desires, particularly those of France. The European initiatives developed by France in 1950 cannot be detached from the already existing French policy to involve the United States in the defence of Western Europe as much as possible. At the same time the integrated command structure of NATO represented a way of organizing a military alliance in peacetime that transcended the intergovernmental frameworks that were common up to that time.

Chapter 6, '*Westbindung*: from Schuman Plan to ECSC', considers the negotiations concerning the plan for a supranational coal and steel community developed by Monnet and his staff in the spring of 1950, in which France and the Federal Republic were to participate on an equal footing. It was evident that both powers would greatly benefit from this plan. Nonetheless, they failed to reach an agreement. The negotiations, in which not only France and the Federal Republic, but also Italy and the Benelux countries participated, had come to a standstill by the end of 1950. Thanks to the United States, which put considerable pressure on the Federal Republic outside the negotiations, as it had taken a strong interest in the plan, the negotiations were at last successfully completed in March 1951.

The seventh chapter, '*Westbindung*: from Pleven Plan to WEU', describes the endless political manoeuvres of France, the Federal Republic and the United States, which started when the latter power, in response to the North Korean invasion of South Korea, began to demand that Western Europe immediately commence with the rearmament of West Germany to strengthen the collective defence of Western Europe. This demand was totally unacceptable to France. For four years France tried to prevent the rearmament of its arch-enemy in every possible way. In October 1950, for example, it launched a plan for a European army. The United States at first rejected the French proposal, but then decided to embrace it in the summer of 1951. However, subsequent negotiations on the European Defence Community (EDC) took an unfavourable turn as far as France was concerned. These negotiations soon focused on the scope of West Germany's military contribution and the supranational framework in which it would have to be incorporated, whereas the contribution *itself* was no longer under discussion. France did sign the EDC treaty in May 1952, but, in August 1954, after two years of political struggle and delaying tactics, it refused to cooperate any further in the project. It was in fact the EDC's supranational character which caused the most resistance in France. Hardly two months after the EDC's downfall France finally resigned itself to West German rearmament within the framework of the intergovernmental West European Union (WEU).

In the eighth chapter, '*Das Junktim*: the EEC and Euratom', I discuss the ultimately successful attempt of the Benelux countries to save 'Europe' after the failure of the EDC. So as not to antagonize France from the very beginning, their plans for an economic community and nuclear energy community, introduced in May 1955, were less supranational in character than the earlier proposals for the ECSC and EDC. The negotiations following this *relance européenne* lasted until March 1957. The main bottleneck was that France was favourably inclined towards Euratom, but not so much towards the idea of an economic community, whereas, for the Federal Republic, it was exactly the opposite. Again, it was mainly thanks to the influence of the United States that France and the Federal Republic finally settled this matter. This had everything to do with the harsh and humiliating way in which the United States called its allies Great Britain and France to order in the Suez Canal crisis. The actions taken by the United States (not to mention those of the Soviet Union) put the importance of further Western European cooperation in a clear perspective. If the Western European powers wished to continue to play an important role in world politics, they would have to join forces. Several months later, France and the Federal Republic successfully completed the negotiations of both treaties.

The last chapter, entitled 'The Continuing Struggle', consists of three parts. The first is a recapitulation of the main lines of argument. The second contains a very brief summary of the developments in European cooperation since 1957. The third part discusses the future organization of European cooperation given the fact that its very foundation, i.e. the division of Germany, fell away in 1990.

Just like science, historiography is based on the art of systematic over-simplification, i.e. the art of leaving out all that might interfere with a clear understanding of the research object (cf. Popper 1982, p. 44).[4] In this book I have therefore disentangled certain matters which are strongly interwoven and can only be understood in relation to each other, and which, at the time, were indeed not considered separately. The London Conference on Germany in 1948 is a good example of this. Although practically all the items on the agenda were largely interdependent as far as their progress was concerned, I try nonetheless as far as possible to discuss the questions concerned individually in Chapters 3, 4 and 5.

Accordingly, I have seen it as my task to explain matters in such a way that some form of logic may be discovered in the organization of Western European cooperation in the period 1947–1957. The reader should take into account, however, that the people involved might never have had a clear perception of this logic, not even at those moments which are now considered 'historic'. After all, 'nations stumble upon establishments, which are indeed the result of human action, but not the execution of any human design'

(Ferguson 1773, p. 205). A historical logic can be devised only in retrospect and much of what now seems familiar and obvious to us was unknown and unclear to those involved in decision-making at the time. Julian Barnes indicates the same when he states with regard to the creation of Géricault's painting *The Raft of Medusa*: 'when we know the final result progress towards it seems irresistible. We start with the masterpiece and work backwards through the discarded ideas and near-misses. We must try to allow for hazard, for lucky discovery, even for bluff' (Barnes 1990, pp. 134–5).[5] Indeed, we should not only allow for hazard, but also for bluff, since in their attempts to convince others, Jean Monnet and Konrad Adenauer, who were the leading figures in the struggle for the organization of Europe, undoubtedly proved to be the biggest bluffers of all.

Notes

1. In a letter to Major Roeder, dated 22 December 1827, Clausewitz stated: 'War is nothing but the continuation of political struggles with the use of other means' (Clausewitz [1832] 1980, p. 1235). Compare Stuurman's characterization of the European integration process as 'primarily the continuation of national politics by other means. The European option was taken where the traditional forms of national politics and international diplomacy did not offer any solution' (Stuurman 1995, p. 150).
2. Just like Mitrany, the father of functionalism, Monnet was a technocrat in the sense that he believed in 'technical self-determination'. It is possible to find an institutional or other type of solution to a certain problem, entirely geared to the nature of this problem and purified of all obfuscating elements, particularly of vested social, bureaucratic and ideological interests (cf. Jansen and De Vree [1985] 1988, p. 119, and De Wilde 1991, pp. 177–8). Thus it is conceivable that a 'political problem' can be solved only if 'politics', which pre-eminently defends vested interests, is excluded. However, unlike Mitrany, Monnet did not believe that the goodwill of the parties involved also implied that precarious political problems could be reduced to innocuous technical matters (cf. Claude [1956] 1964, p. 350, and the discussion of functionalism at the end of the next chapter).
3. Cf. Hume: 'The soldan of EGYPT, or the emperor of ROME, might drive his harmless subjects, like brute beasts, against their sentiments and inclination: But he must, at least, have lead his *mamalukes*, or *praetorian bands*, like men, by their opinion' (Hume 1985, pp. 32–3).
4. Compare Kossmann's statement that 'all of us ought to be so keenly aware of the inextricable complexity of history that we should not criticize a historian for simplifying matters. Of course he does. If he did not he would not be able to say anything meaningful' (Kossmann 1987, p. 232).

5. Compare the quote of historian Wedgwood in Acheson's memoirs: 'history is
    lived forwards but it is written in retrospect. We know the end before we consider
    the beginning and we can never wholly recapture what it was to know the
    beginning only' (Wedgwood 1967, p. 35; cf. Acheson 1969, p. xvii).

2. The States System

1. State and Sovereignty

Two fundamental methodological choices underlie the present analysis of the struggle for the organization of Europe in the period 1947–1957. The first of these, however consequential, is not controversial. It implies that this subject will be studied on the assumption that the relevant actors and factors can be regarded as elements of a *system* – in this case, of course, an international system. A system is then seen as a set of elements that are somehow interrelated. This means that 'the conduct or state of any one of the elements is influenced by the conduct or state of the other elements' (Lieshout 1995, p. 27). As far as these elements are concerned, a distinction will also be made between the *actors* (or the acting units) on the one hand, and the *structure* of the system, on the other.

This systems approach implies that the organization of Western European cooperation, which resulted in such institutions as the European Community for Steel and Coal (ECSC) and the European Economic Community (EEC), will be viewed from the perspective that the actors in the system under consideration are trying to survive by adapting to the system's structure as best as they can. It also means that the manner in which this adaptation process takes place will in turn have consequences for the structure of the system. It should be emphasized that a systems approach does not mean that the behaviour of the actors is determined by the structure of the system. The structure refers to the boundary conditions, which are themselves continuously subject to greater or smaller changes, and which an actor will have to conform to if he is to maintain himself in the system. It is up to the actor to find out what these boundary conditions look like and to decide whether or not he wants to comply with them.

The second methodological choice is at least as fundamental as the first one, but is conversely 'essentially' contested. In the present analysis the *state* is chosen as the actor (the acting unit) in the international system. The struggle for the organization of Europe will be described in terms of a *states system*. This implies that the emergence of such organizations as the ECSC and EEC, as well as the failure of the European Defence Community (EDC), will in the end be reduced to the considerations and decisions of states, and not to those of so-called 'non-state actors', such as multinational corporations, international organizations, labour unions, political parties, or social movements, to name but a few.

This choice for the state as the actor in the international system has everything to do with the fact that the structure of this system is 'anarchical'. This property of the structure will be discussed extensively later in this chapter. For the moment, it is sufficient to point out that the states, thanks to their monopoly of the legitimate use of violence, 'when the crunch comes remake the rules by which other actors operate' (Waltz 1979, p. 94), and, more generally, that the state can be viewed as 'man's foremost practical instrument for getting things done' (Deutsch 1968, p. 39). For this reason it should not come as a surprise that time and again the behaviour of the other participants in the international system attests to their conviction that important international problems cannot be solved without the active collaboration of the states.[1]

Thus it is beyond dispute that the activities developed by the 'Action Committee for the United States of Europe' in the years 1956–1957 had an impact on decision-making with respect to the establishment of the EEC and the European Atomic Energy Community (Euratom). This Action Committee, founded by Monnet, and consisting of prominent representatives from almost all political parties and labour unions from the countries involved in the negotiations on these treaties, was able to exercise a considerable amount of influence, because its members had easy access to the leaders of government and the ministers who had to make the relevant decisions. These ministers and leaders read the letters of the members of the Action Committee and received the authors for a personal interview, but nonetheless the Action Committee's role in the decision-making process went no further than bringing to notice the solutions it propagated.

The state is an abstraction – a 'category of thought' according to Carr (cf. Carr [1939] 1964, p. 150), a 'mental construction' in the words of Goldstein (cf. Goldstein 1996, p. 11) – which fulfils a central function in the discipline of international relations.[2] This abstraction does, however, reflect a reality. It refers to an institution that, with respect to a certain geographical area, claims to have the means at its disposal to enforce, if necessary, the fulfilment of the promises made to one another by individuals living in that area, where this claim is accepted as legitimate by a sufficient number of these individuals (it is not necessary that all individuals in that area accept this claim as legitimate) (cf. Lieshout 1995, p. 111).

The state's dominance of the international system originated on the European continent, when, in the fifteenth century, the then existing order under the spiritual and secular authority of Pope and Emperor, which was not based on territory, was gradually eroded (cf. Spruyt 1994, pp. 42–57).[3] The religious wars that broke out in the sixteenth century dealt the deathblow to the old order with its universalistic pretensions, and heralded the triumph of a new one based on territorially defined units that accepted one another as equals. As sovereign states (in nearly all cases this concerned kingdoms and principalities, with the Dutch Republic and Venice as notable exceptions) they no longer claimed the right to exercise authority on the territory of another state, and denied that any authority could be placed above them. The victory of this new principle for organizing their mutual relations was laid down in the peace treaties signed in Münster in 1648 (Peace of Westphalia). It was most succinctly expressed in the signatories' acceptance of the rule *cuius regio eius religio* ('whose country, his religion') for the settlement of religious conflicts.[4] For this rule 'not only meant that the monarchs of Europe should respect each others' choice of religion. It also implied that *territory* was the key requirement for participation in modern international politics' (Knutsen 1992, p. 71).

Thus, it is characteristic for a state to possess sovereignty. In view of the fact that sovereignty is so much interwoven with the state, it will come as no surprise that sovereignty is also a concept that is far from clear. Sovereignty, too, refers to a situation as well as to a claim to that situation. In precisely the same way as for the state, it is impossible to reduce sovereignty either to a 'brute' empirical fact or to a purely juridical concept. As Bull has observed in this connection:

> The sovereignty of states may be said to exist both at a normative level and at a factual level. On the one hand, states assert the right to supremacy over authorities within their territory and population and independence of authorities outside it; but, on the other hand, they also actually exercise, in varying degrees, such supremacy and independence in practice. (Bull 1977, p. 8)

Sovereignty forms the translation in terms of international law of an actual state of affairs with respect to the effective exercise of authority over a certain territory and the people living there. Most of the time, translation and the actual state of affairs will coincide, but this need not always be the case. The possession of sovereignty, as has already been stated in so many words above, constitutes the certificate of membership of the states system, with all the accompanying rights and obligations. It is possible, however, that under certain circumstances this certificate will be denied to a state by the other states. This denial has very adverse consequences for the effective exercise of authority. This is the reason why sovereignty is more than just a judicial term. It also explains why it was of great importance to the German Federal Republic to acquire sovereignty as soon as possible after its establishment in 1949.

Sovereignty has two aspects. The first is that, with regard to its territory and the population living on it, a state recognizes no authority other than its own. This is called 'territorial integrity' or 'internal' sovereignty. A state can delegate part of its internal authority to an international organization – as did the member states of the ECSC, when they delegated to the High Authority their authority to determine the price of coal and steel. The second aspect is that a state recognizes no authority above it in its international relations. This is called 'independence' or 'external' sovereignty. Independence refers to a state's authority to conduct relations with other states. A state can also delegate part of its external authority to an international organization – as did the member states of the EEC, when they delegated to the European Commission their authority to conduct negotiations in the framework of the General Agreement on Tarriffs and Trade (GATT).

To complicate matters a little, it is possible that a state possessing independence will be very much dependent on other states in respect of its conduct. The relationship between the external aspect of sovereignty and dependence can be illustrated very neatly by comparing the situation in which Finland found itself in the first decade following World War II and that of the Federal Republic in its first one and a half years of existence. Finland was undoubtedly almost as dependent on the Soviet Union as West Germany was on the United States. What it boils down to is that Finland possessed the authority at any moment during that period to adopt a foreign policy that completely disregarded its evident dependence on the Soviet Union. That it would have been very foolish of Finland to adopt such a policy is not the point as far as external sovereignty is concerned. The point is that the Federal Republic, in its first one and a half years of existence, did not even have the authority to adopt a foreign policy that, in view of its heavy dependence on the United States, would have been very foolish. The conduct of the Federal Republic's foreign policy remained with the occupation authorities, one of which was the United States. For this reason it would also have been impossible for West Germany to start negotiations with France on the Schuman Plan if the United States and Great Britain had been against it in their capacity as occupying powers.[5]

As has already been mentioned at the beginning of this section, the states are assigned a motive to act. This is to the effect that a state tries to survive in the states system, or, as DePorte has phrased it, 'the first order of business for any state is to ensure its own survival' (DePorte [1978] 1986, p.1). The question of what means are best suited for realizing this aim – the procurement of weapons, the increase of GDP, the conclusion of alliances, to give but a few examples – will not be further discussed here. However, it will be clear that a state can only survive if it succeeds in obtaining the means to enable it to adapt successfully to the structure of the international system. This structure, as explained above, consists of all other elements in the international system. The conduct or state of these elements is a more or less established fact as far as the state is concerned. No matter how powerful a state is, or how dominant its position in the states system, in the end it cannot escape from, as I have called it elsewhere, 'the dictate of reality' (Lieshout 1995, pp. 35–7).

2. The Internal and External Structure

Until now, I have referred to *the* structure of the states system. Such a general concept of structure, however, is usually not sufficient if one is in search of an adequate description and explanation of events in the states system. This applies in particular to the situation in which one tries to get a hold on the manner in which the states system evolves over time. In that case it is wise to make a distinction within *the* structure between, on the one hand, the internal structure of the states, and, on the other, the external structure of the states system.

The *internal structure* of a state refers to the properties of the state itself. How powerful is the state? How large is its population? What is its position with respect to available natural resources? What is the state's geographical situation? Does the state border on the sea, or is it landlocked? In what manner is political decision-making organized? Is the state a democracy, or is it a dictatorship? A crucial aspect of the internal structure concerns the state's adaptability. This refers particularly to the ways in which the state processes information on the external structure and the changes therein, and its capacity for decision-making, whether collective or not, in order to carry through possibly necessary changes. The better the information, and the greater a state's capacity for decision-making, the sooner a state is able to take advantage of changes in the structure of the international system. The greater ease and success with which the Federal Republic was able to adapt to changes in the external structure in comparison to France can to a large extent be attributed to the chancellor's dominant position in West German constitutional practice, whereas, during the Fourth Republic, French cabinets were at the mercy of permanently changing coalitions of parties, which attached great importance to party discipline, but did not really practise it.

An important aspect of collective decision-making concerns the ways in which government and other organizations collect information, prepare decisions and implement decisions already taken. This aspect refers to organizational routines – the so-called 'Standard Operating Procedures' (SOPs) – and 'action channels'. The latter are particularly important, as these structure the preparation and implementation of decisions by determining which persons and agencies play a role, and which do not: 'most critically, channels determine "who's got the action"' (Allison 1971, p. 170). It is very difficult for persons and agencies not hooked onto the action channel to exert influence on the preparation and implementation of a decision. Usually their role is limited to explaining to anyone who cares to listen that they would have done things in a completely different way. The selection of a certain action channel can be a question of organizational routine and, accordingly, will be more or less automatic, or it can also be the result of a deliberate decision (cf. Lieshout and Westerheijden in Huberts and Kleinnijenhuis 1994, p. 194). The best example of the latter in the history of the struggle for the organization of Europe 1947–1957, and of the momentous consequences of selecting one action channel as opposed to another, is without doubt the decision of French foreign minister Schuman in May 1950 not to entrust his own department with the chairmanship and secretariat of the conference on the Schuman Plan, which would have been natural *qua* organizational routine, but rather Monnet and his staff of the *Commissariat au Plan* (see further Chapter 6). From the point of view of the officials of the foreign ministry – and also many a minister in the French cabinet – this was an experiment that certainly did not merit repetition. The conference on the Pleven Plan, which started in February 1951, was once again in the safe hands of the officials of the *Quai d'Orsay*.

At the end of this brief sketch of some of the important elements of the internal structure, it should be pointed out that the decision to analyse the struggle for the organization of Europe in terms of a states system does not imply that the human individual has no role to play in it. On the contrary, it is very possible that a single human individual can fulfil an important, even decisive role in decision-making processes with far-reaching social consequences – that is to say, if SOPs, action channels and the 'political' entrepreneurship of the human individual (cf. my characterization of the 'political' in Chapter 1), make it possible for him to do so (cf. Russett and Starr [1981] 1996, p. 246). At the same time, this means that the considered judgments of the human individual who finds himself in such a position, but also the preconceived ideas and prejudices he has acquired over the years, can greatly influence the manner in which social processes progress.[6]

The *external structure* of the states system refers to such aspects as the way in which states are positioned *vis-à-vis* one another, the degree of polarity of the states system, i.e. the extent to which power is concentrated in the states system, the degree of stability of the states system, the level of international cooperation (whether on an *ad hoc* basis, or institutionalized in the context of international organizations), the extent of the international division of labour, and the state of technology (e.g. weapon or communication technology). Besides these more or less 'brute' aspects, the external structure also comprises 'soft' aspects such as the states' shared opinions on how foreign policy and diplomacy should be conducted, and their common ideas on the best way for a state to survive in the states system (cf. Bull 1977, p. 13 and Schroeder [1994] 1996, p. x).[7]

The distinguishing characteristic of the external structure of the states system is that it is anarchical. Anarchy constitutes what John Ruggie has called the 'deep structure' of the states system (Ruggie in Keohane 1986, p. 135). This property of the external structure does not mean that chaos reigns supreme in the states system. It implies that the states system lacks an agency (compare my earlier description of the state) that if necessary can force states to keep their promises. The states system is a self-help system. The anarchical character of the external structure of the states system is in fact the equivalent of sovereignty, which is a property of the internal structure of the state. Anarchy and sovereignty are 'mutually constitutive' (cf. Buzan *et al.* 1993).

It goes without saying that an anarchical structure does not increase the chances of successful cooperation between the actors in the system. It seems even more obvious that in an anarchy – in the case of a conflict between two or more actors, for example about the interpretation of a promise – these actors will more easily resort to violence to settle it, than in a hierarchy where they can appeal to an agency that has the means to force the other party to keep its promise. The anarchical structure of the states system has led many authors to describe life in that system in the most gloomy terms. The image they evoke of the situation the states find themselves in corresponds largely with Hobbes' famous depiction of the state of nature in his *Leviathan*. Like Hobbes, they argue that anarchy implies that every state is the potential enemy of every other state, that a division of labour – and consequently, prosperity – is impossible to realize, and that the life of states can be no more than 'solitary, poor, nasty, brutish, and short' (Hobbes [1651] 1947, p. 82).

No matter how much this depiction appeals to the imagination, or how strongly it appears to be confirmed by the horrors of the countless wars the states system has experienced since its inception – particularly those of the two world wars in this century – it is nonetheless one-sided. As Henkin has pointed out, 'violations of law attract attention and the occasional violation is dramatic', and therefore the 'sober loyalty of nations to the law and their obligations is hardly noted', but it is 'probably the case that *almost all nations observe almost all principles of international law and almost all of their obligations almost all of the time*' (Henkin [1968] 1979, p. 47; emphasis in original). Against the Hobbesian image of the states system may be set another image. It is the image of a 'society of states', in which the states:

> recognising certain common interests and perhaps some common values regard themselves as bound by certain rules in their dealings with one another, such as that they should respect one another's claims to independence, that they should honour agreements into which they enter, and that they should be subject to certain limitations in exercising force against one another. (Bull 1977, p. 13)

The 350-year history of the states system shows that states can be unreliable partners, continuously engaged in war or the preparation for war, as well as faithful allies cooperating with one another quite extensively. The Western European integration process makes clear how far cooperation can go between states, the anarchical nature of the external structure of the states system notwithstanding. Besides, one should never lose sight of the fact that anarchy, taken by itself, can never explain why states sometimes do cooperate with one another, and sometimes do not, why certain states regularly wage war upon one another, and others coexist peacefully for centuries. Such differences in behaviour can only be explained by taking into account other aspects of external *and* internal structure.

One aspect of external structure that greatly influences the possibilities for international cooperation concerns the degree of polarity of the states system – the degree to which power is concentrated within the states system. The degree of polarity is usually determined by the number of great powers in the states system. Conventionally, three categories are distinguished: a multipolar system, that is to say, a states system with more than two great powers; a bipolar system, in the case of two great powers; and a hegemonic system, when there is only one great power in the states system. Expectations are that states will cooperate with one another more often and more easily, to the extent that power is more concentrated in the states system, and the number of great powers is smaller (see also Section 5).

3.   Security Dilemma and Balance of Power

A state trying to survive in the states system must rely on its own efforts. The states system does not have an agency that guarantees a state a certain subsistence level or ensures that other states keep the promises they may have made to it, if necessary, by resorting to force. It goes without saying that a state in a system with such a structure behaves circumspectly and worries constantly about its own security. It is also rather obvious that a state in such a situation will decide to arm itself out of self-preservation. At that moment, however, this state is confronted with the problem that what would be the safest situation from the point of view of its *own* security – namely, that it is the only one possessing weapons while all the other ones do not possess them – would be regarded by the other states as the most dangerous one from the viewpoint of *their* security. This follows from the fact that the weapons a state acquires in order to defend itself almost always give rise to the fear in the other states that these might some day be used against them, the result being that the other states, in their turn, start to acquire weapons to increase their security. Although this reaction is totally understandable, it naturally heightens the first state's feelings of insecurity. Consequently, this state decides to increase its weaponry even further, starting the next round in the arms race.

Thus, every state in the states system faces the following dilemma: all states would be better off if all of them chose not to arm themselves, but for each of them individually it would be disastrous to choose not to arm itself and therefore become the defenceless victim of a state that did choose to arm itself (in game theory jargon the latter outcome is called the 'sucker payoff'). For this reason every state decides to resolve this *security dilemma* by arming itself, even though it prefers, just like all the other states, the situation where all states are unarmed to the one where they are all armed. This dilemma, which in this context is called the 'strong' security dilemma, may be represented in the following way:

Figure 1: 'Strong' Security Dilemma

		J	
		C	D
I	C	3,3	1,4
	D	4,1	2,2

There are two states, *I* and *J*, which can choose between two strategies.[8] On the one hand, they can decide not to arm themselves: strategy C; on the other hand, they can decide to do just that: strategy D. (The letters C and D stand for 'cooperate' and 'defect' respectively.) The outcome valued the highest by each individual state is that in which the state in question chooses to arm itself while the other refrains from doing so. This outcome is designated by the number 4 (in the diagram the first entry in the cell signifies I's valuation of the outcome, and the second J's). The second best outcome for each individual state is at the same time best for both of them collectively. This is the outcome in which they both decide not to arm themselves. This outcome is designated by the number 3. The worst outcome for both I and J is that it chooses not to arm itself, whereas the other does. This outcome is designated by the number 1. Each state then prefers the outcome that they both arm themselves, which is designated by the number 2. In such a strategic situation both states choose to arm themselves, although they are fully aware that both of them would be better off if they were to decide not to do so. However, state I, as well as state J, sees itself confronted with the dilemma that, if it were to decide not to arm itself, this decision may lead to the best possible world for them collectively, but also to the worst possible world for that state alone. In view of this dilemma, both states decide to play it safe and to arm themselves.

The 'strong' security dilemma forms an indispensable part of almost every text in which an attempt is made to formulate some kind of model of the states system. This chapter is no exception to this rule. Nonetheless, the relations between France and the Federal Republic during the years 1947–1957 were never such that their respective order of preference with regard to the various European integration projects corresponded with that of a state in a 'strong' security dilemma. (This even holds true in the case of the failure of the European Defence Community in 1954, see Chapter 7, Section 6.) When the game is expanded to include three players, and the United States is included in the analysis, it is also true of the United States that it had an order of preference throughout the period with respect to the European initiatives which differed from that of a state faced with a 'strong' security dilemma.

It should be pointed out that the conflict between the states in the 'strong' security dilemma is not total. The game situation they find themselves in is not that of a 'zero-sum game', i.e. a game in which each gain for one state (for instance, +1) is of the same magnitude as the other state's loss (−1 in this example), with the result that the sum of gain and loss always equals zero. States involved in a 'strong' security dilemma, as opposed to those playing a zero-sum game, are not only one another's potential adversaries, but also one another's possible partners. The states in the 'strong' security dilemma are perfectly aware of having a common interest, but they also realize that the pursuit of this common interest cannot be reconciled with the protection of their self-interest (cf. Schelling [1960] 1980, p. 89).

Even in a situation in which the protection of their self-interest and the promotion of the common interest boil down to the same thing, the states may still fail to realize this common interest. Consider the situation that *I* as well as *J* has for some reason come to the conclusion that its original notion that the best outcome of it being armed while the other is not is a mistake. Both now think that the best outcome would be one in which they were both unarmed. At the same time, each of them sticks to its conviction that the outcome in which both states are armed is preferable to the outcome in which it is the only one without weapons. The order of preference of both states in this 'weak' security dilemma can be represented as in Figure 2.

Figure 2: 'Weak' Security Dilemma

		J	
		C	D
I	C	4,4	1,3
	D	3,1	2,2

In such a situation the natural outcome would seem to be that both *I* and *J* decide not to arm themselves.[9] However, more than forty years ago, Waltz argued that such an outcome is less natural than one would think at first sight. It seems to be common sense to choose C, but whether this choice is indeed sensible depends entirely on the 'rationality' of the other player: 'to allow in my calculation for the irrational acts of others can lead to no determinate solutions, but to attempt to act on a rational calculation without making such an allowance may lead to my undoing' (Waltz [1954] 1959, p. 169). According to Waltz, in such an uncertain situation both states will want to be on the safe side and will decide to arm themselves.

In the 'weak' security dilemma everything depends on trust. The states can escape from the dilemma if each of them trusts the other not to choose strategy D – for any reason, varying from simple inattention to a deliberate trick – consequently saddling it with the 'sucker payoff'. If the states do not succeed in establishing this trust, cooperation will not be achieved, although the states put the highest value on the outcome of both choosing strategy C. This is precisely the situation that occurred in the winter of 1950–1951 between France and the Federal Republic with respect to the coal and steel community (see Chapter 6, Section 3). Both powers preferred the outcome of the community being established to every other outcome, but hardly five years after the war, policy-makers in Paris and Bonn were highly concerned that the other's openly professed attachment to the steel and coal community was no more than a cover for a strategy aimed to ensure – by defecting and accepting a lesser outcome – that the other was left with the worst possible outcome. It was only thanks to the intervention of the United States that a solution was found that gave France and West Germany sufficient trust in one another to dare to take the step of cooperating in the coal and steel pool.

As has previously been observed, the worst possible situation for the largest possible majority of states would be that the smallest possible minority was armed and they were not. For this reason states are very anxious to prevent a situation from materializing in which a single state could establish its hegemony over the other states. One of the activities states engage in to this end is to enter into alliances with other states, intended to enable them to form a counterbalance against the potential hegemon. The latter activity is the subject matter of the centrepiece of classical international relations theory: the theory of the balance of power.

The formation of balances of power is not unique to states. Throughout ancient history, chroniclers of the many wars between city-states, barbarous tribes, kingdoms and empires noted that the protagonists entered into alliances with one another to create a counterweight against a potential hegemon. In his history of the Peloponnesian War (421–404 BC), Thucydides related how the representatives of Corinth succeeded in convincing their allies, including Sparta, of the necessity of fighting the rising Athens by pointing out among other things that:

> Athens is so much stronger than any single state in our alliance that she is capable of standing up to all of us together. So unless we go to war with her not only in full force but also with every city and every nationality inspired by the same purpose, she will find us divided and will easily subdue us. (Thucydides 1954, p. 79–80)

Polybius in turn described in *The Histories* how, in his view, Hiero, the tyrant of Syracuse, acted 'very wisely and sensibly' during the First Punic War (264–241 BC) when he came to the aid of the weaker Carthage against the stronger Rome, since 'we should never contribute to the attainment by one state of a power so preponderant, that none dare dispute with it even for their acknowledged rights' (Polybius [1922] 1954, p. 225).

The observations made by Thucydides and Polybius clearly show that a balance of power does not only exist if all the states in states system are more or less equally powerful. A balance of power can be established while there are great differences in power between the states. In the words of Vattel, one of the first theorists on this subject in the eighteenth century, the balance of power refers to 'an arrangement of affairs so that no State shall be in a position to have absolute mastery and dominate others' (Vattel [1758] 1916, p. 251).

The emergence of a balance of power through which the ambitions of an aspiring hegemon are thwarted accordingly constitutes the most important guarantee states have in their struggle to survive in the states system. But this guarantee is accompanied by some rather nasty side effects. The nastiest is without doubt that war is the most important instrument for maintaining or establishing a balance of power. The many wars fought in Europe between 1713 and 1772, the period generally regarded as the golden age of the balance of power 'in theory as well as in practice' (Morgenthau [1948] 1978, p. 196), are a perfect demonstration of this. Another unpleasant side effect is that the states involved continually try to shift the burdens of establishing a balance of power onto one another. In 1713, with the Peace of Utrecht, the High Contracting Parties had agreed that it was the duty of international society – which they deemed to be identical to the society of European states – to preserve the balance of power (cf. Bull 1977, pp. 37 and 106; also Morgenthau [1948] 1978, p. 186). However, the expectation that the other states could ultimately be trusted to bear the costs of maintaining the balance of power made the states somewhat careless in the execution of their responsibilities in this matter (cf. Schroeder [1994] 1996). This resulted in the states continually letting things get out of hand to such an extent that war was indeed the only means left to stop a potential hegemon.

Furthermore, it is quite possible for the attempts of states to prevent the hegemony of a certain state to end in failure. The balance of power does not always 'work' (the expression that is generally used). There is no guarantee at all that this most important guarantee for the survival of states will actually come into being whenever this is 'really' necessary. It is true that Morgenthau has defended the position that the states' ambition to survive in the international system must out of necessity lead to the establishment of a balance of power that will frustrate the aspiring hegemon (cf. Morgenthau [1948] 1978, p. 173), but this position is untenable. Morgenthau is wrong, because he implicitly equates the states system with a perfectly competitive market, in which an equilibrium price is established without any of the (many) producers aiming to realize this price. In such a market an equilibrium is indeed automatically established without anyone bothering to bring it about.

If, however, an analogy has to be made, then it must be one between the states system and an oligopoly, a market in which the establishment of an equilibrium price requires the constant attention of the leading producers. It also holds true of the states system that a balance of power can only be maintained if the major states are aware of the relevance of their actions to the success or failure of attempts to thwart a potential hegemon. This is a lesson the European states learned with great difficulty at the end of the eighteenth and the beginning of the nineteenth century (cf. Chapter 3, Section 1).

The threat that a certain state may establish a hegemony is in itself not sufficient inducement for the other states to form an alliance to ward it off (cf. Schroeder 1994). After all, the Corinthians had to use all their rhetorical skills to persuade the Spartans and their other allies that the time had come to declare war on Athens. Also, the threat of a Soviet dominance of the European continent did not spontaneously lead the Western European powers to combine in order to create a counterbalance against it. The United States had to work very hard to make the Western European powers realize that it would be worth their while to contribute actively to the establishment of a balance of power in Europe in order to contain the Soviet threat (cf. Chapter 5, Sections 2 and 3).

4.   The Credibility of States

The picture of life in the states system sketched in the previous section does indeed correspond very closely to Hobbes' famous depiction of life in the state of nature. The security dilemma, whether it manifests itself in its 'strong' or 'weak' form, compels states to worry constantly about one another's intentions, and in many cases makes cooperation impossible. The establishment of balances of power is inevitably accompanied by high costs, and provides states only with a precarious security. Nevertheless, thanks to an important factor in the considerations states make when deciding how best to survive in the states system, life in that system is less insecure and dangerous than this picture suggests.

A state will only succeed in concluding alliances with other states with a view to preventing a threatening hegemony, if this state has to some extent gained the reputation of keeping its promises and executing its threats – at least in the opinion of the states it deals with regularly, as the other states are less relevant in this context. To put it somewhat differently, a state will only find allies if it has acquired a certain *credibility* in the eyes of the other states. This factor in the states' considerations constitutes a major deterrent to their breaking their promises at will, even though the states system lacks an agency that can force states to keep them.[10] At the same time, this means that states are prepared to go to very great lengths in order to show that it is not their fault, but rather that of the other state or states, that a certain agreement has not been kept. Witness the antics of the French prime minister Mendès-France in August 1954, aimed at convincing the public that it was not France but the other five signatories to the treaty that were responsible for the failure of the conference on the defence community in Brussels (cf. Chapter 7, Section 6).

It will be clear that, other things being equal, a state with a great degree of credibility will have less difficulty getting its way in the states system than a state with little credibility. Consequently, the former will survive more easily in that system than the latter. The 'weak' security dilemma is an obstacle that can be easily overcome by two states with a reputation for keeping their promises. It is an almost insurmountable barrier for states with poor credibility. (Although it must be said that great credibility is no benefit to states wishing to escape from a 'strong' security dilemma.)

It can be deduced from the observation that greater credibility makes life easier in the states system, that the more weight a state attaches to its credibility, the greater the probability is that this state will act in accordance with the rule that constitutes the basis of all international law, namely *pacta sunt servanda* ('agreements must be kept'). This even holds true in the event that this state, for whatever reason, regrets ever having entered into this agreement, and would be very glad to get out of it. In this way the states' desire for credibility ensures a level of predictability in their mutual relations, and with that the possibilities for cooperation with one another, and lays the foundation for a certain regulation of their relations.[11]

5. Differences in Power and Transaction Costs

It will be clear that the importance states attach to their credibility is a great asset, but also a very vulnerable one. Take, for example, a state that has promised to come to the aid of another state if the latter becomes the victim of armed aggression, and suppose this situation actually occurs. The state that has made the promise is now confronted with the following choice: either it keeps its promise, meaning that it will have to undergo great sacrifices in the short term (providing diplomatic assistance, sending economic and military aid, and perhaps even taking part in the fighting), or it breaks its promise, ensuring that it will have to undergo greater sacrifices in the long term (when it later wants to persuade other states that it is also in their interest to behave themselves more in accordance with its wishes). The state is strongly tempted to let the immediate advantages of breaking its promise prevail over the future advantages gained by keeping it. This temptation is made greater by the realization that, in the past, many states have succumbed to it without this leading to their ruin.

However, in addition to the desire for credibility there is yet another factor that enhances the predictability of relations between states, and as a result increases the importance states attach to their credibility. This factor is that great differences in power exist between states. The more powerful a certain state is compared with the other states in the states system, the more prudent the other states will judge it to be to consider that state's expected behaviour, and the less necessary it will be for that state to consider the expected behaviour of the other states. On the one hand, this means that 'certain international issues are as a consequence settled, the demands of certain states (weak ones) can in practice be left out of account, the demands of certain other states (strong ones) recognized to be the only ones relevant to the issue in hand' (Bull 1977, p. 206). On the other hand, this implies that the states falling within the reach of power of one of the most powerful states in the states system (usually referred to as the 'great powers') will think twice before deciding to break a promise, whether it be to one another or to that powerful state, out of fear of incurring the latter's displeasure.

Just like any other state, a great power tries as much as possible to organize the states system according to its own wishes. To the extent that it succeeds in this – which is naturally a direct function of the power preponderance of the great power *vis-à-vis* the other states – a great power feels itself more responsible for the way things are going in a larger part of the states system, if only to prevent it from being dragged into a conflict with some other great power by the actions of the less powerful states in its sphere of influence. The great powers devise the rules to be followed by the other states, and have both the capabilities and the will to maintain these rules (cf. Keohane 1984, pp. 34–5).

A very important implication of the above is that, the smaller the number of great powers and the greater their preponderance, the more the great powers will act as managers of the states system. The problem with establishing a balance of power discussed in Section 3, namely that the states try to shift the costs involved onto one another as much as possible, with the result that the balance is only established at the very last moment or not at all, becomes less important as the number of great powers in the states system becomes smaller. As Waltz observed:

the smaller the number of great powers, and the wider the disparities between the few most powerful states and the many others, the more likely the former are to act for the sake of the system and to participate in the management of, or interfere in the affairs of, lesser states. (Waltz 1979, p. 198)

Through their efforts to organize the states system as much as possible in their own interests, the great powers increase the predictability of life in the states system for all states. The order the great powers create in the states system has the character of a collective good (cf. Lieshout 1995, p. 75). This means, among other things, that it is not feasible for the great powers, once they have established this order, to prevent the other states also from benefiting from it, even though the latter have made no contribution whatsoever to its establishment.

In his famous essay *Perpetual Peace*, Kant argued that states can ward off the negative consequences of the anarchical structure of the states system, which he portrayed in very Hobbesian terms, by each state adopting a republican constitution. This, however, can only be accomplished 'if Fortune ordains that a powerful and enlightened people should form a republic [as] this would serve as a centre of federal union for other states wishing to join' (Kant [1795] 1903, p. 134). The development described by Kant boils down to what nowadays would be called the establishment of an *international regime* by a great power. As far as Kant was concerned, this was a good thing in the case of revolutionary France at the end of the eighteenth century. However, the establishment of a regime is not always favourably received by the states that 'profit' from it. It is true that the great power acts for the sake of the common interest, but its views on what this common interest entails, and the best way of promoting it, need not necessarily coincide with those of the other states that are part of such a regime. After World War II France had the greatest difficulty with the United States' interpretation of the North Atlantic security regime intended to stop the Soviet Union's advance. This applied in particular to the American demand for the Federal Republic to be rearmed. At the same time, the conflicts between the United States and France never escalated to such high levels that the establishment of the regime and its subsequent functioning were threatened. Furthermore, power relations at the time were such that these, combined with the American presence in Germany as an occupation power, would have enabled the United States to establish a security regime one way or another, if necessary even without the assistance of the Western European states (needless to say that, in that case, the regime would have taken an entirely different shape),[12] whereas the Western European powers would never have succeeded in establishing a security regime on their own. For France this meant that it needed to involve itself with shaping the regime, and for the United States, that it welcomed every contribution to the reduction of the costs of the regime – which, if necessary, it would have borne alone – even if this contribution came from the troublesome French.[13] Just like any other great power, the United States tried as hard as it could to push back the free-rider behaviour of the states which profited from its exertions, but in return it had to pay the price of these states interfering in the shaping and functioning of the regime.

Thus the great powers play a very important role in the establishment of regimes. The possibility cannot be excluded that regimes come into being without great powers playing a role in their emergence, but their assistance increases the chances of success. This does not mean that the undermining of the position of the great power responsible for the establishment of a certain regime also leads to the disappearance of the regime. Once it is functioning, a regime increases the predictability of life for the states taking part in it, or, to use an expression often employed in this context, it decreases their transaction costs. The larger this decrease in transaction costs in the eyes of the participants, the more they are prepared to pay for the continued existence of the regime (cf. Keohane 1984). Yet another factor is involved here, which, following De Jasay, may be called the 'productivity' of the regime (De Jasay 1989, pp. 146–8). The more successful the regime has been in the past in furthering the interests of the states taking part in it, the greater lengths they will go to maintain the regime. Naturally, these are subjects of only minor importance to the present study, which is concerned more with the establishment of regimes than with their continued existence or decline.

6.   An Institutional Realist Analysis

The bleak picture of the prospects of cooperation in the states system sketched in Section 3 corresponds to the one sketched by the adherents of (neo-) realism. The more optimistic picture of the possibilities of cooperation in the states system that emerged in Sections 4 and 5 agrees with the one that is sketched in the work of those whom I have called the institutional realists (cf. Lieshout in Van Deth 1993, pp. 216–7).[14] As may be apparent from the way in which I have set up the argument developed in this chapter, I am of the opinion that institutional realism should be regarded as an improved version of (neo-)realism. Both theories start from the same two basic assumptions. First, that the international system is a states system, meaning that states are the actors (the acting units) in the international system. Second, that anarchy is the most important property of the external structure of the states system. What institutional realism adds to (neo-)realism – and this is the reason why it offers a better understanding of the functioning of the states system – is the perception that institutions can play a crucial role also in this kind of system, as part of the external structure *and* the internal structure (the latter category (neo-)realists tend to lose sight of). Institutions do this by entering into the considerations of states when they decide on the best way to survive in the states system.

My choice in favour of institutional realism as the guiding principle for my analysis of the struggle for the organization of Europe would suggest that it is my opinion that what happened in the years 1947–1957 can be understood with the help of a general theory such as institutional realism. To put this somewhat differently, I am of the opinion that, although admittedly the type of international organizations established in Europe in the 1950s is very rare in the states system, their establishment is not a phenomenon in need of a special explanatory framework (cf. also Risse-Kappen 1996, p. 56).

Moreover, the question remains whether an alternative framework really would be available. The theory in question, (neo-)functionalism, is more in the nature of a normative theory about the method that should be used to attain a world in which war is a thing of the past, than an empirical theory about the way things work in the existing world. (I am very much aware of the fact that my lumping together functionalism and neo-functionalism must come as quite a shock to experts on the differences between the two schools of thought (cf. Cram in Richardson 1996, pp. 41–7).)

Functionalism rests on two assumptions. The first is that the cause of the great frequency with which wars occur in the states system is to be found in the combination of authority and territory that was established with the Peace of Westphalia by the assignment of sovereignty to the members of the system (see also Section 1). The second is that relations between states comprise various activities – such as economic, social, cultural and political – and that it is possible to organize these activities in such a way that they are separated from one another for a certain period of time so that they can no longer influence each other (cf. Claude [1956] 1964, p. 350).

The method functionalism then recommends to establish a world without war, is, in the words of its founder Mitrany, '[to link] authority to a specific activity, to break away from the traditional link between authority and a definite territory' (cf. De Wilde 1991, p. 197). The states should be persuaded to hand over part of their sovereignty to organizations charged with the execution of certain specific tasks, for instance in the field of economics, which at first sight would seem to pose no threat to the states' right to exist. This is when the truth comes out. Once this first step has been taken, these organizations will develop dynamics of their own, which the states will not be able to withstand. Their position will gradually be undermined, and they will ultimately disappear from the world stage, with war in their wake, because they will have become completely superfluous. As Claude has noted: 'functionalism may be regarded as a device of sneaking up on sovereignty, full of hopeful possibilities for establishing the groundwork of international community' (Claude [1956] 1964, p. 351). This irresistible dynamic (the so-called *engrenage*, or 'spill-over effect', see also Section 6.4) results from the constant call for greater jurisdiction on the part of the officials employed by the supranational organizations, and the pressure groups of those who stand to gain from an extension of the authority of these organizations.

This 'implicit determinism' of (neo-)functionalism (De Wilde 1991, p. 180; cf. also Busch in Jachtenfuchs and Kohler-Koch 1996, pp. 282–3) makes it even more difficult to accept this already rather nebulous approach. However, it cannot be denied that the spill-over effect in many ways forms a good characterization of the daily practice of 'Europe', particularly if one takes into account the effects of the rulings of the European Court of Justice (cf. Burley and Mattli 1993). Nonetheless, it is true that every deepening or enlargement of the European regime requiring a fundamental revision of this regime's rules of the game – as was the case with the switch from sector integration (the ECSC) to the common market (the EEC) in 1957, or the decision to establish an Economic and Monetary Union (EMU) in 1991 – can in no way be inter-preted as part of an inexorable process that started with the ECSC coming into operation in 1952. The making of such fundamentally political decisions is the preserve of states, and, for the time being, institutional realism offers the best theoretical framework to understand the conditions under which states are prepared to make these kinds of 'history-making' decision (cf. Peterson 1995, p. 84).

Notes

1. Although these arguments appear to be rather strong, it cannot be denied that this choice of the state as the acting unit in the international system is controversial. Since the beginning of this century, a long series of publications have appeared in which it is argued that, as a result of the dramatic rise in the number of interactions between the units in the international system – i.e. the increase in the 'density' of the international system (cf. Buzan [1982] 1991, pp. 151–3) – characterizations of the state as used by Deutsch no longer apply. Ohmae is one of the most prominent representatives of this school. The statement with which he opened an article in *Foreign Affairs* some years ago on the rise of the region state, is typical in this context. According to Ohmae, 'the nation state has become

an unnatural, even dysfunctional, unit for organizing human activity' (Ohmae 1993, p. 78).

2. It is of course somewhat confusing that the relations between states are usually called inter*national* relations. This has however become so established in practice that it seems best to accept this inconsistency. A nation is also an abstraction used to indicate a group of people who believe that they have a common background and future, who also cherish this communality, and who, moreover, are of the opinion that this distinguishes them from other groups of people. For the most part, they speak the same language and adhere to the same religion.

3. The dissolution of this order had already started at the end of the thirteenth century with the conflict between King Philip IV the Fair of France and Pope Boniface VIII concerning the right claimed by Philip to impose taxes on the churches in his kingdom without the Pope's prior consent. In this conflict Philip's lawyers defended the position that the Pope had no supranational authority in this matter by arguing that *rex est imperator in regno suo* ('the king is ruler in his own realm').

4. The rule that the established religion must be the same as that practised by the ruler had already been laid down with respect to the Holy Roman Empire in the Peace of Augsburg of 1555, which ended the Schmalkaldic War.

5. After March 1951, matters became even more complicated when the occupation authorities permitted the Federal Republic to maintain diplomatic relations with other states, but at the same time reserved all kinds of rights regarding the foreign policy of West Germany (see Chapter 3, Section 4).

6. The role the human individual can play in decision-making processes with great social consequences may be illustrated using the following metaphor. The human individual is an engine driver. Where his train will arrive depends on the position of the many switches and his ability to drive the train. The position of the switches is usually beyond the control of the engine driver, as these react autonomously or are operated by a switchman. Nonetheless, it can happen that the engine driver throws a switch on his own, or convinces a switchman that it is also in his interest to do so. In contrast to regular railway traffic, the route and destination of the train are not clear at the time of departure. It is up to the engine driver to decide at which station he wishes to arrive, but as he has no control over the position of the switches, there is no guarantee at all that he will ever arrive at the station of his choice. Most of the time, the position of the switches will be such that the train is conducted hither and thither, as a result of which an 'impartial spectator' can easily get the impression that the train is no more than a plaything in the hands of the switches. However, it is also possible that a whole series of switches are suddenly in the right position (perhaps thanks in part to the exertions of the engine driver) so that good progress can be made in the direction of the train's destination. It is then the engine driver's job to observe that the positions of the switches are correct, and subsequently to profit from this actively by competently driving the train nearer to the desired station. In a comparable manner, social norms and values, administrative routines and action channels,

other human individuals *and* chance repeatedly create 'positions of switches' for a human individual enabling him to influence the course of social events, sometimes even decisively.

7. As I observed in my *Between Anarchy and Hierarchy*: 'In order to explain the behaviour of states, it is not enough to know – to use a well-known analogy – that states *are* billiard balls. States must also view one another as billiard balls. What matters in particular, is how states learn that they will be better off treating one another as if they were billiard balls, and that this learning process can only proceed by means of trial and error' (Lieshout 1995: 177).

8. The 'strong' security dilemma as described here is identical to the well-known Prisoner's Dilemma. This concerns the dilemma with which two prisoners, suspected of having committed a serious crime, are confronted by the prosecuting attorney who deals with their case. The attorney knows there is not enough evidence to convict them of the crime unless both of them confess. In order to get a conviction, the prisoners are interrogated separately, and each of them is told the following story. If both prisoners remain silent, they can be charged only with a less serious crime, and each of them faces a relatively light sentence of one year in prison. If both of them confess, a sentence of five years in prison for both prisoners would be requested. However, if only one of them were to confess and the other remained silent, a sentence of only three months would be requested for the prisoner who confessed, and the maximum sentence of ten years in prison would be requested for the prisoner who remained silent. The outcome of the game is that both prisoners confess to the prosecuting attorney (cf. Lieshout 1995, pp. 75–6).

9. This characterization of the 'weak' security dilemma implies that the states find themselves in the same situation as the stag hunters described by Rousseau in his *Discourse on the Origin of Inequality* (1755). The hunt will take at least a day, and can only be completed successfully if none of the hunters shirks his obligations. Otherwise the stag will escape. Unfortunately circumstances are such that each of the hunters knows that the others are incorrigible opportunists, preferring the easily caught hare to the stag that takes a whole day's work to catch, even though they find venison tastier than hare. This knowledge causes each of the hunters to chase after a hare as soon as he sees one, without troubling himself for one moment about the success of the hunt (cf. Lieshout 1995, pp. 81–2).

10. Hobbes might actually have agreed with this point, considering his refutation of the so-called 'argument of the fool'. The fool argues that, in the state of nature, every man is concerned only with his own conservation, and that it is therefore not against reason for a man not to keep his part of a convenant if this is to his benefit, even though the other party has performed already. According to Hobbes, however, reason dictates that this man should fulfil his part, seeing that in the state of nature 'there is no man who can hope by his own strength, or wit, to defend himself from destruction, without the help of confederates and therefore he which declares he thinks it reason to deceive those who help him, can in

reason expect no other means of safety, than what can be had from his own single power (Hobbes [1651] 1947, pp. 95–6). Hobbes seems not to have realized that this understanding would have made life in the state of nature less miserable and hopeless than he himself thought.

11. From a certain point of view the states system even offers a more favourable environment for the growth of cooperation between its members than a national system. This follows from the fact that the states system has no more than 200 members, whereas the vast majority of national systems have millions of members. The smaller the number of members in a group, the more quickly it will be noticed if one of them fails to keep his promise, resulting in adverse consequences for the reputation of the member who failed to perform (cf. Lieshout 1995, p. 61 and Keohane 1984, p. 77).

12. This is the fundamental difference between the situation with respect to NATO on the one hand, and the European integration projects on the other. In the case of NATO, if the worst came to the worst, the United States would have been able to produce the collective good on its own, whereas in the other cases the United States would not have been able to do so.

13. A comparable situation occurred with respect to the Netherlands' participation in the conference on the Schuman Plan. The Dutch position was that, in view of the French and German unity regarding the coal and steel community, there was every reason to expect the community to become a reality. In that case, the best thing the Netherlands could do was to take part in the conference in order to try to bend things in its favour as much as possible – something in which the Dutch delegation was rather successful during the first phase of the conference (see Chapter 6, Section 3). France and Germany were not averse to the Dutch participation, as the Netherlands, thanks to its relatively efficient coal and steel industry, would become a net contributor to the community (the Federal Republic would be the other one).

14. In order to avoid possible misunderstanding, I would like to point out that included in my definition of institutional realists are both the American authors who go by the name of 'neo-liberals' or 'neo-institutionalists', with Keohane as their most prominent representative, and the British scholars who are called 'Grotians' since they claim to be inspired by the work of Grotius. Undoubtedly, Bull is the best known representative of the latter school. I have chosen the name 'institutional realism' in order to indicate the 'realist' foundations of both these 'institutional' schools. I may add that, in my view, the perceptions provided by 'social constructivism', as described by John Ruggie (cf. Ruggie 1998, pp. 28–34), are part and parcel of institutional realism. But in all fairness it must be said that in social constructivism there is a stronger emphasis on the 'soft' aspects both of the external structure of the states system and of the internal structure of the states.

3. The German Problem

1. The Destruction of the European Balance of Power

The fact that Poland had ceased to exist as an independent state as a result of three successive divisions of the Polish territory between Prussia, Russia and Austria at the end of the eighteenth century (in 1772, 1793 and 1795, respectively) made clear that the free interplay of forces between the European great powers no longer guaranteed the survival of the other powers that were part of the European states system. A few years later, the French dash for power in Europe under Napoleon showed that the great powers themselves could also no longer count on the salutory operation of the European balance of power. After their crushing defeats, Austria and Prussia were reduced to vassal states of the French empire.

Mainly due to Napoleon's boundless ambitions, the French pursuit of power eventually reached its limit, and when, in 1814 and 1815 France was finally defeated by a broad coalition in which all other European great powers participated, the latter had in any case learned that a balance of power can only be brought about if the great powers in the states system also considered it their common duty to improve and maintain this balance. This insight found its expression in the Concert of Europe, which included England, Russia, Austria, Prussia and also the defeated France. The participating powers agreed that they needed to find widely supported solutions to the problems the European states system was repeatedly confronted with, and that this could best be done through consultation and recognition of the rights of great *and* small European powers.[1]

As a result of this Concert, the European balance of power functioned reasonably well for a number of decades. After the great Prussian victory over France in the war of 1870–1871, the Concert was faced with a problem for which it was ultimately unable to find a solution: the rapidly increasing power of the German empire (which had been proclaimed at the Versailles Palace in 1871).

World War I constituted the first phase of the decline of the European balance of power. In 1914, Germany's policy to encourage its ally Austria-Hungary in taking a hard line *vis-à-vis* Serbia (which was supported by Russia) following the assassination in Sarajevo of the successor to the

Austrian throne was partly based on the German policy-makers' view that, at this juncture, Germany was offered what one would now call a 'window of opportunity'. Great Britain and France, two of Germany's main opponents, were in decline, and although Russia was rapidly becoming an influential power – and certainly was considered a potential threat to Germany – it was not yet strong enough to constitute any real threat. In economic terms, the United States was already more powerful than the German empire in 1914, but because of its policy of non-interference as far as European matters were concerned, it did not feature very prominently in the calculations of European rulers.

In the last two years of World War I, the 'German problem' manifested itself to its full extent. The German empire, with Austria-Hungary as its junior partner, was winning the battle against the powers of the *Entente*. The other major European powers were apparently unable to hold off a German hegemony, so that a European balance of power could no longer be established. In the spring of 1918, after Russia had had to sign the humiliating Peace Treaty of Brest-Litovsk and subsequently fell prey to civil war, Germany prepared itself to defeat Great Britain and France decisively. However, the German spring offensive did not lead to the desired breakthrough. This failure turned out to be fatal to Germany as United States' participation on the side of the *Entente* tipped the scales in its favour in the course of 1918. The United States had declared war on Germany by 1 April 1917, but it took a considerable time to mobilize the American war potential. Germany finally capitulated in November 1918, even before the allies could launch their attack on German territory.

After the war, the United States rapidly withdrew its forces from Europe. As many authors have pointed out, the somewhat paradoxical result was that, after the Treaty of Versailles, Germany was in a better strategic position *vis-à-vis* Great Britain and France – the powers that had to guard the new European balance of power – than before World War I, even though it had to give up some of its territory and pay reparations. To quote Haffner:

> The disarmament and obligation to pay war reparations indeed meant that Germany had been encumbered with two heavy mortgages, which would have to be redeemed at some time. But otherwise it gradually proved that the position of the German empire – which had lost parts of its territory in the west, east and north, but was still intact – had by no means become weaker after 1914; on the contrary, it had become stronger. (Haffner [1987] 1989, p. 180)

It was only a matter of time before Germany would take advantage of this improved strategic position.[2]

In the 1930s, under Hitler's rule, Germany decided to undo the decisions taken in Versailles, while France and Great Britain were unable to defend them. The events which followed successively were: the remilitarization of the Rhineland (1936), the *Anschluss* or incorporation of Austria into the German *Reich* (1938), Czechoslovakia's cession of Sudetenland to Germany (after the Treaty of Munich in 1938) and the occupation of the rump state of Czechoslovakia, followed by the establishment of the protectorate Bohemia-Moravia (1939). In a last attempt to contain Germany's expansionism, France and Great Britain guaranteed the Polish borders in the spring of 1939. However, the events of the previous years had tarnished the credibility of both powers to such an extent that any deterrent effect this declaration of guarantee might have had was undermined from the very start. Germany invaded Poland in September 1939. When it subsequently ignored the ultimatum issued by France and Great Britain, both powers declared war on Germany, marking the beginning of World War II.

Again, Germany could only be beaten with the help of the United States. However, this time the German defeat was complete. In accordance with the decision that British Prime Minister Churchill and American President Roosevelt had taken at their conference in Casablanca in January 1943, Germany was forced to surrender unconditionally, which it did in May 1945. The entire German territory was subsequently occupied and divided into occupation zones. In June 1945, the victors proclaimed that they would exercise supreme authority in Germany for the duration of the occupation period. The solution to the German problem now seemed close at hand. At the same time, it was clear to all those involved that this solution could not be found within the context of a European balance of power. For there were only two possible solutions. The first was that the German threat would be rendered harmless by a Soviet hegemony over Europe; the second that a renewal of German aggression would be prevented by the United States' active involvement in establishing a balance of power in Europe. This solution required the Americans to keep their forces in Europe for a considerable period of time. However, in the first years after the war, it was not clear whether the United States would be prepared to do so. At the Yalta Conference in February 1945, Roosevelt had announced that American troops would only remain in Europe up to two years after the German capitulation.

2.   The Contours of a Solution: 1945–1948

2.1. Introduction
France was also one of the occupying powers. When the provisional French

government claimed this status, the United States and the Soviet Union initially were not prepared to satisfy this French demand.[3] It was thanks to the British who laboured for the French cause at the Yalta Conference – 'Churchill and Eden "fought like tigers for France"' (Young 1984, p. 8) – that France was finally allocated an occupation zone and became a member of the allied Control Council, the body that would have to coordinate the policies in the various occupation zones. It was of the utmost importance to Great Britain that France would again become a strong power on the European continent. Churchill, for example, defended the British proposal by arguing that 'the French must grow strong again to help check a revived Germany'. It was also his opinion that 'the French had had long experience in occupying Germany and [that] they would not be lenient'. Initially, Stalin was against France being given a seat on the Control Council. He was afraid that France 'would [soon] demand that de Gaulle attend the Big Three's conferences' (Willis [1965] 1968, p. 12). After further consultations, the Big Three nevertheless decided that part of the zones occupied by the Americans and British should be allocated to France – which was incidentally a much smaller zone than France had had in mind – and that it would have a seat on the Control Council.[4]

At the Yalta Conference, the Big Three confirmed that they did not want to divide Germany and that they intended to govern it as a unity. In spite of this intention, the Soviet Union annexed the area around Königsberg (Kaliningrad) and withdrew part of its occupation zone from the control of the Control Council by placing these *Ostgebiete* under Polish administration as a compensation for the Russian annexation of the Polish territory to the east of the Curzon Line. Moreover, little came of governing Germany as a unity. This was in the first instance not a question of political unwillingness as far as the American, British and Soviet occupation authorities were concerned. The zones were rather different in nature. For example, the British zone was mainly industrial, whereas the Soviet zone was predominantly agricultural. Furthermore, each of the powers introduced its own administrative tradition in their respective zones. This, combined with the fact that the Control Council could only take measures for the entire German territory if all four occupying powers agreed, and also depended on the occupation powers as far as the implementation of these measures was concerned (the Control Council lacked an administrative apparatus of its own), led to considerable differences in administrative practice. The situation became even more confused because the Big Three had not developed a clear view on the future of Germany. Only France had such a clear view: Germany would have to be partitioned. However, to its great chagrin, France was not invited to the Potsdam

Conference in August 1945, where Great Britain, the United States and the Soviet Union confirmed their intentions as formulated in Yalta.[5]

In the first months of the occupation, there was no open conflict regarding Germany's future between the Western allies and the Soviet Union. In the Control Council, the United States and the Soviet Union tried to establish a common approach to deal with the problems. It was France that frustrated the activities of the Control Council, in protest against the decisions taken in Potsdam, by relying regularly on its right of veto.[6]

2.2. A Rapid Economic Recovery: American and British Policies with Respect to Germany

The two world wars had thoroughly convinced the American security community that the greatest threat to the security of the United States was the dominance of one power in Europe. Following the defeat of Germany, military leaders and diplomats therefore considered it their most important task to prevent this from ever occurring again.[7] In their opinion, the most appropriate way to achieve this was by restoring the European balance of power. This restoration was, however, seriously threatened by the desperate situation in which the Western European powers found themselves. It was in any case necessary to prevent the Soviet Union from extending its power any further in Europe. This did not mean, however, that the American policy-makers thought that the Soviet Union was about to establish its hegemony over Europe by force; on the contrary, they were actually convinced that the Soviet Union lacked the military means to do so. What they feared most was that the European continent would simply fall into the Soviet Union's lap as a result of the deplorable situation in Western Europe. It was not inconceivable that the economic chaos might lead to coups by local Communist parties in various countries, and that these parties would subsequently turn to the Soviet Union for support (cf. Leffler 1984, pp. 363–4).

Thus, the American policy of restoring the European balance of power could be translated into a policy aimed at raising the Western European standard of living as quickly as possible. Moreover, the Americans were of the opinion that such a policy could succeed only if Germany was helped to a rapid recovery, as this country was after all the driving force behind the European economy. The American policy-makers were therefore facing a dilemma. On the one hand, Germany should be kept weak as long as possible to prevent it from ever dominating Europe again, but on the other, a rapid recovery by Germany was essential to avert the threat of a Soviet domination over Europe. The first years following the war displayed a shift in American priorities in this respect. This may be illustrated by the instructions the

American Chiefs of Staff gave to the American Commander-in-Chief in Europe in April 1945 (JCS 1067) and July 1947 (JCS 1779), respectively. Whereas the former were still focused on preventing a renewal of German aggression, which entailed that 'you will take no steps (*a*) looking toward the economic rehabilitation of Germany, or (*b*) designed to maintain or strengthen the German economy' (Ruhm von Oppen 1955, p. 21), the latter mainly related to measures facilitating the German contribution to the reconstruction of Europe since 'an orderly and prosperous Europe requires the economic contributions of a stable and productive Germany' (Senate Committee on Foreign Relations 1950, p. 552).

The point of departure of British policy in the first year of the occupation was that an undivided Germany – naturally minus the areas annexed or allocated to Poland by the Soviet Union[8] – would be governed by the four occupying powers, which had to ensure that reparations be paid and were also responsible for the economic and, perhaps more importantly, moral regeneration of Germany. Great Britain's main objective was the same as that of the United States: to make a renewal of German aggression impossible. Unlike the Americans, the British regarded the Russian policy towards Germany as resulting from a justified fear of German aggression and much less from the desire to expand the Russian sphere of influence as much as possible in Europe.

Initially, Great Britain wished to assume an active role in the reconstruction of Europe, but not a year had passed before it became clear that it would be unable to play such a role. Apparently, all the British could do was to wait and react to American and Soviet initiatives. The main reason for this passive attitude lay in the costs of the occupation zone, which constituted an unacceptable burden on Great Britain. During the war, 'the British had insisted on taking the zone which was the largest in population, the most industrialized and the most destroyed' (Ellwood 1992, p. 53). So now they were reaping the bitter fruit, also in part because the Soviet Union, contrary to the Potsdam agreements, exported food from its zone to the British zone in very small quantities. It soon became clear to Great Britain that it would take considerable time before the industry in its zone was sufficiently restored to bring in the foreign currency needed to pay for the import of food. For the time being, Great Britain itself would have to furnish this foreign currency (cf. Watt in Scharf and Schröder 1979, p. 16). It seemed the world was turned upside down. Instead of Great Britain receiving reparations from Germany, as should have happened, it had to pump vast amounts of money into its occupation zone. Besides, the British economy would not be able to provide the required amounts much longer. The best solution to this problem seemed to be to merge the British zone with one or more of the other zones; however, this was not seriously considered at the time. The British government had high hopes that an agreement with the Soviet Union on the German question would soon be reached. However, this hope completely evaporated when, at the Paris conference of the foreign ministers of the occupying powers in the spring and summer of 1946, the Soviet Union rejected the plan for a treaty between the four powers on Germany's disarmament drawn up by James Byrnes, the American Secretary of State.

In the winter of 1945–1946, the situation in Germany rapidly deteriorated. The main reason for this was the lack of cooperation between the occupying powers. The French and, to a lesser extent, the Russians continually obstructed the decision-making process in the Control Council so that it practically came to a standstill. The Byrnes Plan aimed to take away the French and Russian resistance to the reconstruction of Germany – and to overcome the impasse – by offering France and the Soviet Union certain guarantees against a renewal of German aggression. It provided for a treaty between the four occupying forces that would guarantee Germany's disarmament for twenty-five years. All this time, American forces would remain stationed in Europe. As early as December 1945, Byrnes submitted this plan informally to Stalin, who was not unfavourably disposed towards it. However, during the first round of the conference of the foreign ministers, it turned out that Russian foreign minister Molotov found it somewhat premature to discuss such a treaty. Only after Germany was completely disarmed and demilitarized would such a plan be considered (cf. Krieger 1987, p. 153). As far as France was concerned, the plan would only be considered in the light of the French *desiderata*.

In May, the military governor of the American zone, General Clay, managed to convince Byrnes that measures needed to be taken as quickly as possible, otherwise 'the whole edifice [in Germany] will come crashing down on our heads' (Yergin 1977, p. 229). The best solution was, of course, that the occupying powers would after all treat Germany as a unity. If this could not be achieved, Clay proposed to merge the American and British zones.

On the eve of the second round of the conference of foreign ministers, Byrnes and British foreign minister Bevin agreed that the moment of truth had come. If the Soviet Union persisted in opposing the Byrnes Plan, they would no longer have any doubt that 'the Russians were bent on further westward expansion, and that for this reason they wanted to aggravate economic paralysis and political disintegration in Germany' (Yergin 1977, p. 230). On 9 and 10 July 1946, Molotov made two speeches in which he once again rejected the plan. He clung to the view that Germany should be totally disarmed and demilitarized (and should remain so for at least forty years), that the Ruhr Basin must be placed under the control of the four powers, and that a satisfactory solution to the problem of the reparations ought to be found. In passing, he also rejected the French plans for the division of Germany. The day after Molotov's second speech, Byrnes informed the other foreign ministers that the United States was prepared 'to enter into agreement with any other delegation for the treatment of their two Zones as an economic unit' and that he had instructed the American representatives in Germany 'to concert immediately with the representatives of any other Power to set up the administrative organization necessary for this purpose'. Great Britain was the only occupying power willing to accept this American offer. In early December 1946, after several months of negotiations in which the British tried in vain to shift a large part of the expenses of their zone on to the Americans, the agreement on the integration of the two zones was signed. This took effect on 1 January 1947.

An important consequence of the establishment of the Bizone was the failure of the British Labour government's plans to socialize the coal and steel industries in the British zone in much the same way as it was trying to do in Great Britain. In October 1946, Bevin had stated in the House of Commons: 'our intention is that these industries should be owned and controlled in the future by the public. The exact form of this public ownership is now being worked out' (Lister 1960, p. 148). The United States, however, did not like these plans at all. According to American authorities, the lack of coal in Germany could partly be blamed on 'a British obsession with questions of ownership rather than production' (Milward 1984, p. 143).[9] France too had considerable objections to the British socialization policy. In the eyes of the French, socialization meant nothing more than that a future German government would become the owner of the German heavy industry, and that was, of course, absolutely out of the question. The United States put so much pressure on Great Britain that, given its dependency on the former, it had no choice but to yield.[10] Hardly a year after Bevin's statement, the British abandoned their socialization policy as far as Germany was concerned.

Everyone's attention was fixed on the Soviet Union's rejection of the Byrnes Plan, but, as has been mentioned above, France also did not react very enthusiastically. It was only willing to study the plan in the light of its own programme. At the conference of foreign ministers, France emphasized again and again that it could only agree to a joint government of Germany if the other occupying powers complied with the French demands that the Rhineland and Ruhr Basin should no longer be part of Germany and the Saarland become French. These demands were not in line with the agreements the Big

Three had made in Potsdam. Their main aim was, of course, to prevent Germany from ever becoming a threat to France again, but, according to the United States, the policy of obstruction that France pursued in support of these demands only helped the Soviet Union. One week after the conference of foreign ministers had ended, General Clay wrote a memorandum in which he once again emphasized the disastrous effects of the policy of obstruction on the economic situation in Germany – and consequently on that in Europe. This memorandum formed the basis for a speech that Byrnes made in Stuttgart at the beginning of September (cf. Gimbel 1972). In this speech Byrnes denounced the impasse in the Control Council which meant that 'the Control Council is neither governing Germany nor allowing Germany to govern itself', and tried to persuade France and the Soviet Union towards more cooperation. On the one hand, he showed himself willing to consider the Soviet Union's wishes while, on the other, he dashed all France's hopes that its policy of obstruction would ever lead to the desired result. Byrnes thus emphasized that the United States, as agreed in Potsdam, would support the annexation of Königsberg at the coming peace conference, and that it was not entirely unsympathetic towards a revision of the Polish–German border in favour of Poland. The French demands, however, he resolutely rejected, except for the French claim on the Saarland: 'except as here indicated, the United States will not support any encroachment on territory which is indisputably German or any division of Germany which is not genuinely desired by the people concerned' (Ruhm von Oppen 1955, pp. 159–60).

According to Clay, another obstacle that prevented the much desired economic recovery of Germany was the continuing uncertainty regarding the duration of the American military presence in Europe. This led to a defeatist attitude among German officials and politicians. They constantly asked themselves why they should exert themselves for the reconstruction of Germany if the Soviet Union was soon to gain control over Germany anyway. As the Soviet Union had rejected the Byrnes Plan, which provided for an American presence in Europe for a period of twenty-five years, the Germans needed to be given certainty in some other way (cf. Krieger 1987, pp. 164–5, and Yergin 1977, p. 232). At Clay's instigation, Byrnes therefore assured his audience in Stuttgart: 'We are not withdrawing. We are staying here. As long as there is an occupation army in Germany, the American armed forces will be part of that occupation army' (Ruhm von Oppen 1955, p. 158). The United States accepted for the time being that its military presence was essential in order for its policy of economic recovery to succeed, so that this might eventually lead to the establishment of a new European balance of power, which would no longer require its presence in Europe.

2.3. The Largest Reparations Possible: Soviet Policy with Respect to Germany

The Soviet Union's policy was first of all aimed at creating the conditions that would make it impossible for Germany ever again to become a military threat to the Soviet Union. The Soviets' quest for security was characterized by four aspects. The first was the complete disarmament and demilitarization of Germany. The second concerned the creation of secure frontiers through a considerable extension of its territory towards the west. The Soviet Union clung to its conquests of 1939, resulting from the agreements of the Molotov–Ribbentrop Pact (Estonia, Latvia, Lithuania and part of Poland), and also annexed parts of Germany, Czechoslovakia and Rumania in 1945. The third aspect was the erection of a *cordon sanitaire* of satellite states between Germany and the Soviet Union. Finally, the fourth aspect concerned the Ruhr Basin, which the Soviet Union wanted to place under the control of the four occupying powers. In addition to this defensive objective of safeguarding national security, the Soviet Union also wanted to achieve an offensive objective with respect to Germany: it tried to bring the whole of Germany within its own sphere of influence as quickly as possible (cf. Mastny 1996, p. 24, and Gaddis 1997, p. 116). This is the reason why the Soviet Union was so much in favour of German unity. If Germany as a whole were to opt for the Soviet Union, the latter would gain a decisive advantage over the United States in the struggle for power over Europe. Given the enormous sacrifices it had made in the war against Hitler's Germany, the Soviet Union thought it held a good position to gain the favour of the German population. Its own occupation zone constituted a sound base for achieving this ultimate goal. The Soviet Union was convinced that the Communist Party of Germany (KPD) could play a crucial role in this context. It would have to run the new socialist unity party (SED), in which the KPD and the East German Social Democratic Party (SPD) were to merge. This SED 'would then solicit the allegiance of Social Democrats and other sympathetic Germans in the west, and by these means bring about unification' (Gaddis 1997, p. 116).

However, the struggle of the German Communist leaders for the favour of the German population was a lost cause from the very beginning. The fact that Soviet soldiers plundered the country and raped the women on a large scale in the first two years of the occupation certainly did not enhance the Soviet Union's popularity. Nor were the Germans very pleased with the Soviet Union handing the 'Eastern Territories' over to Poland (cf. Gaddis 1997, pp. 116 and 119).

Moreover, economically speaking, the Soviet Union had the handicap that it had nothing to offer Germany. This was mainly due to the third objective of the Soviet policy towards Germany, i.e. to obtain the largest reparations possible for the recovery of the Soviet economy. Insofar as the Soviet Union depended on the cooperation of the other occupying powers in this respect, this meant that it stubbornly clung to its view that no progress could be made in the negotiations concerning the German question as long as no agreement was reached on the amount and distribution of the reparations. Where the Soviet Union itself had full control over this matter, i.e. in its own zone, this policy led to the large-scale dismantling of the existing industry and infrastructure. Naturally, this had very serious consequences for the standard of living in the Soviet zone and, subsequently, for the Soviet Unions's chances of success in winning Germany over to its cause. Although bringing the whole of Germany within the Soviet sphere of influence was a long-term ideal, it was very doubtful whether this could actually be realized. As for the means with which the Soviet Union might restore its economy, these were literally there for the taking in its own occupation zone. This was a temptation it could not resist. In actual practice, the objective of obtaining the largest reparations possible soon prevailed. During the first years after the war, the Red Army's main occupation was the dismantling and transportation of railway equipment, machines, installations and even complete factories for the reconstruction of the Soviet Union (cf. Kennedy-Pipe 1995, pp. 95–6 and 134–5), although the Soviet Union had assured the East German Communist leaders in January 1947 that the reparations would be cancelled if they hampered the economic recovery in the Soviet zone (cf. Mastny 1996, p. 25).

2.4. Security through Subordination: French Policy with Respect to Germany

The French policy with respect to Germany in the first years after World War II can be characterized as a determined attempt 'to escape from history', as Furniss so adequately put it (cf. Furniss 1960, p. x). The memory of the century and a half in which France fell into decline and Germany rose to prominence had to be obliterated by making the now smaller and decentralized Germany, which also had to pay considerable reparations, subordinate to France. The destruction of the German unitary state, the separation of the Rhineland from Germany, the internationalization of the Ruhr Basin and the French annexation of the Saarland were all part of a policy aimed at restoring France to its rightful position as the most important Western European power and the Rhine as the 'natural' border of France.[11] In the French view, the occupation zone was primarily there to be exploited. The French were certainly very successful in doing so in the early years of the occupation.

France initially tried to gain support for its policy towards Germany by setting itself up as a mediator between the Soviet Union and the United States in the hopes of obtaining the appreciation of one or, even better, of both of them (cf. Lerner and Aron 1957). However, France totally lacked the power to play that role convincingly. Moreover, France's policy of subordination and partitioning could not be brought into line with what the two powers had in mind for Germany. After Byrnes had rejected the French policy in the speech he delivered in Stuttgart, Molotov did the same at the conference of foreign ministers in Moscow. At the end of March 1947, he criticized plans that 'have as a goal the destruction or the weakening of the German state' and distanced himself from the idea of a federal Germany. Molotov also rejected France's claims on the Saarland (cf. Wall 1991, p. 66). From that moment on, France grudgingly began to seek a rapprochement with the United States. As things stood, the French view was that the subordination of Germany could still be realized by a rapid restoration of the French economy and military potential. As far as economic and military support was concerned, the French knew very well that they could expect much more from the United States than from the Soviet Union.

A central issue in the French policy of economic recovery was the plan for the modernization of the French economy as formulated by a group of civil servants under the supervision of Monnet. This plan was aimed at improving the international competitive position of the French economy, particularly with respect to Germany. The French coal and steel industries were two of the spearheads in the plan. However, the objectives for these sectors could be realized only if France was to succeed in making the German coal and steel industries subservient to its needs – 'far from being based on a liberal internationalism, the Monnet Plan was based on the crudest possible expression of mercantilist principles. It was aimed at seizing German resources in order to capture German markets' (Milward 1984, p. 137; cf. Lynch 1984 and Milward 1992, pp. 334–5).[12]

3. An Unintended Outcome: the Foundation of the Federal Republic of Germany

In the course of 1947, relations between the Soviet Union and the other occupying powers deteriorated more and more. Consequently, the chances of signing a peace treaty with Germany in the short term became very slim. In mid-January 1948 Great Britain took the initiative and called for a Six-Power conference (the United States, France, Great Britain and the Benelux countries), at which the whole spectrum of German long-term and short-term problems would be discussed (cf. Ireland 1981, p. 62). This conference was held in London at the end of February 1948. It actually consisted of three subconferences. At the first, the parties discussed the way in which the Marshall Plan should be implemented (see Chapter 4, Section 3). At the second, they mainly concerned themselves with the establishment of a Western European security system (see Chapter 5, Section 2). And at the third subconference – which will be discussed in this section – they tried to find a solution for the position of Germany.

The most important subjects of discussion at the third subconference were the possible integration of the French occupation zone into the Bizone, the position of the Ruhr Basin, and the future political structure of that part of Germany which had been placed under the authority of the Western allies. Negotiations on these questions revolved around the old familiar problem of 'how Germany – or at least the western zones – might contribute to the recovery of Europe without at the same time becoming an economic and political threat again to the neighbouring countries' (Krieger 1987, p. 329). The United States wanted Germany to be given control over its own affairs again as soon as possible. Great Britain agreed to such a policy,[13] but simultaneously tried to protect its own heavy industry from German competition. France was, of course, vehemently opposed to the American policy. The entire conference on the position of Germany – which would drag on until the end of December 1948 – in fact consisted of a series of French rearguard actions meant to save as much as possible of the earlier French policy aimed at subordinating Germany.[14]

France initially refused to negotiate on the integration of the French zone into the Bizone. According to the French, the parties concerned should first reach agreement on the internationalization of the coal and steel industries in the Ruhr Basin (at least as far as management was concerned; the French regarded the question of ownership as something that could be dealt with later). The United States, however, did not agree. If France was not prepared to start negotiations on the integration of the zones, the United States threatened to exclude the French occupation zone from Marshall aid. At the same time, however, the United States and Great Britain met France's demands with respect to the internationalization of the Ruhr industry to the extent that they agreed to the establishment of an international authority which would gain control over the distribution 'between German consumption and export' of the coal, coke and steel produced in the Ruhr Basin. The International Authority for the Ruhr (IAR) would have to safeguard 'adequate access to supplies of these products, taking into account the essential needs of Germany'. In this control body, each of the three occupying powers and

Germany were to have three votes (for the time being, however, Germany would be represented by the occupation authorities) and each of the Benelux countries one vote. Resolutions would be adopted by majority vote (cf. Department of State 1973, p. 286). Furthermore, the IAR would begin to operate before the formation of a provisional West German government. In response to the American-British proposal, and with a view to a rapid integration of the zones, France agreed that the military governors would start talks on how they should harmonize their economic policies, and that currency reforms would be carried out in the three zones, which was something the French had always opposed.

However, France did find a willing ear for its objections to that part of the American-British proposal aimed at forming a provisional West German government for the three zones as quickly as possible. The United States and Great Britain adopted the French view that such a government could only be formed after a legislative assembly had drawn up a constitution.

On 1 June 1948, negotiations in London were concluded with the signing of a number of agreements. The French government, however, feared the final results would find no mercy in the eyes of the French public.[15] It therefore initially refused to sign the agreements. After the United States and Great Britain had put pressure on it, the French government decided to submit the agreements to the National Assembly, where they were subsequently ratified by a bare majority.

The day after the French parliament had approved the results of the London Conference on Germany, currency reforms were announced in the three western occupation zones, with the exception of Berlin. In response, the Soviet Union declared that it would also implement monetary reforms in its zone, including Berlin. The Western allies thereupon decided that the new West German currency could also be used as legal tender in their Berlin zones. The very next day, Soviet troops blocked all the railways and roads leading from the Western zones to Berlin. This blockade was to last for almost a year, without the Soviet Union gaining anything from it.

The implementation of the measures which needed to be taken to transform the three western occupation zones into a single West German entity did not go very smoothly. It was only in December 1948 that the United States, Great Britain and France started negotiations on the integration of the French zone into the Bizone and an occupation statute, which would be in force until a peace treaty was signed with Germany. It was not until April 1949 that the Western allies finally reached agreement on the conditions for the integration and the text of the statute. An allied High Commission consisting of one American, one Frenchman and one Briton would have supreme authority over

West Germany. The West German government to be formed would be given full legislative, executive and judicial power – within the limits of the new West German constitution – over all those matters that did not fall within the competence of the occupation authorities. The powers of the High Commission were extensive. The Western allies furthermore agreed that the Occupation Statute would be reviewed within one and a half years of its coming into force with a view to a further extension of the powers of the West German authorities.

Negotiations on the IAR also proceeded with considerable difficulty. It was only in November 1948 that the powers involved came together again in London to find a way out of the impasse that had arisen due to the fact that the French National Assembly, when it ratified the London agreements, had stipulated that the French government should reopen the discussion on the internationalization of the management of the mines and basic industries of the Ruhr Basin at meetings where the details of the IAR agreement would be worked out. However, the United States and the other powers involved did not want the IAR to be anything more than a control body. At the many formal and informal meetings France only managed to win agreement that a number of concessions were made with respect to minor issues. In the last week of December the exhausted negotiators finally approved the draft statutes of the IAR. Nonetheless, they reopened the negotiations in January as there were still various details that needed to be settled as well as many differences of interpretation concerning certain parts of the text that had been approved in December.[16] The final settlement was reached at the end of April 1949; the IAR was subsequently established in Düsseldorf at the beginning of August.

Drawing up a constitution for West Germany also proved a difficult and time-consuming affair. On 1 July 1948, the military governors submitted the directives regarding the future political organization of Germany to the prime ministers of the West German *Länder*. It soon became clear that the prime ministers were not entirely happy with the idea of West Germany having its own constitution. Their greatest fear was that such a constitution would mean the *de facto* division of Germany. For the same reason they disapproved of submitting it to the West German population for approval. The compromise finally reached between the Western allies and the West German authorities was that, instead of a Legislative Assembly drawing up a constitution, a Parliamentary Council would lay down a Basic Law. They also agreed that the outcome of the deliberations should be submitted to the parliaments of the *Länder* for approval. The Parliamentary Council first met in September 1948 and chose Adenauer as its chairman.

The final text of the Basic Law was approved by the Parliamentary Council on 8 May 1949, and subsequently accepted by the military governors on 12 May. On that same day, the latter also promulgated the Occupation Statute, which would take effect as of 21 September 1949. The formal signing of the Basic Law by the prime ministers of the federal states took place a few days later. At the beginning of September 1949, Heuss was elected as the first president of the Federal Republic, and Adenauer as the first chancellor.[17]

The first official meeting between the allied High Commission and a delegation of the new West German government led by Adenauer took place on the Petersberg near Bonn on 21 September. The atmosphere there was tense, particularly because the High Commission wanted to make it very clear to Adenauer that 'he was completely dependent on the more or less good intentions and decisions of the three Western powers' (Baring 1969, p. 66). But that was something Adenauer already entirely understood. In his first government policy statement in the *Bundestag*, he emphasized that 'the only way to regain our freedom is by trying to extend our freedom and powers step by step in consultation with the allied High Commission' (Baring 1969, p. 63).

The Russian answer to the foundation of the Federal Republic was the transformation of the Russian occupation zone into the German Democratic Republic, founded on 11 October 1949. Thus, the division of Germany became an established fact.

The American policy aimed at restoring the German economy as quickly as possible and the Russian policy of exploiting that economy to the fullest extent led to a solution of the German problem which no one had in mind in 1945. As a result of the partition, Germany no longer constituted a threat to the independence of the powers that were part of the European states system. However, the fall of Germany also brought down the European balance of power, for the bipolar balance that replaced it was partly supported by a non-European power: the United States.

4. The Position of the Federal Republic of Germany in International Law

4.1. A State without Central Authority

The last thing I want to do is to deny the fundamental importance of general theoretical notions of why things are as they are in international politics for getting *some* grip on the development of the Western European cooperation in the period 1947–1957 – no matter whether these concepts are stated explicitly, as in the previous chapter, or remain implicit, as is the working method of most historians. However, it should be noted that it is virtually impossible to get an *adequate* grip on this process using only these notions. This can only be achieved if one takes into account the idiosyncratic circumstance that the Federal Republic was not a sovereign state throughout that entire period.[18] My historical account of the struggle for the organization of Europe would therefore not be complete without my paying some attention to the position of the Federal Republic in international law. This position is a derivative of the position allocated to Germany by the victorious allied powers following its unconditional capitulation on 8 May 1945 and the occupation of the German territory by the United States, the Soviet Union, Great Britain and France. On 5 June 1945, in the Declaration of Berlin, the occupation authorities confirmed Germany's unconditional surrender and announced that they would assume supreme authority over Germany. They subsequently established the Control Council by proclamation on 30 August 1945. To this body they transferred supreme authority with respect to matters concerning Germany as a whole.

Experts on international law are generally of the opinion that Germany continued to exist as a state, despite its unconditional surrender, military occupation and division into four occupation zones. There are three arguments that seem to justify this interpretation. The first is that the situation had never been such that the authority of the state was completely dissolved. Although government had been terminated at the national level, it nevertheless remained operative to some extent at the local level. Moreover, almost immediately after the beginning of the occupation, local government was reorganized at the level of the *Länder*. In addition, the question remains whether a temporary suspension of a state's authority during an occupation period will inevitably lead to the end of that state. This was not the case in Austria in the period 1938–1945, nor in Poland in the period 1939–1945. The unconditional surrender had no effect on the existence of Germany. The preamble of the Declaration of Berlin revealed that the occupying powers intended to place Germany under their 'trusteeship' (cf. Van Ooijen *et al.* 1996, p. 11).

The second argument is that the German people and German nationality continued to exist. Other states continued to recognize German nationality. In 1946, for example, the English Court of Appeal ruled that the German state existed and that the German complainant Küchenmeister therefore had no case, as he was still considered to be an enemy alien.

The third argument used to prove that Germany continued to exist as a state is that, following the unconditional capitulation, the territory of the German *Reich* had not become the territory of the occupying powers. With the exception of the area around Königsberg in East Prussia, no part of the German territory had been annexed. Of course, the allies did decide in

September 1944 that Germany would have to give up the territories that it had annexed itself since 1938. When the occupation authorities spoke of 'Germany', they meant Germany as it existed 'within the borders of 31 December 1937'.

4.2. The Occupation Statute

The Occupation Statute, which was promulgated on 8 April 1949 and implemented on 21 September 1949, had to create some room for the West German state to function independently without affecting the foundations of the occupation as laid down in the Declaration of Berlin. In this statute the United States, Great Britain and France first confirmed that supreme authority would remain theirs and that the occupation was to continue. They subsequently declared that they intended to allow the German people the greatest possible degree of self-government insofar as this was reconcilable with the occupation. Furthermore, they clung to their role of 'trustee'. 'In order to ensure the accomplishment of the basic purposes of the occupation', they reserved for themselves certain powers with respect to a whole list of policy areas. These policy areas were specified in Article 2 of the statute. These involved disarmament and demilitarization, supervision of the Ruhr Basin, decartelization and deconcentration (see Chapter 6), compensations and reparations, foreign affairs and foreign trade, refugee problems, security of allied troops, reimbursement of the costs of the occupation and defence of the Basic Law and constitutions of the *Länder*. Within these limits, the Federal Republic and the participating *Länder* would possess 'full legislative, executive and judicial powers in accordance with the Basic Law and with their respective constitutions' (Article 1). At the same time, the occupation authorities reserved for themselves the right 'to resume, in whole or in part, the exercise of full authority if they consider that to do so is essential to security or to preserve democratic government in Germany or in pursuance of the international obligations of their governments' (Article 3) (cf. Van Ooijen *et al.* 1996, p. 15). This was a clause that filled Chancellor Adenauer with dread, as I will explain in the following section.

Finally, the occupying powers stipulated in Article 9 that, no later than eighteen months after the implementation of the Occupation Statute, they would evaluate its effects with a view to extending the powers of the West German authorities. This 'small revision' took place in March 1951. One of the results of this revision was that the Federal Republic regained the responsibility for the conduct of foreign relations.

5. Reconciliation through Integration and Equality

If ever there was one person in the history of the struggle for the organization of Europe for whom the decision-making process had been so pre-structured (cf. Chapter 2, Section 2) that he was time and again in the position to change its course decisively in the direction he deemed desirable, it was West German Chancellor Adenauer. The Federal Republic's 'German policy' in the period 1949–1957 was largely Adenauer's policy. Adenauer's 'window of opportunity' was the result of the role West Germany's Basic Law had assigned to the chancellor and the role he had to play according to the High Commission in its relation to the Federal Republic.

In the light of experiences with the Republic of Weimar, those who drew up the Basic Law intended to strengthen the government's position *vis-à-vis* both the president and parliament. Furthermore, they gave the chancellor a dominant position in the government. It is for this reason that Baring typifies the Federal Republic as a 'chancellor democracy' (cf. Baring 1969). The chancellor determined and bore the responsibility for policy guidelines (*Richt-linienkompetenz*). In accordance with these guidelines, each of the ministers had his own responsibility for managing his department independently. Parliament could not bring down individual ministers. It could only bring down the chancellor. This it could do by means of a 'constructive motion of no confidence'. This procedure required that the parliament could dismiss the chancellor only if it had been able to appoint a successor.

In foreign policy, the chancellor's position of power became even stronger, because the High Commission regarded him as the sole intermediary in all matters concerning the Federal Republic as a whole, such as foreign relations. In these matters, Adenauer, therefore, had in fact full control over the action and information channels between the High Commission on the one hand and the Federal Republic on the other. All communication lines between West Germany and other countries, which officially fell under the authority of the High Commission, ran accordingly via the chancellor. Following the small revision of the statute in March 1951, Adenauer still managed to maintain a full grasp on West Germany's foreign policy for a number of years by combining the position of chancellor with that of minister of foreign affairs up to one month after the termination of the occupation regime on 5 May 1955.

It was Adenauer's firm belief that the recovery of West Germany could only take place within the context of a European policy containing the following three elements, which were inextricably linked: reconciliation with France, *Westbindung* ('binding to the West') and *Gleichberechtigung* ('equal treatment'). Of these three elements, reconciliation with France certainly had the highest priority for Adenauer. Thanks to his. determination to bring about the Franco-German reconciliation, his European policy did more than just seek the gratification of West Germany's self-interest. In this respect, the Chancellor fully understood France's quest for security. As he stated in a speech in March 1946, 'a solution to the German question had to be found that was organic and natural and that would therefore be durable; a solution which would reassure our western neighbours and give them a feeling of lasting security' (Adenauer 1966a, p. 36). At the same time, Adenauer was of the opinion that this reconciliation could succeed only if it took place within strong institutional frameworks in which the Federal Republic would participate on an equal footing with the other Western European powers.

The *Westbindung*, i.e. the incorporation of the Federal Republic in institutional arrangements enabling the other Western European powers to exert control over it, might then be used as a means to satisfy the justified desire for security, and, ultimately, to take away the distrust which many countries nourished with respect to the Federal Republic. The *Westbindung* also served a purpose from which West Germany might benefit: it would make it impossible for West Germany to fall back on the traditional *Schaukelpolitik* ('seesaw policy'), which it used to play East and West out against one another, and which Adenauer saw as the true cause of Germany's downfall (cf. Baring 1969, p. 57).[19] For the same reason, Adenauer did not think the time was ripe to discuss the reunification of the two Germanies. He was convinced that a reunified Germany would cease to be a threat to peace only after the *Westbindung* had been fully realized, making a seesaw policy forever impossible.[20] In this respect, Hanrieder rightly speaks of the confluence of 'necessity and choice' (cf. Hanrieder 1989, p. 337). Given the political constellation in Europe in the fifties, the Federal Republic had no choice but to integrate into Western Europe, but Adenauer would not have wanted it any other way.

A very important additional reason for Adenauer attaching so much value to the *Westbindung* was the following. His greatest fear was that, after some time, the victors would come to a mutual agreement at the expense of the Federal Republic and subsequently force the result of the negotiations upon it, having come to the conclusion that the question of the German peace treaty was an obstacle to settling other more important matters, and that the whole affair had dragged on long enough (cf. Joffe in Macridis [1958] 1989, p. 83). In the light of the text of the Occupation Statute, such a development was not inconceivable. It has already been mentioned above that, in Article 3, the occupation authorities had left open the possibility that they would resume, in whole or in part, the exercise of full authority, not only if the security or democracy in Germany was threatened, but also if the international obligations of their governments necessitated it. (Is it too far-fetched to think in this respect of obligations resulting from an agreement on Germany with the Soviet Union?) In Adenauer's view the deep embedding of the Federal Republic in Western Europe was also meant to reduce the chances of such a disastrous outcome as much as possible. By means of the *Westbindung*, the West German rump state could convince the Western allies of its great value as an ally, so that they would think twice before sacrificing the Federal Republic in order to reach an agreement with the Soviet Union on Germany as a whole (cf. Niedhart 1986, p. 169).

The third element in Adenauer's 'German policy' was the *Gleichberechtigung*, which also implied regaining the status of sovereign state. Of the three elements, this was the most obvious one, and therefore also often created considerable difficulties in the negotiations with the other states. This was undoubtedly so because this element could be directly related to West Germany's self-interest. However, Adenauer insisted on *Gleichberechtigung*, although he was willing time after time to interpret this objective in its broadest sense (see for example Chapter 7, Section 5 and Chapter 8, Section 3). In the new institutions to be formed, which had to bind the Federal Republic to Western Europe, it was to participate on an equal footing with the other powers and not from a subordinate position: without equality there would be no 'self-binding', and without 'self-binding' no reconciliation.

Notes

1. To those who are familiar with Schroeder's *The Transformation of European Politics 1763–1848*, it will be clear that the previous two paragraphs were inspired by this work (cf. Schroeder [1994] 1996).
2. From this point of view, World War II was certainly 'by far the fundamental international event of the twentieth century. Europe has been adapting to its consequences ever since' (DePorte [1978] 1986, p. 19). In line with this view, there is also a great deal to be said in favour of the idea of regarding the two world wars as one great world war, interrupted by an exceptionally long truce of more than twenty years in which there was a continuous threat that the hostilities would be resumed and in which the powers involved dragged themselves from crisis to crisis (cf. Carr's introduction to international relations *The Twenty Years' Crisis, 1919–1939*; Carr [1939] 1964). Moreover, this point of view seems to be the most compelling one with the passing of the years. Davies even speaks of 'the seventy-five years' European civil war of 1914–1989' (cf. Davies 1996, p. 14).

3. At the Tehran Conference in November 1943, Roosevelt and Stalin came to the conclusion that 'France after the war could not be restored to Great Power status. For Stalin the Vichy regime represented the "real" France; FDR agreed, and declared that no Frenchman over age 40 should be allowed to participate in the administration of his country: They were all corrupt. "The first necessity for the French, not only for the government but for the people as well, was to become honest citizens"' (Wall 1991, p. 27). Krieger too points out that the United States 'saw the collapse of France in 1940 as a major example of a serious threat to Europe. The defeat of France was not just regarded as a consequence of "Munich", that is to say, as the foreign policy of an expansionist dictator, but also as a result of defects in the internal structure of France' (Krieger 1987, p. 17).

4. At the beginning of April 1945, France stated its demands with respect to the size of the French occupation zone: the left bank of the Rhine up to Cologne, plus the federal states of Hessen-Nassau, Hessen-Kassel, Hessen-Darmstadt and Baden. Eventually, the British and Americans reached agreement with the French on the following. France would get the Saarland, the Palatinate, the former Rhine province up to Remagen, southern Baden and southern Württemberg, the Lindau district, which connected the French occupation zone in Germany to the one in Austria, and the four districts of Hessen on the right bank of the Rhine.

5. At this conference Great Britain and the United States also accepted the Soviet Union's annexation of the area around Königsberg in East Prussia and, in anticipation of a final peace treaty, they resigned themselves to the Soviet Union handing part of its occupation zone over to Poland.

6. Cf. Yergin: 'Although it is a point befogged by the haze of recollections and the scrambling of chronologies, Germany, the most important of all European questions, did not become a subject of real contention until well into the spring of 1946' (Yergin 1977, p. 226; cf. Mastny 1996, p. 24).

7. According to the prominent diplomat George Kennan, it was essential for the United States that 'no single Continental land power should come to dominate the entire Eurasian land mass. Our interest has lain rather in the maintenance of some sort of stable balance among the powers of the interior, in order that none of them should effect the subjugation of the others, conquer the seafaring fringes of the land mass, become a great sea power as well as land power, shatter the position of England, and enter – as in these circumstances it certainly would – on an overseas expansion hostile to ourselves and supported by the immense resources of the interior of Europe and Asia' (Kennan [1951] 1952, p. 11).

    More than thirty years later, on the basis of a study of the relevant archives, Leffler came to the conclusion that 'from the closing days of World War II, American defense officials believed that they could not allow any prospective adversary to control the Eurasian land mass. This was the lesson taught by two world wars. Strategic thinkers and military analysts insisted that any power or powers attempting to dominate Eurasia must be regarded as potentially hostile to the United States' (Leffler 1984, p. 356).

8. In the autumn of 1945, Great Britain was, however, in favour of an independent

Ruhr state under international supervision, as advocated by France. Six months later, it reconsidered this position. In mid-April 1946, the British cabinet decided not to support the French demands after all. The most important reasons for this change was, firstly, that support for the French plan would lead to a conflict with the United States and the Soviet Union, only to result in an extension of the occupation – whereas the costs of the occupation already threatened to get out of hand – and, secondly, that the disintegration of Germany involved great dangers, which France would not be able to ward off, as it was too weak to do so (cf. Greenwood 1983).

9. An additional complication was that the United States regarded the possible fast recovery of the German coal and steel industries mainly in relation to the general interest of European reconstruction, whereas Great Britain – and the same goes for France – was primarily concerned with its own coal and steel industries, for which it was important that the German competitors would remain cut out as long as possible.

10. Cf. Lademacher: 'Nothing was actually so perfectly clear as the pressure exerted by the Americans, who were not afraid to resort to threats, pressed for a compromise, but aimed at making the British give up the idea of socialization. The British succumbed to this pressure, or rather, had to succumb to it' (in Scharf and Schröder 1979, p. 91).

11. For the sake of completeness: the French view was that the Rhineland north of Cologne should be placed under Belgian, Dutch and British authority. In September 1945, General de Gaulle, the leader of the French provisional government, justified the French demands by arguing that 'Germany was amputated in the east but not in the west. The current of German vitality is thus turned westwards. One day German aggressiveness might well face westwards too. There must therefore be in the west a settlement counterbalancing that in the east' (Willis [1965] 1968, p. 15). In that same month, in a memorandum sent to the other occupation authorities, France referred to 'the great importance it attaches to the fact that the Rhineland-Westphalia region will in future no longer form an arsenal, a corridor or point of departure for Germany to attack its western neighbours. It is of the opinion that the final separation between that region (including the Ruhr) and Germany, necessary to protect the French border, constitutes, among other things, the essential condition for the security of Europe and the whole world' (Ruhm von Oppen 1955, p. 68).

12. Duchêne partly agrees with Milward and Lynch when he observes that France's diplomats had indeed entertained the idea that 'France should fill the industrial void left by Germany's defeat and become the manufacturing core of continental Western Europe', but that Monnet and his staff 'never seem to have invested in such ideas. The steel targets of the Monnet Plan of November 1946, though with an appetite for Ruhr coal and coke, were not consonant with ambitions to replace its heavy industry' (Duchêne 1994, pp. 183–4).

13. In February 1948, in Frankfurt, the United States and Great Britain established the *Wirtschaftsrat* ('Economic Council'), which would be responsible for economic

policy in the Bizone. This council consisted of an executive and legislative body in which the 'democratic' parties – the CDU/CSU and FDP – had a majority.

14. The Soviet Union strongly objected to the deliberations in London. At a meeting of the Control Council at the end of March, Marshall Sokolovski, who was chairman of the Council at the time, asked for some explanation. General Clay, who had just returned from London, refused to honour this request. In response to this, Sokolovski stated that 'the Control Council is no longer a government body' and left the meeting 'without formally declaring the meeting closed' (Krieger 1987, p. 343).

15. At the end of April, Georges Bidault, the French foreign minister, had already explained it to the American ambassador in Paris: 'Don't make it too hard for me. I'll have to face the Assembly and given the attitude of the Communists, the Gaullists, and the Socialists, I don't know how we will come out. Tell your government I am on your side and in the long run we will work something satisfactory out, but at the same time I must think about public opinion here' (Yergin 1977, p. 370).

16. The duration and complexity of the negotiations made Milward remark: 'As for the constitution and powers of the International Authority for the Ruhr, few bodies can have been argued about for so long which in the end did so little' (Milward 1984, p. 153).

17. Adenauer was elected by a majority of one vote: his own. In his memoirs he commented: 'anything else would, of course, have been hypocrisy' (Adenauer 1967, p. 222).

18. It may perhaps surprise the reader that I do not consider the Federal Republic to have been a sovereign state, even after the termination of the occupation regime in May 1955. This interpretation seems to me justified given the fact that the United States, France and Great Britain at the time reserved for themselves certain rights with respect to: (1) stationing troops in Germany, (2) Berlin, and (3) Germany as a whole, including the reunification of the two Germanies and a peace treaty. Moreover, it is in my opinion supported by the text of Article 7 of the Treaty of Moscow 'on the final settlement with respect to Germany' of September 1990. In the first paragraph of this Article, it is stated that the Soviet Union, France, the United States and Great Britain 'terminate their rights and responsibilities relating to Berlin and to Germany as a whole', and subsequently in the second paragraph that 'the United Germany shall have accordingly full sovereignty over its internal and external affairs' (Van Ooijen *et al.* 1996, pp. 39 and 47).

19. As Herbert Blankenhorn, one of Adenauer's closest associates during this period, wrote in his memoirs: 'He knew that he would only succeed if Germany did not fall into the old mistake of pursuing a "seesaw policy" between West and East and thus isolate itself by creating suspicion all around. For the same reason he rejected the neutralization of the country; despite all guarantees, a vacuum in Central Europe would in his opinion not be able to remain free and independent' (Blankenhorn 1980, p. 50).

20. Cf. Joffe: 'In 1966 Adenauer was asked: "Let us assume, though, that a reunified and neutral Germany had been possible, would you have wanted it?" Adenauer's answer was an emphatic "No, never." As curt as this reply was, it probably contains the most concise explanation for the course of West German foreign policy in his thirteen-year tenure' (Joffe in Macridis [1958] 1989, pp. 80–1).

4. The Might of the Dollar: from Marshall Plan to OEEC

1. The Marshall Plan

The idea of an Organization for European Economic Cooperation (OEEC) originated in the spring of 1947 when American policy-makers had become convinced that the economic situation in Europe had deteriorated so dramatically in the winter of 1946 – particularly in France and Germany – that any hope of a lasting European recovery was about to be shattered. The Americans feared that the terrifying vision of Western Europe falling like a ripe fruit into the lap of the Soviet Union would become reality. The American administration decided to take action on the basis of two reports – one written by William Clayton, the American Under-Secretary for Economic Affairs, after a visit to Europe, and the other drawn up by the so-called Policy Planning Staff of the State Department under Kennan's supervision. Aid to the suffering European economies would no longer be provided on the basis of *ad-hoc* decisions, but within the context of an extensive, structured aid programme scheduled for several years.

In the American plan it was crucial that the European powers themselves should take the initiative in drawing up the programme and formulating priorities – although the United States did state that it was prepared to lend a helping hand in the process. As, in the American view, the reconstruction of Germany was essential to the economic recovery of Europe (see Chapter 3, Section 2), the United States also demanded that the German occupation zones be included in the programme. Furthermore, it stipulated that the offer applied to the whole of Europe, including the Soviet Union. This condition was mainly intended to make clear to the public, in the event that the Soviet Union rejected the offer – which many American policy-makers expected or hoped – which of the two powers would be responsible for the division of Europe: not the United States, which had offered aid, but the Soviet Union, which had rejected the offer (cf. Janis [1972] 1982, p. 162).

The American invitation to the European states to draw up an extensive aid programme themselves, for which the United States would furnish the funds, was extended by Secretary of State Marshall on 5 June 1947 almost as an aside in a speech delivered during a graduation ceremony at Harvard

University. The invitation was deliberately low-key – 'something between a hint and suggestion', as Marshall later remarked (cf. Ellwood 1992, p. 86) – to prevent it from immediately arousing opposition in Congress, given the large amount of American tax money involved (cf. Young 1984, p. 63). The wish to let sleeping dogs lie was so strong that, when Marshall began to speak, very few knew that he would make this offer to the European governments. To ensure that Marshall's speech would not go unnoticed, the British embassy was informed at the very last moment that Marshall was going to say something very important.[1]

The condition that the European states first had to reach agreement among themselves on the content of the programme before the United States would make the funds available was seen by the Americans as the ultimate means for creating a situation in which the Europeans could no longer get round taking the first steps towards economic integration. For the Americans it was almost an open-and-shut case: economic integration was the panacea for Europe's ills. American policy-makers saw the absence of a large European internal market as the obvious reason for that continent being plagued by an incessant stream of conflicts and a lasting economic weakness (cf. Hogan 1982, p. 277). For example, Republican senator Dulles had impressed on his audience at the beginning of January 1947 that 'a Europe divided into small compartments could not be a healthy Europe' (Hogan 1982, p. 275).[2] The United States expected to be able to put the European states on the right track towards economic integration by demanding that they jointly formulate the European economic priorities when elaborating the Marshall Plan. The European powers certainly needed an incentive in this respect, because they would do little of their own accord to bring about European integration. They were preparing themselves for a new period of competition and struggle, and were entirely preoccupied with their ambition to restore their own economies and make their own position *vis-à-vis* the other European powers as strong as possible (cf. Ellwood 1988, p. 104).

2. American Ambitions and Western European Wishes

In response to Marshall's speech, Georges Bidault, the French foreign minister, invited his counterparts Bevin and Molotov for consultations in Paris, which started on 27 June 1947. It soon became clear that these would lead to nothing. The condition that the European powers had to formulate priorities together was unacceptable to the Soviet Union. It considered this an interference in its internal affairs that could not be reconciled with its position as a sovereign power. Molotov argued that it would be better if each of the

European powers determined for themselves how much American aid they needed and subsequently negotiated bilaterally with the United States on the conditions under which this aid might be provided. Bevin and Bidault rejected the Soviet point of view and, after a few days of fruitless discussion, Molotov broke off the talks on 2 July. On the following day, the British and French ministers of foreign affairs invited the other European states to send delegations to Paris for a conference on how Marshall's offer might be realized (cf. Young 1984, p. 64 and Hogan 1982, p. 284).

Notwithstanding their willingness to start negotiations on a joint European request for aid in response to the American offer, the French and British authorities actually harboured the same feelings about the plan's multilateral aspects as their Soviet counterparts.[3] At the preparatory talks for the Paris conference, the French and British delegations soon agreed that the main purpose of the conference should be to render the far-reaching American plans for Europe as harmless as possible without jeopardizing the provision of aid (cf. Milward 1984, p. 66).

The conference of the Committee of European Economic Cooperation (CEEC) started on 12 July and was chaired by Bevin. According to the deputy head of the French delegation, Marjolin, the sixteen participating countries did not have any well-defined ideas about what to do at the time (cf. Marjolin 1989, p. 182).[4] Nonetheless, a far-reaching decision was made on the opening day. The participants agreed with the American point of view that reintegration of the German economy into Europe was a prerequisite for raising the level of prosperity in Europe, and that the Western occupation zones therefore had to be incorporated in the European recovery programme. At the same time, however, they decided that the occupation zones should not be represented in any way at the conference (cf. Milward 1984, p. 70).

The differences between the Americans and the Europeans became very clear during the negotiations. In the first few weeks after Marshall had made his speech, the American policy-makers elaborating the plan came to the conclusion that the Europeans needed an additional incentive to realize a united Europe. Therefore, the United States set the additional condition that the American aid programme could only be implemented once the European powers agreed to establish a permanent organization to be entrusted with the coordination and promotion of European economic cooperation. However, the Europeans did not want to have anything to do with American ambitions concerning Europe. The only thing the sixteen European conference particip-ants had in common was that they had all come to Paris to carry off as many American dollars as possible for their own economies. In this context they were prepared to pay lip-service to the American European ideal, for want of a better alternative, but that was as far as they would go. The worst possible outcome for the United States would be that the whole aid programme did not get off the ground, whereas the European countries preferred not to receive any aid at all if it meant that they had first to establish a supranational organization.

Since the United States lacked any further credible means to make the European conference participants change their minds, it is quite understandable in the light of the above-mentioned orders of preference that the United States failed to bring the European countries into line and that it was forced to make a compromise. In early September, it became clear that the conference participants were moving towards submitting a common request for aid to the United States, one that, in reality, consisted of sixteen separate shopping lists for a total amount that largely exceeded the American estimate and did not leave any room for a permanent organization (cf. Milward 1984, pp. 80–1, and Wall 1991, p. 91). The United States refused to accept this outcome. It demanded that the conference draw up a new report better to meet the American conditions. The conference participants refused to do this. By the end of September, after a few weeks of heated discussions, the parties finally managed to reach a compromise. This involved the American negotiators accepting the report – in which only minor points had been revised – in exchange for the European countries' promise that they would establish a permanent European organization once the bill that regulated the aid programme had been passed by the American Congress.

3.   The First Permanent European Organization

At the London Conference on Germany which started at the end of February 1948 (see Chapter 3, Section 3), the participants confirmed that the West German occupation zones would be incorporated into the European aid programme. The participating European delegations also repeated their promise to establish a permanent European organization. The American Congress agreed to the recovery programme in April on the condition that it would be implemented only after the permanent organization had actually been established. A few days later, the sixteen countries involved reached agreement on the organizational structure and subsequently established the Organization for European Economic Cooperation (OEEC).

The first permanent European organization was entirely intergovernmental in nature. The decision-making body was the Council of Ministers, which could only make decisions by unanimous vote. An Executive Committee, in which the ministers were represented by officials, was charged with the day-to-day management. There was also a Secretary-General, but he was subordinate to the Council and the Executive Committee, and his principal duty was to see to it that the decisions made by these two bodies were executed properly. The United States would, of course, have liked to see this done differently. In the negotiations on organizational structure, France too argued in favour of introducing a certain supranational element. It proposed giving the Secretary-General some powers of his own and taking decisions by a majority of votes. However, Great Britain rejected every proposal in that direction. Consequently, France did not really insist on it. Whether or not the new organization would have any power was a question hardly anyone worried about now that all obstacles were removed and the Marshall aid programme could finally be implemented.

The American attempt to realize the much desired European unity had utterly failed, even though the United States had threatened to call off the proposed aid programme if the Europeans were not prepared to take the first steps in that direction. From a conversation which Chancellor Adenauer and High Commissioner McCloy had in October 1949, one may deduce that at least one prominent American policy-maker had learned something from this exercise in humility. When Adenauer remarked that 'the United States could force the European nations to unite by wielding its economic power', McCloy answered that 'No one would regret it more than he did if this unity could not be established; he believed, however, that the American dollar was not so mighty as to bring this about' (Blankenhorn 1980, p. 69).

Notes

1. Acheson, who was Under-Secretary of State at the time, wrote in his memoirs: 'Whether the General [i.e. Marshall] discussed the speech with the President and, if so, what they said, I do not know. It is hard to believe that they did not discuss it. It will also surprise many that the Secretary of State went off to deliver so momentous a speech with an incomplete text and never informed the Department of its final form' (Acheson 1969, p. 233). Kennan also belonged to those who were not informed beforehand. It was in the next day's papers that he learned of Marshall's speech (cf. Janis [1972] 1982, p. 167).
2. Cf. Ellwood: 'In the final analysis integration for the Europeans was the right solution to their problems because it had worked in America' (Ellwood 1992, p. 94).
3. Bevin in particular was opposed to the multilateral character of the plan. When Clayton came to London in June to explain the American initiative, a rather shocked Bevin told him at their first meeting that the new American policy 'of

providing aid to Western Europe as an integrated bloc rather than individual countries would mean that Great Britain would now be "just another European country"' (Milward 1984, p. 62). At their second meeting, Bevin again advocated a separate status for Great Britain. If Great Britain was to be nothing more than part of a common programme, this would mean the sacrifice of 'the little bit of dignity we have left' (Milward 1984, p. 63).

4. The following countries sent a delegation to the conference: France, Great Britain, Belgium, the Netherlands, Luxembourg, Denmark, Norway, Iceland, Sweden, Ireland, Switzerland, Austria, Portugal, Italy, Greece and Turkey. Poland and Czechoslovakia had announced that they would also attend, but they eventually declined due to pressure from the Soviet Union (cf. Gaddis 1997, pp. 41–2). The United States and Canada sent observers to the conference.

5. From Treaty to Organization: the Creation of NATO

1. Introduction

The North Atlantic Treaty Organization (NATO) has existed for so many years and has been so successful that nowadays Western Europeans as well as Americans cannot imagine a military alliance being formed any other way. The continuous, institutionalized consultations between the parties to the Treaty about the course to follow and the integrated command structure of NATO forces are now so familiar that hardly anyone realizes how different the organizational structure of NATO is from that of most other military alliances. Almost all such alliances involve loose coalitions of states, which usually last no longer than a few years and in which the participating states eventually decide for themselves how they will contribute to the realization of their common goal. NATO, however, represents a fundamental innovation in the field of international cooperation, as it is characterized by a considerable degree of collaboration and harmonization. Also, as a result of the integrated command structure, the implementation of policies has strong supranational elements. Ironically enough, this was the last thing the Americans had in mind when they signed the North Atlantic Treaty in Washington in April 1949. Entirely in accordance with American views, this Treaty was much more traditional in nature – and therefore much more noncommittal – than the organization that gradually took shape in the ensuing twenty months.

Before discussing how the Treaty of Washington came into being and how this 'traditional' treaty led to such an unusual organization as NATO, it may be useful to outline briefly how the strategic position of Western Europe was assessed by American, British and French policy-makers in the first years after World War II in the unlikely event of an attack by the Soviet Union, and what they thought would be the best response if such a calamity should take place.

The general opinion was that prior war efforts had affected the Soviet army's strength to such an extent that the Soviet Union could not possibly be preparing for an invasion of Western Europe. Nonetheless, the possibility could not be ruled out that the Soviet Union might

65

underestimate the American willingness to defend Western Europe and risk it anyway. If Soviet troops were to cross the River Elbe more or less 'by accident', it was thought that there were insufficient troops in Western Europe to hold off such an advance. There were, for example, only two American army divisions stationed in West Germany, which had been primarily assigned police tasks, and the United States had just one single division in reserve (cf. Osgood 1962, p. 29). The scenarios developed by the United States in 1947–1948 all provided for a withdrawal to a defence line in the Pyrenees, simultaneous air raids on targets in the Soviet Union and – if these could not force the Russians to their knees – landings in Western Europe similar to those carried out during World War II, with Great Britain and French Algeria serving as the main military bases. These actions would be the first steps towards the liberation of Western Europe.

The British shared the American view that the strategic position of Western Europe would be quite hopeless in the event of a Russian invasion. There were also not enough British troops to oppose a possible Russian offensive. France, however, refused to adopt such a passive attitude. As Henri Queuille, the French Prime Minister, stated to the American press in the early spring of 1949:

> We know that, should Western Europe be occupied, America would come again to our aid, and in the end we would again be liberated. But the consequences would be terrible. The next time you would probably be liberating a corpse, and civilization would probably be dead. No, invasion, if against all probability it should arise, must be stopped even before it begins. If we can count on sufficient force to prevent the Russian army from crossing the Elbe, then European civilization can breathe again. (Furniss 1960, p. 34; cf. Osgood 1962, p. 37)

The prospect of another occupation and another liberation was more than France could stomach.[1] It therefore would not countenance an initial withdrawal to the Pyrenees. France demanded that Western Europe be defended on German territory and that a substantial American military force play an active role in this defence (cf. Wall 1991, p. 132). The United States eventually agreed to the French demands, but the price that France had to pay was high. It had to accept the principle that West German troops would take part in the defence of Western Europe.

2. The Treaty of Brussels and the Vandenberg Resolution

2.1. A British Initiative

After the foreign ministers of the occupying powers again failed to reach agreement about the German question at their conference in November–December 1947, Bevin contacted Marshall on 17 December. The British minister not only proposed to his American colleague to start tripartite consultations between the United States, France and Great Britain about the future of Germany (see also Chapter 3, Section 3), but also to study how the United States could be more involved in the defence of Western Europe. During that same conversation, Marshall suggested proceeding in much the same manner as during the prior drafting of the European recovery programme, i.e. by developing a joint European initiative. Such an approach would certainly increase the chances of the American Congress responding favourably to such a request (cf. Young 1984, p. 79).

The multilateral approach proposed by Marshall was again received unfavourably by the British. When, in his speech to the British House of Commons at the end of January, Bevin advocated the need for a 'Western Union' to withstand the Soviet threat, he also indicated that such a union should be based on a network of bilateral treaties on mutual military assistance between, in the first instance, Great Britain, France and the Benelux countries (cf. Jansen and De Vree [1985] 1988, p. 76).[2] These treaties should basically have the same contents as the Treaty of Dunkirk signed by France and Great Britain in March 1947 to prevent a resurgence of German aggression.[3]

France responded favourably to Bevin's proposal, but the other intended parties to the Treaty, the Benelux countries, were opposed to it. They advocated the institution of a multilateral regional organization for collective self-defence in accordance with the Charter of the United Nations and modelled after the Treaty on Mutual Assistance signed by the American powers in September 1947, also known as the Rio Pact (cf. Spaak 1971, p. 147). The first American reactions to Bevin's ideas were, of course, negative. At a meeting with the head of the European Affairs Section of the State Department, the British ambassador was informed that the United States supported a European security pact modelled on the Rio Pact and that it would give sympathetic consideration to a European request for American participation in such an organization. The most important reason why the Americans took this stance was that the obligation to assist in Article 3 of the Inter-American Treaty on Mutual Assistance had been formulated so that, if any member state were the object of an armed attack, the others must provide this member state with assistance, regardless of who the attacker was (cf. Department of State 1974, pp. 10–11).[4] Unlike Great Britain's proposed network of treaties modelled on the Treaty of Dunkirk, a European security pact therefore did not have to be specifically aimed against Germany. This would make it easier in future to involve Germany in the defence of Western Europe – an objective that Bevin could fully endorse (cf. Department of State 1974, p. 5).

2.2.   The Treaty of Dunkirk: a Relic from the Past

After World War II, both the British and the French supported a mutual assistance treaty to counter renewed German aggression. However, conflicts over the Middle East and, in particular, Germany made the conclusion of such a treaty impossible at that moment. The French-British conflict over Germany had two aspects. The first concerned the British refusal to consider the French demand that such a treaty only be signed after Great Britain had accepted the French 'thesis' of a permanently subordinate, smaller, decentralized Germany (see Chapter 3, Section 2) (cf. Young 1984, p. 44). The second aspect was the amount of coal that France received from the British occupation zone. France wanted to see this amount considerably increased. To the French this aspect was eventually considered the most important.

During a consultation with the British ambassador at the end of December 1946, Léon Blum, the French Prime Minister, had emphatically stated that 'everything depended upon coal as far as France was concerned' (Greenwood 1983, p. 58). At the beginning of January 1947, he dropped the demand that Great Britain must first accept the French 'thesis' before a mutual assistance treaty could be signed. By making this goodwill gesture, he hoped to get Great Britain to adopt a less reserved attitude towards France's desire for larger coal supplies. However, the British negotiators saw the signing of such a treaty mainly as a gesture to prevent Great Britain having to supply extra coal to France. Blum was therefore unable to extract any promises from the British in this respect (cf. Greenwood 1983, p. 60).

Even though these beginnings did not bode well, the British and French negotiators reached an agreement on the content of the Treaty in just a few weeks. To avoid antagonizing the Soviet Union needlessly, they based the text of the Treaty on the texts of the mutual assistance treaties that Great Britain and France had concluded with the Soviet Union in 1942 and 1944 respectively. They also stated in the preamble that the Treaty was concluded in anticipation of a treaty between all the powers 'having responsibility for action in relation to Germany with the object of preventing Germany from again becoming a menace to peace' (Jansen and De Vree [1985] 1988, p. 75).

The Treaty was signed in Dunkirk on 4 March 1947. As the above explanation of the Treaty's background shows, it would be wrong to see the Treaty of Dunkirk as a first step towards the organization of Western European cooperation. The tenor of the Treaty was absolutely traditional. As a product of the 'old way of thinking' about how to achieve international cooperation, the Treaty was certainly no harbinger of a new approach. In the winter of 1946–1947, France and Great Britain had other things to think about (i.e. coal) than laying the foundations for a European institutional structure in which Germany would also be a partner.

2.3. The Prague Coup and the Brussels Conference

With respect to the organization of the Western Union proposed by Bevin, the views of Great Britain and France on the one hand, and those of the United States and the Benelux countries on the other, were so different that there were serious doubts as to whether the enterprise would succeed. However, the communist take-over in Czechoslovakia at the end of February 1948, known as the 'Prague Coup', soon brought the two camps together.

Since the 1946 elections, Czechoslovakia had been ruled by a coalition between the Communist Party and several democratic parties, with the Communist Gottwald as Prime Minister. As a protest against the appointment of eight Communists to key positions in the police by the Communist Minister of the Interior, a majority of eleven ministers tendered their resignation to President Beneš in February 1948 (the Social Democrats remained in office). Under pressure from demonstrating anti-Communist groups on the one hand and Communist action committees occupying public buildings in Prague on the other – all of whom were increasingly violent – Beneš accepted the ministers' resignation on 25 February and instructed Gottwald to form a new government. That very same day, Gottwald had already put together a cabinet dominated by Communists. The course of events was also greatly influenced by the fact that Zorin, the Russian Deputy Minister of Foreign Affairs, was in Prague and continually speculated aloud about possible armed intervention if the job of forming a new government were not given to a Communist.

In the eyes of the Western Europeans and Americans, the developments in Prague underscored not only the reality of the communist threat, but also

Western Europe's inability to cope with this threat on its own. The negotiations concerning the Western Union gained momentum after France made clear that it no longer insisted on a network of bilateral treaties. On 2 March, the American ambassador Caffery informed Marshall that Bidault 'has changed his point of view about treaties along the Dunkirk model and at this juncture is not particularly concerned about sticking to that formula'. According to the French foreign minister, it was of crucial importance at this point to form 'a concrete military alliance (against Soviet attack) with definite promises to do definite things under certain circumstances' (Department of State 1974, pp. 34–5).

The negotiations were initially carried on in the margin of the London Conference on Germany (see also Chapter 3, Section 3) and were subsequently completed in Brussels. On 17 March 1948, the Treaty of Economic, Social, and Cultural Collaboration and Collective Self-Defence – better known as the Brussels Treaty – was signed by France, Great Britain and the Benelux countries. The negotiations mainly revolved around the French demand that the Treaty make explicit reference to the German threat, even though France no longer objected to the obligation of mutual assistance being formulated in terms similar to those in the Rio Pact. The rather colourless compromise the negotiators finally reached was that the need to resist renewed German aggression was indeed mentioned, namely in the preamble and Article VII of the Treaty,[5] and that Article IV, the crucial article laying down the obligation of mutual assistance, was formulated in general terms. In this article, the signatories promised that, if one of them should 'be the object of an armed attack in Europe', the others would provide 'all the military and other aid and assistance in their power' (Van Ooijen *et al*. 1996, p. 52).

On the day the Treaty was signed, President Truman announced in a speech to the American Congress that he fully supported this initiative and that he was convinced 'that the determination of the free countries of Europe to protect themselves will be matched by an equal determination on our part to help them to do so' (Department of State 1974, p. 55). He also confirmed the line of policy which Byrnes had proclaimed in Stuttgart a year and a half earlier (see Chapter 3, Section 2). The United States would keep its occupation forces in Germany 'until the peace is secure in Europe' (Ireland 1981, p. 91). That same day, Bevin and Bidault sent a telegram to Marshall in which they stated that the foundations had been laid for a 'wider arrangement in which other countries including the United States might play a part', and expressed their willingness to start talks on how to fulfil Truman's promise (Department of State 1974, pp. 55–6).

2.4. The Preparations of the Vandenberg Resolution

Five days after Truman's speech to the American Congress, the first of a series of top-secret meetings between the representatives of the United States, Canada and Great Britain took place in Washington, in which they discussed the form the American military aid to Western Europe should take.[6] The previous standpoint that a treaty would be the best solution proved to be controversial within the State Department. The Policy Planning Staff was of the opinion that it would suffice if the president of the United States unilaterally declared, as in the Monroe Doctrine of 1823, that the United States thenceforth considered an attack on Western Europe as an attack on itself (cf. Department of State 1974, p. 59). Kennan and his officials had, however, been sidetracked in the negotiations with Great Britain and Canada. The same applies to the talks between Robert Lovett, the Under-Secretary of State, and Arthur Vandenberg, the Republican chairman of the Senate Committee for Foreign Relations, which started around mid-April as a continuation of the consultations with Canada and Great Britain, and in which they discussed the conditions under which the Senate might give broad support for greater American involvement in the defence of Western Europe.

One of the most important results of the series of top-secret meetings between the United States, Canada and Great Britain was that the latter agreed that a 'regional security arrangement in the North Atlantic Area' could best be laid down in a treaty, particularly as a treaty 'would have much greater political effect than a mere declaration of intent, no matter how strongly worded' (Department of State 1974, p. 72). In his first meeting with Lovett, however, Vandenberg proved 'cool on the formal guarantee of a pact'. He did state his willingness to examine how a procedure might be developed in the short term for providing military aid to back up the Western European powers' own efforts (Department of State 1974, p. 84). Later that month, Vandenberg nonetheless accepted that a treaty, if based on the principle of 'mutual aid and self-help', had the advantage – as opposed to a noncommittal attitude – that it would also stipulate the Western European allies' obligations. Thus the costs of building up a Western European defence would not be borne unilaterally by the United States. At the end of April, there were consultations between Lovett and Marshall on the one hand and Vandenberg and his Republican colleague Dulles on the other. 'After a great deal of discussion', they agreed to take the following course.[7] The State Department would request the Senate Committee for Foreign Relations to prepare a resolution in which the Senate declared itself openly in favour of participation in regional collective security organizations. Once the resolution had been passed by the Senate, the Brussels Pact countries would approach the United States to start talks on how such an organization could be established. The President would subsequently respond by issuing a statement in which he expressed his willingness to start talks if these were held on the basis of 'effective self-help and mutual aid' (State Department 1974, p. 107).

On 11 June 1948, the Vandenberg Resolution, passed unanimously by the Senate Committee for Foreign Relations almost a month earlier, was finally accepted by the Senate by 64 votes to 4. This resolution informed President Truman of 'the sense of the Senate' that the government should pursue, among other things, the following two aims within the framework of the United Nations Charter:

> Progressive development of regional and other collective arrangements for individual and collective self-defense in accordance with the purposes, principles, and provisions of the Charter.
>
> Association of the United States, by constitutional process, with such regional and other collective arrangements as are based on continuous and effective self-help and mutual aid, and as affect its national security. (Department of State 1974, pp. 135–6)

3.   The North Atlantic Treaty

3.1. The Exploratory Talks in Washington

Within two weeks after the Vandenberg Resolution had been passed, tensions in Europe reached a new high when the Soviet Union blocked all access roads to Berlin (see also Chapter 3, Section 3). To boost the morale of the Western European powers, the United States sent 60 B-29 bombers to Great Britain in July. These atomic bombers, which, once stationed in Great Britain, could reach targets in the Soviet Union,[8] symbolized American determination to defend Western Europe against Soviet aggression.

Also in July, the United States, Canada and the five Brussels Pact countries started exploratory talks in Washington about how the former two countries could be more deeply involved in the defence of Western Europe. The United States attached great importance to the exploratory character of the talks, and repeatedly stressed that these could not bind the participants in any way whatsoever. The first phase was concluded at the beginning of September with a memorandum, the so-called Washington Paper, in which the delegations informed their governments about the results achieved up till then. Even though they stated that the memorandum 'represents no firm conclusions' (Department of State 1974, p. 238), they nonetheless felt so much progress had been made in the previous months that a treaty for a North Atlantic security system was now feasible.

In the first two months of deliberations, one prevailing issue was discussed in many different ways: the credibility of the future parties to the Treaty. Would they be prepared to fulfil their promises and carry out their threats? The protagonists in this verbal contest were the United States on the one hand and France on the other. Neither power had any use for high-sounding formulas, and both were looking for concrete gestures. At the same time, both feared that the other party would pay no more than lip-service when the crunch came. The French believed a treaty with the United States would antagonize the Soviet Union. Should this lead to war with the Soviet Union, France would pay the price, as it would already have been overrun by the Soviet army by the time American mobilization was well under way. France therefore stressed the need for immediate and extensive arms supplies to restore the strength of the French army. The United States argued that the mere presence of the American troops in Germany was a firm guarantee that it would come to the aid of Western Europe in the event of Soviet aggression. As things stood, the United States was saddled with responsibility for the defence of Western Europe. It was high time that the Western Europeans showed their willingness to take up the joint defence of their territories. What steps had the members of the Brussels Pact taken so far to bring their defence up to standard? And what progress had they made in harmonizing their defence efforts? If the Western Europeans could not provide such 'proof of good conduct', the United States would not be prepared to take on any further obligations. Also, arms should only be supplied within multilateral frameworks. France's appeal for arms for the French army made the Americans suspect that France ultimately attached little value to the parts of the Treaty of Brussels that were devoted to the importance of European cooperation.

The United States' scepticism about the true value of the promises made by its Western European partners may well have been justified. On the other hand, the Americans certainly did not improve their own credibility by declaring that the manner in which the obligation of mutual assistance was formulated in Article IV of the Treaty of Brussels was unacceptable. To the Americans, this obligation was pushing things too far. They could not be party 'to any Treaty which would provide that the United States would automatically be at war as a result of an event occurring outside its border or by vote of other countries without its concurrence'. In their opinion, Article 3 of the Rio Pact provided sufficient guarantees that such an undesirable development would not occur (Department of State 1974, p. 211).

To the Americans as well as the Canadians, the Treaty of Brussels also went too far in another respect. They did not want anything to do with Articles I and II of the Treaty, which referred to the stimulation of Europe's economic recovery. In another respect they considered the Treaty of Brussels too limited. As the Americans saw it, the United States could only enter into an agreement if it led to an 'adequate increase in its security'. Given the small number of signatories, the Treaty of Brussels would certainly not result in such an increase. The Americans therefore advocated the formation of a North Atlantic community, of which not only the United States, Canada and the Brussels Pact countries, but also Iceland, Norway, Denmark, Portugal and Ireland would be part. Separate arrangements might be made later for Italy and Sweden.[9]

After the Washington Paper had been accepted, the exploratory talks were temporarily suspended for a period of about three months. Presidential elections were looming in the United States and France was struggling with the after effects of the fall of the Schuman cabinet in July (it would become clear in September that this cabinet could not be reconstituted and that a new government would have to be formed). Meanwhile the parties to the talks did take various measures to increase mutual trust. For example, the Brussels Pact countries established a permanent defence organization in London in September, and the United States decided to release equipment to bring three French divisions up to fighting strength.

After the Western European powers had announced at the end of October that, in their opinion, the Washington Paper provided a sound basis for negotiations concerning the North Atlantic Pact, the exploratory talks were resumed in the second half of December. By Christmas a first draft of the Treaty had already been drawn up. The largest stumbling block proved to be the phrasing of the obligation of mutual assistance in Article 5, paragraph 1, of the draft treaty. The text ran as follows:

> The Parties agree that an armed attack against one or more of them within the area defined below shall be considered an attack against them all; and consequently that, if such an armed attack occurs, each of them, in exercise of the right of individual or collective self-defense recognized by Article 51 of the Charter of the United Nations, will assist the party or parties so attacked by taking forthwith such military or other action, individually and in concert with the other Parties, as may be necessary to restore and assure the security of the

North Atlantic area. (Department of State 1974, p. 335)

Although this was already rather non-committal wording and the Western European powers, at an earlier stage, had pressed for a more binding text in line with Article IV of the Treaty of Brussels, the Senate nonetheless considered the wording undermined the authority of Congress. Under the American Constitution, only Congress has the right to declare war. At a meeting with the new Secretary of State, Acheson, Senator Vandenberg and Tom Connally, the latter's Democratic successor as chairman of the Senate Foreign Relations Committee, said that:

> the language used gave an impression of crescendo and haste which perhaps overstated the problem. It implied that the United States was rushing into some kind of autonomous commitment. The Senators wanted the Pact to avoid overstatement or rhetoric. There would be preliminary talks, there would be plans, but the ultimate action would depend upon the decision of each member country. (Department of State 1975, p. 74)

The participants in the exploratory talks had no other choice but to find a formulation that would take full account of American constitutional practice. The text that eventually proved acceptable to all those involved stated that the parties themselves were to determine what action they deemed necessary to withstand an armed attack: 'The Parties agree that (each of them) will assist the Party or Parties so attacked by taking forthwith, individually and in concert with the other Parties, such action as it deems necessary, including the use of armed force' (Van Ooijen *et al.* 1996, p. 60). In strict logic, this last addition was of course superfluous, because 'the first clause included the second', but was included anyway 'to leave no doubt that armed force was contemplated' (Acheson 1969, p. 281).

Another question which still caused some problems in the last months of the exploratory talks concerned the scope of the Treaty. A few days before the draft treaty was completed, France had demanded that French Algeria also be included. The French argued that 'Algeria was a part of France and in the same relation to France as Alaska or Florida to the United States' (Department of State 1974, p. 325).[10] The Americans opposed this territorial expansion for a long time as they could not see how they would benefit from it in terms of their own security. However, when the French threatened to opt out of the whole project, the United States decided to give in to their demands at the end of February (cf. Department of State 1975, p. 131).

By the beginning of March 1949, the exploratory talks had made so much progress that the eight participating powers – Norway had meanwhile joined the original seven – invited Iceland, Denmark, Portugal and Italy to come to Washington to take part in the last phase of the discussions on the establishment of a North Atlantic security community.[11] These negotiations were successfully completed on 4 April 1949 when the Treaty of Washington was solemnly signed.

3.2.   A Political Framework for Security

Strictly speaking, the obligation of mutual assistance laid down in Article 5 of the Treaty of Washington did not add anything substantial to the existing relationship between the United States and Western Europe *vis-à-vis* the Soviet Union. Had there been no such article, it would still have been in the interest of the United States to come to the aid of the Western European powers in the event of Soviet aggression. Nor did this article change the fact that the United States itself would determine when this interest was at stake and, if so, what measures it would take to defend it. Also unchanged was the fact that the best available guarantee of the American determination to defend Europe was the presence of American troops in Germany. In this sense the Treaty was indeed a superfluous exercise and only seemed to vindicate those who, in the spring of 1948, saw very little point in a treaty; Kennan and his staff, for example, had deemed the declaration of a Monroe Doctrine for Europe sufficient to meet the Western European wish for more security. According to Senator Vandenberg, this was precisely what the Treaty implied. During the discussions on the ratification of the Treaty in the Senate, he took the view that this was an instrument enabling the United States to add the North Atlantic area to the territory for which the Monroe Doctrine was originally intended (cf. Osgood 1962, p. 41, and Ireland 1981, pp. 145–6).

It thus appears that, given the existing military situation in Europe, the whole of Article 5 – and hence the whole Treaty – was just as superfluous as the inclusion of the phrase in that same article stating that the use of armed force was one of the measures that parties to the Treaty could take to respond to an armed attack. However, this interpretation does not do justice to the Treaty. For one thing, Article 3, in which the 'effective self-help and mutual aid' required by the Vandenberg Resolution are regulated, and Article 9, which, in line with the Brussels Pact, provides for the formation of a Council that will monitor the implementation of the Treaty, contain provisions which would be totally incompatible with a unilateral declaration such as the Monroe Doctrine. For another – and this is especially important – this view does not acknowledge the great psychological value of the gesture made by the United States in entering openly, and on an equal footing, into an agreement of mutual assistance with the Western European powers. More than anything else, the signatories wanted to create a political framework that would increase the sense of security in Europe (cf. Richardson 1972, p. 604). In this sense, Article 5 can be seen as a political and psychological counterweight to the large number of Soviet troops in Eastern Europe (cf. Osgood 1962, p. 30). However, this does not mean that all the signatories considered this counterweight sufficient. France, in particular, had quite different views on the subject.

In any case, the Treaty did not change the appalling strategic situation in post-war Western Europe. A Soviet offensive would still not meet any real resistance on the ground, and could in the first instance only be repelled from the air. In this respect, the fact that the Strategic Air Command (SAC), responsible for carrying out the long-range bombing necessary to force back the Soviet troops, remained solely an American affair is illustrative of the situation that then prevailed (cf. Osgood 1962, p. 32).

4. The North Atlantic Treaty Organization

4.1. The Military Assistance Programme and the Organization of a Collective Defence

After the Treaty had been signed, France and the United States pursued their search for concrete gestures relentlessly. Whereas France used Article 3 to hammer home the need for as much military assistance as possible as quickly as possible,[12] the United States, referring to Article 9, kept insisting on measures which would show that the Western European powers were indeed trying to achieve a collective defence of their own territories.[13] The main condition to be fulfilled before the extensive American military assistance programme could be initiated was that the North Atlantic community had to make the necessary organizational arrangements for such an integrated defence.

Setting up a credible defence against a Soviet attack was, however, not the sole objective of France and the United States. To France it was just as important that American arms supplies under Article 3 would substantially reinforce France's position *vis-à-vis* West Germany, which was excluded from the military assistance programme. The United States attached just as much value to the consultative bodies provided for in Article 9, because these would give it the opportunity to work gradually towards general acceptance of the idea of West Germany joining the North Atlantic Pact.

One day after the Treaty of Washington had been signed, the Brussels Pact countries submitted to the United States a request for military assistance. Behind the scenes, the State Department had been involved in drawing up this request. It therefore contained all the formulas that the Americans wanted to see included. The Western European powers stated that they were developing a collective defence programme founded on 'entire solidarity between them'. In addition, they gave their assurance that the build-up of their armed forces would take place on 'a coordinated basis in order that in the event of aggression they can operate in accordance with a common strategic plan'. They were forced to appeal to the United States for support, because, given their deplorable economic situation, they simply could not set up a credible defence without damaging their objective of a quick and successful economic recovery (Department of State 1975, pp. 286–7).

At the end of July 1949, less than a week after the Senate ratified the Treaty of Washington by a very large majority, Congress began discussing the legislation on which the Mutual Defence Assistance Programme would be based. It soon became clear that Vandenberg and Dulles could not agree to the programme unless the bill stated that the purpose was only 'to assist common defense plans made by the treaty council', and unless the North Atlantic Council and the Defence Committee provided for in Article 9 had already commenced with their activities (Ireland 1981, p. 155). The bill was promptly amended in accordance with the Senators' wishes, and the first meeting of the Council of Foreign Ministers of the North Atlantic Pact took place in the middle of September. At this meeting, the parties reached agreement on the structure of the alliance.[14] The Military Assistance Bill was passed by the American Congress at the beginning of October. Implementation of the bill was postponed until the allies had drawn up a strategic plan for the integrated defence of the North Atlantic area to which the United States could fully agree.

At the fourth meeting of the Council in London in May 1950, the North Atlantic Pact was finally transformed from a traditional alliance based on a mutual assistance agreement into an organization for collective self-defence. According to Acheson, this was the meeting which placed 'the "O" in NATO' (cf. Acheson 1969, p. 399). The most important element was the decision to set up a permanent body of deputy members of the Council, the so-called Council of Deputies, which would be responsible for the further development of the collective defence.

One may therefore agree with Osgood that, on the eve of the North

Korean invasion of South Korea, military cooperation between the countries of the North Atlantic Pact had already reached a level 'unprecedented among peace-time coalitions' (Osgood 1962, p. 47). At the same time one should not forget that, in the spring of 1950, there was still no integrated command structure for the armed forces of the alliance and that there still was no sign of American involvement in the defence of Western Europe becoming permanent (cf. Ireland 1981, p. 183).

The results of the meetings in London, however far-reaching for the integration of the defence of Western Europe, were nonetheless entirely overshadowed in terms of publicity by another Western European integration initiative, launched in Paris a few days earlier: the Schuman Plan. This plan involved a proposal by the French government to place the whole French and German coal and steel production – as well as that of other European powers willing to participate – under a joint High Authority. This initiative, developed by Jean Monnet and his staff at the *Commissariat au Plan*, had a clear security aspect to it – namely, gaining control over West Germany's existing and future defence industry (see also Chapter 6, Sections 1 and 2).

4.2. A Question that Cannot Come up

As explained in Section 2, the most important reason why the State Department took such a strong interest in a security pact modelled on the Rio Pact and was unfavourably disposed towards a network of bilateral treaties on mutual assistance as desired by France and Great Britain was that a security pact would make it easier in future for Germany to play a part in the defence of Western Europe. The French newspaper *Le Monde* was therefore quite right when, referring to the debates in the French National Assembly about the ratification of the Treaty of Washington, it stated that 'the participation of Germany is contained in this pact like the germ in the egg' (trans. *New York Times*; Ireland 1981, p. 159). Nonetheless, foreign minister Schuman swore to the representatives during these debates at the end of July 1949 that the possibility of Germany joining the Pact was a question that

> cannot come up, either now or even in the future. Germany still has no peace treaty. It has no army, and it must not have one. It has no weapons, and it will have none. The basic concern of the peace-loving nations is precisely the disarmament of Germany. Well then, to be disarmed is to be excluded from the Pact. (Willis [1965] 1968, p. 57)

In the autumn of 1949, this question did nonetheless play an important part in the discussions of the Defence Committee of the North Atlantic Council, which was to draw up the integrated defence plan desired by Vandenberg and Dulles. By insisting that American arms supplies would only commence after submission of a strategic plan that the United States could approve, the Senators hoped to ensure that the allies, in drawing up the plan, would become thoroughly convinced that West Germany was essential to a successful defence of Western Europe and thus to commit the French to German participation. The French government, on the contrary, saw the talks as a way of making the United States accept that, once the French army had been restored to its full strength and American troops were actively involved in the defence of Western Europe, any contribution from West Germany would be completely unnecessary (cf. Ireland 1981, p. 177).[15]

This delicate issue was totally ignored in the integrated defence plan, on which the Defence Committee reached agreement at the beginning of December 1949 and which was approved by President Truman at the end of January 1950. This contained little more than a confirmation of the existing segregation of duties in the defence of Western Europe. Should a party to the Treaty become the victim of armed aggression, 'the hard core of ground forces [was to] come from the European nations' in the first phase of the battle, while the United States would carry out strategic bombing (Ireland 1981, p. 167).

Although Vandenberg and Dulles' plan failed, the rearmament of West Germany remained an item on the agenda. While the defence ministers were drawing up an integrated defence plan, the General Staff of the U.S. Army proposed the formation of a number of West German divisions. After the U.S. National Security Council had ordered a committee to carry out a complete reassessment of American strategy in the early part of 1950, leading in mid-April to the publication of a memorandum (NSC-68), which recommended a substantial increase in the American defence efforts, the American Chiefs of Staff decided to lend their support to the proposal by the General Staff (cf. Richardson 1966, p. 18).

As the North Atlantic Council met in London in May 1950, it was clear to the foreign ministers of the alliance that practically all the military experts saw the rearmament of West Germany as a prerequisite for the credible defence of Western Europe (cf. Osgood 1962, p. 49; see also Wielenga 1989, p. 95). At the same time, it was obvious to them that this military necessity could not be reconciled with the fact that this issue had been declared a taboo subject in French politics. In their view, the military experts had failed to realize that, given the position of French politicians on the rearmament of West Germany, even raising the issue would only weaken the alliance at that point in time.[16] They therefore went to great lengths to spare French susceptibilities in this respect. This consensus was, however, shattered when North Korea invaded South Korea on 25 June 1950.

4.3.   The American 'One Package Proposal'

As a first response to the North Korean invasion of South Korea, the United States drastically increased military aid to its Western European allies. In addition to the $1.4 billion released under the military assistance programme at the beginning of the year, the United States made another $4 billion available in August. At the same time, the Americans stepped up arms production and called on their allies to do the same. In this connection, they also wanted to look at how West German industrial potential could best be utilized for this purpose. The Americans did not, of course, leave it at that. On 31 July, Acheson gave Truman the State Department's views on the rearmament of West Germany. He repeated the familiar standpoint that everything centred on the question of 'how this could be done without disrupting anything else we were doing', and he then came up with a solution

> along the lines of the possible creation of a European or a North Atlantic army under a Central European or North Atlantic command. In such an arrangement, Germans might be enlisted in a European army which would not be subject to the orders of Bonn but would follow the decisions reached in accordance with the North Atlantic procedure. (Department of State 1977, p. 168)

Thus the State Department appeared to be on the right track. Earlier that day, David Bruce, the American ambassador in Paris, had consulted a number of people including France's Prime Minister Pleven and Minister of Defence Moch. In the course of that consultation, Moch had stated: 'The common approach is the only formula under which the French people could be brought to accept participation of Western Germany in NAT defense effort' (Department of State 1977, p. 171). Also, Moch had made it clear that the question of West German involvement in the defence of Western Europe – whether or not at a collective level – had no priority whatsoever in the eyes of the French. At the time, the French were only interested in sending American and British troops to West Germany as quickly as possible to help repel the first waves of a possible attack (cf. Osgood 1962, p. 71).

A few weeks earlier, Lewis Douglas, the American ambassador in Great

Britain, had already argued in favour of greater involvement of the United States in the defence of Western Europe. In his view, this was to be achieved by sending extra troops, which would then become part of an international armed force with a common command structure and an American in supreme command. Acheson submitted these proposals informally to Louis Johnson, the Secretary of Defense, who was favourably disposed towards them. Encouraged by Johnson's attitude, the State Department drew up a memorandum in mid-August, which laid the foundation for the American 'one package proposal' to strengthen the defence of Western Europe, presented a few weeks later. The basic assumptions in the memorandum were firstly that there was no question of the Federal Republic getting its own army, and secondly that the United States would be fully involved in the defence of Western Europe. The American divisions would have to be part of a European defence force to be formed within NATO, in which, in addition to the American divisions and those of the Brussels Pact countries, West German divisions would be included. This European army would be a supranational affair, serving as the 'driving force towards further unification in Western Europe', with its own American commander and its own general staff, in which Germans might also occupy a position. However, West German generals should not be given command over more than a single division, and the armed forces of the Federal Republic would be the only ones without a general staff of their own (cf. Department of State 1977, pp. 213–17).[17]

It is very doubtful whether the ideas about the role of West Germany in the defence of Western Europe as developed by the State Department would have been acceptable from the point of view of *Gleichberechtigung*. Moreover, many Germans in the Federal Republic envisaged a totally different West German contribution to the defence of Western Europe, given their expectations of how a Communist attack would take place. In their view, events in Korea made it clear that the Soviet Union would want to keep out of harm's way and would leave the dirty work to its satellites. Applied to the German situation, this meant that it would not be the Red Army that crossed the Elbe to 'free' the Federal Republic, but the East German *Volkspolizei* ('People's Police'), trained by the Soviets (cf. Baring 1969, p. 81).[18] In the second half of August, Chancellor Adenauer asked the High Commission for permission to set up a West German federal police force, which, as he explained two weeks later, 'would in any case have to be big enough to be capable of effective resistance to the People's Police' (Adenauer 1966a, p. 282).

Great Britain accepted the West German proposal, but the United States and France rejected it. The United States was against it because it was incompatible with its own plans for the defence of Western Europe, whereas France rejected it because it involved a *federal* police force, and much too large a one at that. In September 1950, the occupation authorities therefore only gave the Federal Republic permission to set up a *Bundesschutzpolizei* (federal constabulary) with no more than 30,000 men and composed of contingents from various German states.

Even though the proposal for a federal police force was not accepted, the critical international situation offered sufficient opportunities to improve the position of the Federal Republic. The Chancellor presented the High Commissioners with two memoranda at the end of August. The first stated that the Federal Government was prepared to provide troops for a European army (see also Chapter 7, Section 1). The second stated that a West German contribution to the defence of Western Europe would only be possible if 'Germany's relations with the occupying powers are placed on a new footing'. Accordingly, the Federal Government demanded that the foreign ministers of the occupying powers, when meeting for mutual consultations in September prior to the NATO Council meeting in New York, should declare that the state of war was over, that the future purpose of the occupation was to improve the defence of the Federal Republic against external threats, and that relations between the occupation authorities and the Federal Republic would be 'progressively replaced by a system of contractual agreements' (cf. Adenauer 1966a, p. 281).

At the end of August, President Truman asked the Departments of State and Defense to draw up a joint memorandum in preparation for the consultations between Acheson, Bevin and Schuman and the subsequent NATO Council meeting. This memorandum should indicate the best way to reinforce the defence of Western Europe and the possible contribution by the Federal Republic. As it happened, this joint memorandum entirely reflected the views of the State Department, but with one crucial difference. The State Department's memorandum had not specified when West Germany's military contribution should commence, whereas this latest memorandum stated that 'we should proceed without delay with the formation of adequate West German units since they will require time for organization, training and equipping, during which time the appropriate framework for their integration into a European defence force both in peace and in war can be developed'. It would be pointless for the United States to send extra divisions to Western Europe, set up a European army, and supply an American Commander-in-Chief, unless a start was also made on setting up West German units (Department of State 1977, pp.

275–6).[19] If the allies could not agree to the measures necessary for West German involvement, the United States would withdraw its offer. When, at the first meeting of the North Atlantic Council, Dirk Stikker, the Dutch foreign minister suggested that the allies had a choice between deployment of more American, British and Canadian troops in Western Europe or West German involvement in the defence of Europe (see also Wielenga 1989, p. 98), Acheson quickly disabused him: 'alternatives suggested by the Netherlands were not in fact alternatives. Both courses suggested by the Netherlands would be necessary to build sufficient strength' (Department of State 1977, p. 309).

At the Council meeting there was soon an impasse regarding the rearmament of West Germany, with France on the one side and the other member states on the other. Given fierce French opposition to West German participation in a European army, the United States endeavoured to make them at least accept the American analysis that West German units were indispensable to a successful defence of Western Europe. The French, however, were completely unwilling to do so. When Acheson suggested that France and the United States might approve of a formula accepting the principle of West German rearmament, but also agreeing 'to keep German rearmament lagging behind that of the other powers' (Department of State 1977, p. 299), the only compromise Schuman was willing to make was that it might become opportune one day to set up West German units. According to the French minister of foreign affairs, that day would only come once Europe's armed forces were strong enough to operate effectively (cf. Department of State 1977, p. 339) – in other words, once a West German contribution to the defence of Western Europe was no longer necessary!

The Americans did not succeed in breaking down French resistance. Eventually, they only got France to agree to look at how West Germany might contribute to the collective defence of Western Europe. The final communiqué stated that the Council had ordered the Defence Committee to examine, 'from the technical point of view', the methods by which the Federal Republic could most usefully contribute to a successful defence of Western Europe, 'bearing in mind the unanimous conclusion of the Council that it would not serve the best interests of Europe or of Germany to bring into being a German national army or a German general staff' (Department of State 1977, p. 352). At the time, the United States reconciled itself to the impasse forced by the French, but Acheson told Bevin and Schuman that if the Europeans came over in October [for the Defence Committee meeting; RHL] and said they would not do anything about German participation, we would then have to review the whole thing. If they came over in October and said it was still unsettled and they did not know what they would do, we would also have to take another look into the whole problem. (Department of State 1977, p. 1393)

At the end of September, the High Commission notified the German Chancellor of the decisions that the foreign ministers of the occupying powers had taken in response to the Federal Government's memorandum about the conditions under which West German participation in a European army might be achieved. The High Commissioners informed Adenauer that the occupation authorities were prepared to end the state of war as soon as possible, but that for the time being they wished to continue the occupation. The next day, the American High Commissioner McCloy also warned Adenauer that 'the inclusion in the international armed force must in no case be allowed to become the subject of a deal. The Federal Republic must not make political conditions for membership' (Adenauer 1966a, p. 290).

4.4. The French Counterproposal: the Pleven Plan

During a break in one of the many NATO Council meetings concerning the American 'one package proposal', wrote Acheson in his memoirs, he was once taken aside by Bech, his Luxembourg opposite number, who implored him 'to be more relaxed' as 'Paris was working on a European military system based on the Schuman Coal and Steel Plan. When I asked why Schuman did not tell me so, he answered, "He doesn't know it yet"' (Acheson 1969, p. 444). At the end of the Council, however, Schuman did seem to be in the know. He told Acheson confidentially how important it was that France would no longer 'be "drag on the end of a chain" in this matter' and that 'perhaps the best way to do this was for the French and Germans to come to some sort of agreement, and he was now thinking what he could do to lead the development' (Department of State 1977, p. 353).

Exactly one month later, Prime Minister Pleven launched his plan for a European army in the French National Assembly. Under European supreme command, this army would take up the defence of Western Europe together with American and British divisions within the framework of NATO. Gradually, West German troops would also be incorporated into this European army, but only 'on the level of the smallest unit possible'. This Pleven Plan was largely the creation of Monnet and his staff, as witness the condition that the talks on such a European army should only commence after the European Coal and Steel Community Treaty had been signed (see also Chapter 7, Sections 1 and 2).

Given the content of the French plan, it would probably not have had a positive impact on Acheson's thinking if it had actually been announced during the NATO Council meeting. According to the American Secretary of State, the plan was 'hopeless' anyway. The clause referring to the Schuman Plan confirmed his suspicion that the French were only using the plan as a vehicle to delay the issue of German rearmament. Marshall, the former Secretary of State who had succeeded Johnson as defence minister at the end of September 1950, shared Acheson's views in this matter. The plan 'would raise problems necessitating almost endless negotiations and delay' (Department of State 1977, p. 411).[20] American suspicions about the plan were not allayed when the phrase 'the smallest unit possible' turned out to mean a battalion, whereas, in the American view, anything smaller than a division could not be an effective fighting unit.

At the Defence Committee meeting in October, Marshall stated that the United States could not help set up an integrated command structure and supply a Commander-in-Chief as long as it was not clear what measures NATO proposed to take to involve West Germany in the collective defence of Western Europe. His British colleague Shinwell increased the pressure on France by stating that Great Britain, under the given circumstances, would not be prepared to send extra troops to the Continent. Moch, however, was adamant. If West German involvement was desired, the Pleven Plan would be the only negotiable option and the involvement of entire German divisions remained out of the question. There was thus a complete impasse with respect to the 'one package proposal' (cf. Department of State 1977, pp. 415–16 and 423–5).

4.5.   The American-French Compromise: the Spofford Plan

As Acheson had anticipated that the Defence Committee meeting would not lead to any tangible results, he had already begun to look for a way out of the French-American conflict in the middle of October: 'it may be that delay in creation of the integrated force will not appear to be in the best interest of the United States' (Department of State 1977, p. 382). A month later, the outlines of a compromise gradually emerged. After weeks of intensive negotiations in the Council of Deputies, a final compromise was reached in December. The most important feature of this compromise – known as the Spofford Plan after the American chairman of the Council of Deputies – was that, on the one hand, the Americans would support the

French proposal to convene a conference at which the interested European powers would discuss how the Pleven Plan could be implemented, and that, on the other hand, the French would no longer oppose measures in preparation for West German involvement in an integrated North Atlantic defence force – possibly as part of an European army – and would no longer delay these in anticipation of successful completion of talks on the Pleven Plan. Moreover, initiation of these talks was no longer dependent on the signing of the ECSC Treaty. A second feature was France's concession that the smallest possible unit would not be a battalion, but what was called a 'regimental combat team'. The United States for its part maintained the position that the division was the smallest effective fighting unit, but accepted that, before divisions could be set up, regiments must first be formed, and that further examination might subsequently prove whether or not these were functioning satisfactorily.

During the NATO Council meeting at the end of December 1950, no further complications arose with respect to the Spofford Plan. The Council subsequently decided to set up a Supreme Headquarters Atlantic Powers in Europe (SHAPE) and unanimously recommended General Eisenhower as the first Supreme Allied Commander in Europe (SACEUR). Eisenhower was given this post before the end of that very day. On that occasion, Truman also announced that the United States proposed to send a number of divisions to the Federal Republic to reinforce the defence of Western Europe.

5.   Tired but Involved

At the end of his book *Creating the Entangling Alliance*, Ireland concludes that

> because there could no longer be any doubt that the United States would participate in the initial defense of Europe, the constitutional safeguards written into the treaty no longer applied. Although the vast majority of senators ultimately faced up to the new responsibilities of the cold war and approved Truman's action, it was clear that a great departure had taken place in the conduct of American foreign policy; from then on, the security of the United States was unmistakably linked with that of Western Europe. (Ireland 1981, p. 225)

At the end of this chapter, it should come as no surprise to the reader that I basically agree with Ireland's conclusion. However, I am much less happy about an earlier passage in his book in which he states that

American plans to send extra divisions to Europe as well as an integrated defence force and an American Commander-in-Chief 'were greatly influenced by the American desire to gain French acceptance for German rearmament, thereby giving the U.S. commitment a shape and permanence it might otherwise not have assumed' (Ireland 1981, p. 215). As I hope to have proved, these plans were predominantly based on a desire to convince the Western European powers that the sacrifices the United States demanded from them in order to withstand Soviet aggression would not be in vain from the very outset. The idea that the policy outlined by the United States might also have reassured the French as to the dangers of West German rearmament is, in my opinion, unfounded. As clearly illustrated above, the French were not in the least reassured by this policy.

The American policy should be understood as that of a great power which, in attempting to further its own interests – in this case by ensuring Western Europe would not fall like a ripe fruit into the lap of its rival the Soviet Union – was prepared to provide a collective good (see Chapter 2, Section 5). United States' insistence on West German involvement should primarily be seen as part of its attempts to prevent the Western Europeans from getting a free ride. American determination in this respect can subsequently be explained by the fact that it was 'fundamentally un-contested' among American policy-makers that this free-rider behaviour would not occur if the Europeans were only willing to learn from their past mistakes, give up their age-old feuding, and unite (cf. Chapter 4, Section 3).

If the above lines suggest that the Americans were rather tired of the Western Europeans, I can only say that, in my opinion, such a feeling did indeed exist. On the other hand, one should not forget that American policy-makers were also very much involved with the European continent. In this respect, the American attitude towards the European continent differed completely from the traditional attitude of the British. In contrast to the United States, Great Britain always remained a 'flank power', which was not really interested in the Continent and tried to avoid any involvement with it (cf. Schroeder [1994] 1996). A typical example of this difference in attitude is the correspondence between the Americans and British in the initial phase of the process that eventually led to the 'entangling alliance'. At the end of January 1948, Bevin tried to convince his American counterpart that all plans for closer Western European cooperation would prove ineffective and unreliable 'unless there is assurance of American support for the defence of Western Europe' (Department of State 1974, p. 14). In his answer, Under-Secretary of State

Lovett did not refute Bevin's analysis. He could, however, not resist making a subtle reference by noting Bevin's statement that, for their part, the British government 'were not yet in a position to give firm assurances as to the role Britain intends to play in operations on the continent of Europe' (Department of State 1974, p. 18).

Notes

1. At the end of April 1948, Kennan sent a memorandum to Under-Secretary of State Lovett, in which he spoke of 'the dual catastrophe of Russian invasion and subsequent military liberation' (Department of State 1974, p. 109).

2. Our familiarity with the current form of European cooperation makes it hard for us to imagine nowadays that the 'Western Union' as envisaged by Bevin was to be based on a collection of bilateral treaties. Bevin, however, saw Western European union exclusively as a 'spiritual union', which would be 'more of a brotherhood and less of a rigid system' (Jansen and De Vree [1985] 1988, p. 76). Within a few years, it would turn out that Bevin's lofty ideal of Western European unity could not be reconciled with the daily political routine of British non-alignment (cf. Young 1984, p. 82).

3. Greenwood points out that, during the preparations for the Treaty of Dunkirk in the early spring of 1947, the British and French negotiators had also considered the possibility of concluding a similar treaty with the individual Benelux countries, but 'the issue was raised only to be dropped on the grounds that "more harm than good may be caused by trying to go too quickly"' (Greenwood 1983, p. 61).

4. The first paragraph of Article 3 runs as follows: 'The High Contracting Parties agree that an armed attack by any State against an American State shall be considered as an attack against all the American States and, consequently, each one of the said Contracting Parties undertakes to assist in meeting the attack in the exercise of the inherent right of individual or collective self-defense recognized by Article 51 of the Charter of the United Nations' (Department of State 1970, p. 560).

5. The preamble mentions 'steps as may be held to be necessary in the event of a renewal by Germany of a policy of aggression', while Article VII refers to 'a renewal by Germany of an aggressive policy' (Van Ooijen *et al.* 1996, pp. 52–3).

6. A French delegation had not been invited. At the beginning of the meeting, the British delegation insisted that the French should take part in the talks as soon as possible. The Americans were of the opinion that French participation would entail a security risk and therefore could better be postponed. The British and Canadian delegations deferred to the American standpoint, but only for the time being (cf. Department of State 1974, pp. 59–60).

7. At this meeting Dulles stated (cf. Chapter 4, Section 3) that an agreement with the Western European powers 'should also be designed to further the basic concept of ERP (the European Recovery Programme) to the end of ultimate union or fusion among the Western European countries. He emphasized that any attempt to freeze the Western European countries in their old habits of thought, association and economics would be futile and, in his opinion, against our national interest' (Department of State 1974, p. 106).

8. It was only in 1949–1950 that these bombers were converted to carry atomic bombs. It was not until the second half of 1951 that they were equipped with such bombs (cf. Botti 1987 and Mastny 1996, p. 49).

9. During these talks the participants referred several times to the need for future German involvement in the North Atlantic security system, without this leading to any protests from France. The Washington Paper does not mention anything about this except that 'the ultimate relationship of Western Germany to a North Atlantic security arrangement must eventually be determined but it would be premature to attempt to do so at this time' (Department of State 1974, p. 242).

10. At the same meeting France proposed that Italy should also be one of the signatories to the North Atlantic Treaty. The Americans argued that, from a military point of view, this would not be such a good idea. They acknowledged, however, that such a gesture might have great symbolic value. For various reasons the other countries also showed very little enthusiasm for the French proposal.

11. Ireland did not receive an invitation. In an earlier phase, it had informally been approached with a view to possible participation. However, when it turned out that Ireland deemed participation possible only after Northern Ireland was reunited with the Irish Republic, the parties refrained from approaching Ireland officially.

12. Article 3 of the Treaty of Washington reads: 'in order more effectively to achieve the objectives of this Treaty, the Parties, separately and jointly, by means of continuous and effective self-help and mutual aid, will maintain and develop their individual and collective capacity to resist armed attack' (Department of State 1975, p. 282). This article is the only one that does not originate from the Rio Pact or the Brussels Pact (cf. Ireland 1981, p. 107).

13. Article 9 reads as follows: 'The Parties hereby establish a council, on which each of them shall be represented, to consider matters concerning the implementation of this Treaty. The council shall be so organized as to be able to meet promptly at any time. The council shall set up such subsidiary bodies as may be necessary; in particular it shall establish immediately a defense committee which shall recommend measures for the implementation of Articles 3 and 5' (Department of State 1975, p. 283). In his memoirs, Paul-Henri Spaak, the Belgian Prime Minister, observed that it was Article 9 that 'gave the Atlantic Alliance a new character and made the treaty an effective instrument' (Spaak 1971, p. 152).

14. It was decided to establish the following bodies: a Defence Committee, consisting of the Defence Ministers, a Military Committee, consisting of the chiefs-of-staff from the participating countries (as it had no army, Iceland was allowed to send a civilian representative) and five regional planning groups. A so-called Standing Group was formed to function as the executive body of the Military Committee. This Standing Group consisted of representatives from the United States, Great Britain and France.

15. In doing so, the French government was faced with the problem that the need for West German rearmament was undisputed among French military leaders (see also Chapter 7, Section 4). General Béthouart, the French High Commissioner in Austria, for example, asked Marshall on 5 November 1948, much to the latter's surprise, 'whether or not we should have some plans for the arming of Western Germany in case of a Soviet breach of the peace' (Department of State 1974, p. 676).

16. On the authority of their respective governments, the High Commissioners did issue a statement at the end of the North Atlantic Council meeting of 22 May – after being invited to do so by the government of the Federal Republic at an earlier stage – in which they declared that 'an armed attack on the western occupation forces in Germany would be considered as an armed attack on all parties to the treaty and that article 5 immediately would be brought into play. As long as the occupation forces remained, the Federal Republic was protected by the North Atlantic Treaty. As a further assurance, the high commissioners stated that "the three Allied Powers have no intention in the present European situation of withdrawing their occupation forces from Germany"' (Ireland 1981, p. 176).

17. According to McGeehan, this last condition ensured that the West German troops would be little else than 'the modern equivalent of cannon-fodder' (McGeehan 1971, p. 43).

18. This police force trained by the Soviet army had a paramilitary character and was estimated to total 150,000 men in 1951. In an American protest note of 23 May 1950, which was sent to the Soviet Union, it was objected that these forces, the so-called *Bereitschaften*, were not an ordinary police force and that they also did not perform any regular police tasks. They were units that received 'basic infantry, artillery, and armored training' and were equipped with 'military weapons, including machine guns, howitzers, anti-aircraft cannon, mortars, and tanks', and 'must be regarded, therefore, as a military force' (Ruhm von Oppen 1955, p. 493).

19. Acheson wrote in his memoirs that 'the Defense Department required no persuasion that the defense of Europe needed, in their phrase, "beefing up", nor did its officers doubt that the beef would have to be provided by increased allied forces, increased American troops and military aid, the inclusion of armed German units, and – to integrate and direct the whole effort – a unified command. But – and here came the rub – they wanted all of these elements in (their phrase again) "one package". They would not recommend any more

American forces in Europe, or the responsibility of this country's assuming the unified command, unless the whole scheme should be made a viable one. To do this required wholehearted German cooperation. I knew that this was the stiffest fence on the course. To make it the first and the *sine qua non* of the rest seemed to me to be going about the project the hard way with a vengeance' (Acheson 1969, pp. 437–8).

20. In the Defence Committee meeting at the end of October, this view was challenged by Moch. He impressed on his colleagues that 'if French intend to be dilatory subordination would be to ratification [of the ECSC Treaty; RHL] instead of to signature' (Department of State 1977, p. 416).

6. *Westbindung*: from Schuman Plan to ECSC

1. Introduction

The Schuman Plan was a surprising and daring initiative, which caused quite a sensation when it was launched on 9 May 1950. It did not just appear out of the blue, however. In the first years after World War II, there were already many ideas circulating about how peace and security in Europe could be advanced by integrating the French and West German coal and steel industries in some way or other.

In February 1948, at the London Conference on Germany, ambassador Douglas had already suggested placing not only the Ruhr Basin but also comparable areas in Western Europe under the envisaged international authority. Douglas acknowledged that 'his suggestion might be too ambitious and might look too far into the future' (Department of State 1973, p. 99). Nonetheless, the Americans clung to the idea of using the International Authority for the Ruhr (IAR) as a means to further the economic integration of Europe. Kennan, for example, wrote a memorandum in the early spring of 1949 in which he reserved exactly this role for the IAR (cf. Lademacher in Foschepoth 1985, p. 250). Also, at a press conference in mid-October 1949, McCloy stated that the IAR might be a stepping stone to a confederated European construction – based of course on 'competitive and unrestricted free enterprise' – which then would be responsible for the heavy industries of Great Britain, France, the Federal Republic, Saarland and Luxembourg (cf. Lademacher in Foschepoth 1985, p. 250).

The British historian Milward even takes the view that the Schuman Plan 'did not emerge like a *deus ex machina* from the Planning Commissariat in spring 1950. It was in essence already there at the end of the London Conference' (Milward 1984, p. 164). Milward is referring here to the memoranda written in December 1948 by the officials of the *Quai d'Orsay* (the French Ministry of Foreign Affairs) concerning the endless negotiations about the statutes of the IAR (see also Chapter 3, Section 3). In these memoranda the proposition was defended that it would be an illusion to think that France could prevent the recovery of West Germany.

93

The French policy of constantly raising new obstacles in order to delay this recovery as long as possible was therefore pointless; worse, it was counter-productive. The continual lodging of objections, which the French government would in any case eventually have to give up, weakened the French position even more. It would be much better to accept the reality of West German recovery and to try to solve the German problem within a European framework – for example, by establishing a European steel pool in which the Germans and French would be represented on an equal footing and would jointly control the production of steel in Europe. According to the *Quai d'Orsay* officials such an initiative to involve Germany in Europe would only succeed if it were launched before 'our neighbour has regained its sovereignty' (Poidevin in Foschepoth 1985, pp. 135–6).

In his speech to the High Commission on 21 September 1949, on the occasion of the entry into force of the Occupation Statute, Adenauer too stated that, according to the government of the Federal Republic, the IAR provided an opening 'for creating a positive and viable European federation', at least if 'the control of the Ruhr would cease to be a unilateral arrangement' (Adenauer 1966a, p. 184).[1] There can be no doubt, however, that the Chancellor was actually much more interested in another plan, which he mentioned on several occasions in the months that followed. This involved the United States making capital available to France, which in turn would have to use this capital to acquire an interest in the Ruhr industry. This would enable France to achieve its ardent wish to gain some control over this industry and also obtain the security it rightly demanded (cf. Blankenhorn 1980, p. 68, and Lademacher in Foschepoth 1985, p. 252).

Even though the idea of integrating the French and German coal and steel industries was hanging in the air, two key features of the Schuman Plan deviated completely from all that had been considered in this respect up to the spring of 1950. It was exactly these two features that captured people's imagination. I am referring to the supranational aspects of the plan and the technocratic interpretation of these same aspects.[2] Moreover, Milward completely overlooks the fact that the *Quai d'Orsay* officials were deliberately ignored during the preparation and introduction of the Plan and were also excluded from the negotiations concerning the plan later on. The action channel (see Chapter 2, Section 2) ran from Schuman via his *directeur de cabinet*, Clappier, to Monnet and his staff at the *Commissariat au Plan* (cf. Duchêne 1994, pp. 205–6).

2. The Launch of the Schuman Plan

In the spring of 1950, there was much pressure on France to come up with some form of initiative. In September 1949, in the margin of the North Atlantic Council, Acheson (also speaking on behalf of Bevin) had entrusted Schuman with the task of developing a common policy with regard to Germany (cf. Monnet 1978, p. 299). At the end of October Acheson returned to this question in a private letter to Schuman and urgently requested his French colleague to make a proposal. He assured Schuman: 'now is the time for French initiative and leadership of the type required to integrate the German Federal Republic promptly and decisively into Western Europe. Delay will seriously weaken the possibilities of success' (Schwabe 1988, p. 219). Schuman was very much aware of the importance of French leadership and had consulted various people on the subject, but in the end he did nothing (cf. Monnet 1978, pp. 284–5 and Marjolin 1989, p. 272). Any proposal which so much as hinted at the rehabilitation of the Federal Republic was certain to provoke a storm of criticism in France. In the spring of 1950 there were signs that the Americans were beginning to lose patience, and the French knew that the United States might well take advantage of the North Atlantic Council meeting in May (see Chapter 5, Section 4) to propose its own initiative regarding the role of the Federal Republic within the framework of the North Atlantic Treaty. On the eve of that meeting, therefore, Schuman had to come up with something. Luckily, Monnet helped him out at the very last moment.

Since 1946, as head of the Planning Commissariat, Monnet had been responsible for implementing the plan drawn up under his supervision for the modernization of the French economy, and that of heavy industry in particular. The plan's aim was to restore France to its rightful position as the dominant power in Western Europe (see Chapter 3, Section 2). While trying to accomplish his task, Monnet was confronted with two considerable problems, which were intimately connected. The first was that it might take so much time to overcome the stagnation and lethargy which had characterized the French economy under the Third Republic, that France would not succeed in keeping ahead of the reviving West German economy. This would, of course, have been fatal to French ambitions. The second problem was that the United States was actually very anxious for the West German economy to recover as soon as possible, in view of the conflict with the Soviet Union. Another complicating factor was that the French steel industry in Lorraine depended heavily on West German coke (see, for example, Willis [1965] 1968, Milward 1984 and Dedman 1996).

However, what worried Monnet most in the spring of 1950 was the general sense of resignation he encountered among his compatriots (as he revealed in his autobiography). Whoever he talked to seemed to have already resigned themselves to a German recovery, another period of Franco-German conflict and French inability to counter such gloomy prospects (cf. Monnet 1978, pp. 289–90).

At the beginning of April 1950, Monnet thought up a means of escaping from this ominous vicious circle: France and the Federal Republic would pool their coal and steel production. A supranational body, in which France and West Germany would be represented *on equal terms*, would run this pool.

Throughout April, Monnet and his staff worked on the text of a memorandum in which this solution was incorporated. The text was finally submitted to Schuman at the beginning of May. Schuman approved it – 'I've read the proposal. I'll use it' (Monnet 1978, p. 299) – and submitted it to his French cabinet colleagues on 9 May. Despite all the advantages the plan seemed to offer France, Schuman deemed it wise to defend the proposal at the cabinet meeting in a manner which was 'even more elliptical and less audible than usual'. Schuman's vague presentation did not cause any harm to the plan. It was accepted, 'even if most members of the Cabinet learned its precise terms only from the next day's press' (Monnet 1978, p. 303). That very same afternoon, Schuman made the plan public at a press conference. He stated that the French government was willing to take action concerning 'a small but decisive point' and therefore proposed

> to place all of French and German coal and steel production under a joint High Authority, in an organization open to participation by other European countries.
>
> By establishing a joint basic production and setting up a new High Authority whose decisions will be binding upon France, Germany and the countries that join, this proposal will lay the first concrete foundations of a European federation which is essential for the preservation of peace. (Van Ooijen *et al.* 1996, pp. 62 and 63)[3]

The Schuman Plan could therefore be seen first of all as a new method of giving France control over West German recovery. Nonetheless, on the morning of 9 May, when he was informed about the content of the plan, Adenauer immediately notified Schuman that he approved 'wholeheartedly' of his initiative (cf. Adenauer 1966a, p. 257). It was in some way to be expected that the chancellor would respond so swiftly and positively. As the *Quai d'Orsay* had already concluded in December 1948 (see the previous section), the Federal Republic, as long as it was not a sovereign state, would have very little objection to participating in supranational European institutions. For Germany, in contrast to the other Western European powers, participation in such institutions did not mean relinquishing sovereign rights. For example, the High Authority provided for in the Schuman Plan would assume rights which the Federal Republic could not exercise at that time anyway (cf. Joffe in Macridis [1958] 1989, p. 78).

More fundamentally, the Schuman Plan was in keeping with the three key features of Adenauer's German policy (see also Chapter 3, Section 5): (i) it was in line with his objective of bringing about a reconciliation between Germany and France; (ii) to this end, it entailed the incorporation of the Federal Republic into Western European organizations; and (iii) it accepted the condition, which he considered crucial, that this reconciliation through 'self-binding' could only be achieved if it was on an equal footing.

The plan would foster such reconciliation, as it satisfied the French desire for security. Schuman also highlighted this point in a private letter to Adenauer, which he sent along with an official letter and the text of the plan. In this letter he emphasized that:

> the purpose of his proposal was not economic, but eminently political. In France there was a fear that once Germany had recovered, she would attack France. He could imagine that the corresponding fears might be present in Germany. Rearmament always showed first in an increased production of coal, iron, and steel. If an organization such as he was proposing was to be set up, it would enable each country to detect the first signs of rearmament, and would have an extraordinarily calming effect in France. (Adenauer 1966a, p. 257; cf. also Monnet 1978, p. 303)

This shows that the *Westbindung*, which the plan provided for by placing the whole French and West German coal and steel production under the High Authority, also had to ensure that France and the Federal Republic would gain so much control over each other's war industries that future wars between the two countries would be not only unthinkable but also impossible. From the point of view of *Gleichberechtigung*, another attractive aspect of the plan was that the Federal Republic would participate in the proposed High Authority on the basis of equality with the other participating powers and not from the subordinate position of an occupied state, as was the case in the IAR. While the High Authority enabled France to gain more control over the West German coal and steel industries, the same went for West Germany!

At the end of May, Monnet and Adenauer met for the first time to discuss further details of the plan.[4] At this meeting, Monnet emphasized once again that the aim of the French proposal was 'essentially political' (Monnet 1978, p. 310). He therefore asked Adenauer not to send any technical experts to the coming conference but 'persons with a wide economic horizon and European convictions. The last aspect was the most important. It was also necessary that these representatives be in a position to draft and to discuss agreements in constitutional and international law' (Adenauer 1966a, p. 263; cf. Blankenhorn 1980, p. 104).[5] Adenauer, for his part, wondered whether it would not be wiser for France and the Federal Republic to reach agreement first, before inviting the other powers to participate in the coal and steel pool. However, Monnet was able to convince the Chancellor that such a procedure would be undesirable, 'as it would have aroused the distrust of the other countries and soon created a state of mind which was opposed to the plan' (Schwabe 1988, p. 135).

The United States also greeted the Schuman Plan with approval. When Acheson, who was visiting Paris on the eve of the North Atlantic Council meeting, was informed of the content of the plan, he at first adopted a reserved attitude – 'all sorts of questions at once arose. To begin with, was the plan cover for a gigantic European cartel?' (Acheson 1969, p. 383). In a telegram he sent to his deputy in Washington the day after the plan was launched, however, he emphasized that 'it is important that French be given credit for making a conscious and far reaching effort to advance Franco-German *rapprochement* and European integration' (Department of State 1977, p. 695). The State Department shared his view. In the telegram it sent in reply, it agreed that the French deserved to be complimented for their leadership, initiative and constructive approach (cf. Department of State 1977, p. 696). The Economic Co-operation Administration (ECA), the American organization supervising the implementation of the Marshall Plan, even commented very favourably on the Schuman Plan. The ECA greeted it as a bold and ingenious initiative and an important step towards free trade. After all, it provided for immediate abolition of the existing tariff walls between the participating countries. The ECA also felt that the dangers of a cartel, although real, should not be exaggerated. The aim was to achieve the highest possible production levels, and Monnet had assured the ECA that less effective producers would therefore have to disappear (cf. Department of State 1977, pp. 702–3). Given the positive responses from the State Department and the ECA, President Truman decided as early as 18 May to support the French initiative openly.

Although he repeatedly professed his favourable inclination towards

Europe and was fully aware of the advantages of European unity –
particularly for France and Franco-German relations – Bevin rejected the
plan. This response was no doubt partly motivated by a certain resentment
of the fact that France had not informed Great Britain in advance about the
initiative it was to launch. This resentment grew even stronger when it
turned out that the French had notified the United States beforehand,
through Acheson (cf. Young 1984, p. 150, and Milward 1984, p. 400).
Mainly, however, this negative response was based on the idea – which
British policy-makers regarded as an established fact – that Great Britain
could not participate in projects aiming at European union (such as the
Schuman Plan), since it was not part of Europe. Relinquishing their
sovereign rights might help the European powers to recover, but it was
unthinkable that such a great power as Britain would ever need to do so.

Illustrative in this respect was the brochure *European Unity* published by
the National Executive Committee of the Labour Party in June 1950, which
Bevin had initiated in April (cf. Young 1984, pp. 143–4). This brochure
expressed the old familiar view that Great Britain was favourably inclined
towards expanding intergovernmental cooperation with Europe, for
example, within the OEEC, but that it rejected further cooperation if this
were to mean relinquishing part of its sovereignty. Far more than just a
rational analysis of the British position on Europe, this document was an
expression of the anti-European sentiments harboured by the Labour Party.
It complacently stated that 'in every respect except distance we in Britain
are closer to our kinsmen in Australia and New Zealand on the far side of
the world than we are to Europe. We are closer in language and in origins,
in social habits and institutions, in political outlook and in economic
interest' (Monnet 1978, p. 315). The Labour Party was not alone in this
opinion. It had also taken root in the Foreign Office. The permanent under-
secretary, for example, did not have any problems with the content of the
brochure. He declared that *European Unity* 'in its main thesis [is] along the
true lines of British policy' (Young 1984, p. 160). This view was also
undisputed within the Conservative Party. As early as September 1946, in
his famous Zurich speech, in which he called for the establishment of a
United States of Europe, Churchill stated that Great Britain and the
Commonwealth could only play the role of a well-disposed outsider in this
process – a point which many failed to notice at the time.[6]

After intensive talks with Monnet and other French representatives, the
British cabinet was eventually prepared to negotiate about cooperation as
far as coal and steel were concerned, but it refused to agree in advance to
the establishment of a High Authority with supranational powers. For

Schuman and Monnet, however, this point was not negotiable. On 1 June, Schuman gave the British an ultimatum: by eight o'clock the following evening, Great Britain must state whether or not it would take part in the negotiations (the basic assumption being that the pool was to be supranational in character). Schuman was not afraid to bring things to a head – much against the will of the French ambassador in London (cf. Young 1984, p. 154) – because he had already obtained the support of the Federal Republic and the plan was mainly focused on laying a new foundation for Franco-German relations. The following day, the British government decided not to take part in the negotiations, because 'no British government could be expected to accept such a commitment without having had any opportunity to assess the consequences which it might involve for our key industries, our export trade and our level of employment' (Milward 1984, p. 404). On 3 June this parting of the ways was made public. Both France and Great Britain issued a communiqué, in which each gave its own version of the reasons underlying this split. That same day a third communiqué was published, which stated that the Federal Republic, the Benelux countries and Italy had accepted the French invitation and would attend the conference on the Schuman Plan, which was to be convened in Paris a few weeks later (cf. Young 1984, p. 157). However, it should be borne in mind that, at the beginning of June 1950, no one interpreted the British withdrawal as a gesture that would have far-reaching consequences. There was, after all, no guarantee that the negotiations concerning the Schuman Plan would be successful. Everyone expected that Great Britain would join the negotiations on cooperation in coal and steel production once the French supranational initiative came to nothing, but then, of course, only on an intergovernmental basis. Only after some years did it become clear that this had been a true watershed (cf. Bullen in Schwabe 1988, p. 207, and Young 1984, p. 148).

3.   Negotiations on a Coal and Steel Pool

3.1. The First Phase of the Negotiations: June–August 1950
The so-called Conference of the Six started on 20 June 1950. Schuman was chairman of this conference, but left the actual work to Monnet and his staff. Monnet who was – as it was stenographically reported – 'anxious idea not become lost in myriad of problems to be worked out' (cf. Department of State 1977, p. 699), proposed that the negotiators limit themselves in the first instance to achieving agreement on a general framework treaty for the establishment of a High Authority. These

negotiations would have to be completed before the summer recess of the national parliaments; this was a plan that Adenauer fully supported (cf. Adenauer 1966a, pp. 263–4 and Monnet 1978, p. 320). Only then would all the tiresome technical details be discussed. In Monnet's view, these could be left to the High Authority or be the subject of further negotiations between the participating powers (cf. Monnet 1978, p. 321). In the latter case, he deemed it advisable for these to take place under the supervision of an international arbitrator who had the 'power to resolve deadlocks' (Department of State 1977, pp. 703–4).

Monnet's intentions were almost immediately thwarted by the attitude of the Dutch and Belgian delegations. 'Accepting the principle of a High Authority with real powers' might have been 'the entry ticket to the Schuman talks' (Duchêne 1994, p. 202), but once they were in, both countries immediately started trying to get their money back. The Dutch and Belgian position was that they were not prepared to sign anything at all before all the political, economic and social consequences of the entire enterprise had been put down on paper. France and the Federal Republic might already be convinced of the value of a supranational authority, but Belgium and the Netherlands certainly were not.[7] As Max Suetens, the head of the Belgian delegation, remarked in response to the French opening statement, 'you see the solution to our problems through the High Authority. We see the High Authority through our problems and their solutions' (Milward 1992, p. 65 and Duchêne 1994, p. 210)

In the following weeks, Belgium and the Netherlands concentrated their fire on the technocratic aspects of the Schuman Plan and the working document based on the plan, presented by Monnet two days after the conference had started. What particularly disturbed them was that, according to the original plan as well as the working document, the High Authority would operate in a political vacuum. They found it unacceptable that neither the responsibilities nor the accountability of the High Authority were clearly outlined. Dirk Spierenburg, the leader of the Dutch delegation, stated emphatically that the Netherlands wanted the governments of the participating countries to have some control over the High Authority's activities. He proposed that a Special Council of Ministers be established in addition to the High Authority. This council would have the power to coordinate the policies of the High Authority and those of the member states. He also proposed that this council should have a certain controlling power over the High Authority's performance. This last idea was, of course, out of keeping with the Schuman Plan, as its ultimate consequence would be to degrade the High Authority to little more than an international executive secretariat of the Council of Ministers, similar to that of the OEEC (see Chapter 4, Section 3). Monnet soon realized that he could not keep politics out of the proposed community and would have to accept some sort of Council of Ministers, but the second component of what became known as 'the Dutch formula' was completely unacceptable to him. This would undermine the whole *raison d'être* of the Schuman Plan.

In his negotiations with the Benelux countries, Monnet was hampered by the fact that he lacked broad support in his own country. In fact, he was in a rather isolated position. *Quai d'Orsay* officials felt they had been ignored and there was a great deal of opposition in the French cabinet to the whole idea of a supranational organization. In particular Maurice Petsche, the French Minister of Finance, did not want anything to do with the Schuman Plan (cf. Bossuat in Deighton 1995, p. 26). He approached his British counterpart Cripps about this in June. On that occasion he fulminated 'in very bitter terms against M. Monnet's successful attempt to rush ministers into decisions without adequate time for reflection' (Duchêne 1994, p. 205) and even asked Cripps to help him find a way for Great Britain to wreck the conference. Cripps, however, was not prepared to do so.

After consulting Spierenburg, Monnet put forward a compromise proposal at the meeting of delegation leaders on 12 July. It provided for a Council of Ministers with coordinating powers, but also for a High Authority with its own supranational powers, which therefore, on certain well-defined issues, would not need the approval of the member states. Spierenburg did not accept Monnet's compromise straight away. He clung to the idea that the High Authority should be an executive body of the Council of Ministers. However, when it turned out that the West German delegation, in the person of Hallstein, fully supported the proposal – the *Westbindung* could not be tampered with – Spierenburg finally gave in (cf. Monnet 1978, pp. 332–3, and Kersten in Schwabe 1988, pp. 294–5).[8]

As a result of this compromise, the powers of the High Authority needed to be defined very precisely. This meant that the procedure envisaged by Monnet, i.e. a brief period of negotiations concluding with a framework agreement on the establishment of a High Authority, had to be abandoned. In the subsequent weeks, the negotiators became bogged down in technical details, much as Monnet had feared, and continued with unflagging zeal in their attempts to reduce the supranational aspects of the Community to an absolute minimum. Monnet was forced to chair many more lengthy sessions at which his main function was to prevent the powers of the High Authority from being whittled down to the point where it could no longer operate independently (cf. Monnet 1978, p. 333).

Although it fully supported Monnet's compromise proposal, the West German delegation adopted a rather reserved attitude in the first phase of the negotiations. This was largely due to an event that had taken place five days after the start of the conference – the North Korean invasion of South Korea. When he heard the news on the afternoon of 25 June, Monnet immediately realized that this development would seriously threaten the successful completion of his project. He guessed – quite correctly, as shown in the previous chapter – that this clear expression of aggressive intentions on the part of the Communists would prompt the United States to demand a larger contribution to the defence of Western Europe from the Western European powers and, consequently, a contribution from West Germany (cf. Duchêne 1994, p. 226). This would obviously lead to a shift in the balance of power between France and the Federal Republic in favour of the latter and thus the Schuman Plan would lose much of its appeal in the eyes of the West Germans as far as *Gleichberechtigung* was concerned.

These developments in international politics were not the sole reason for the reserved attitude of the West German delegation. Another reason was the fact that, as in France, the whole enterprise was a fairly controversial issue in the Federal Republic. Although Adenauer was a staunch supporter,[9] his government had only a small majority in the *Bundestag* and was also internally divided on the issue. The SPD, the largest opposition party, which had almost as many seats as Adenauer's CDU/CSU, was firmly opposed to the Schuman Plan. According to its leader, Schumacher, it could only lead to 'Europe Inc.' under the directorship of 'the four Ks': '*Kapitalismus, Klerikalismus, Konservatismus* and *Kartelle*' (Adenauer 1966a, p. 329 and Monnet 1978, p. 319). Within the actual Federal Government, Ludwig Erhard, the Minister of Economic Affairs, was not very enthusiastic.[10] He feared the plan would protect the coal and steel industries from the world market, whereas he was convinced that these industries would benefit much more – as would the entire Western European economy – if they were to be part of it (cf. Willis [1965] 1968, p. 126).

In early August, the delegations reached agreement on the basic institutional design of the coal and steel community. This primarily consisted of a High Authority with supranational powers and a Council of Ministers with coordinating powers. The member states would be represented on an equal footing in both bodies. They also agreed on the establishment of a parliament, known as the Common Assembly, to which the High Authority was to report on its activities,[11] as well as a Court of Justice, which would settle disputes concerning the functioning of the common coal and steel market.

Subsequently, negotiations were suspended to enable the delegations to consult their governments back home about the results achieved. Far-reaching and exceptional as these results may have been in the context of international cooperation, there was so little left of the original French working document that it had no longer any relevance except from a historical point of view, as one member of the West German delegation pointed out (cf. Gillingham in Schwabe 1988, p. 416).

3.2. The Second Phase of the Negotiations: September 1950–March 1951

After the conference had been reopened in early September, the negotiations continued in working groups. However, the negotiators made very little progress. In October, there was even the threat of a deadlock over two draft articles drawn up by the French delegation in consultation with the American embassy, which were to form the basis for the Community's anti-cartel policy (cf. Duchêne 1994, p. 213).[12]

The fact that so little progress was made had to do with four mutually reinforcing developments. The first involved the delegations' continuing offensive aimed at strengthening the position of the Council of Ministers and limiting the powers of the High Authority. The second was that all the participating countries were trying to safeguard their own industries against the blows they were expected to suffer as a result of competition. They were trying to do so in all kinds of ways, some of which even conflicted with the accepted principle of a common coal and steel market. The Belgian delegation was particularly ingenious in inventing ways of protecting the heavily subsidized coal and steel industries in the Walloon provinces, and defended these with great tenacity (cf. Milward 1992, pp. 73–4).[13] The third development was that the West German delegation became less and less inclined to make compromises. Now that it was clear that the United States was keen to encourage the formation of a European army in which West German troops would also take part, the idea that time was on its side had obviously taken root in the Federal Republic. At one of the joint meetings of the foreign and defence ministers of the three occupying powers in New York, Schuman observed that 'there was a marked slowdown in general Schuman Plan discussions since start of talks on European defense force due to question in German mind as to necessity of making efforts in economic field if they become equals militarily' (Department of State 1977, p. 339). The final development was directly connected with the previous one. Particularly in the first weeks of

September, Monnet was too taken up with the complications surrounding impending German rearmament to pay much attention to the negotiations.

In the course of the following month Monnet was again free to devote all his attention to the conference. A steering group under his chairmanship was given the task of finding solutions to all the important questions the working groups were unable to resolve (cf. Duchêne 1994, p. 213). This was no easy matter. The main obstacles were Belgian policy aimed at protecting the inefficient Walloon coal and steel industries as much and for as long as possible, and West German resistance to the proposed anti-trust articles. It would take until the beginning of December for the draft text of the treaty to be completed, although the West German delegation continued objecting to the two anti-trust articles. As late as January 1951, Hallstein suggested to Monnet that it might be best after all to remove these articles from the text.

The West German refusal to accept these two articles had to do not so much with their specific content as with the considerable dissatisfaction in the Federal Republic about another issue that was intricately linked with the Community's future anti-cartel policy, but could not be regulated by the treaty itself. In the middle of December, Acheson received a memorandum in which he was informed about how the negotiations were developing:

> Finally, the Germans appear to be on the verge of demanding that they be relieved of the requirement to deconcentrate the Ruhr coal and steel industries, as a condition of joining the Plan. This position has not yet fully emerged, but it is becoming more prominent in comments from Frankfurt and Paris. (Department of State 1977, p. 766)

This memorandum referred to the policy laid down by the High Commission in Law No. 27 on 16 May 1950, exactly one week after the Schuman Plan was launched; this aimed 'to decentralize the German economy for the purpose of eliminating excessive concentration of economic power and preventing the development of a war potential' (*Official Gazette* 1950, p. 299), and to bring about the decartelization and deconcentration of the West German coal and steel industries. Apparently, the West Germans would not accept these two articles as long as the High Commission clung to this policy (cf. Schwabe in Schwabe 1988, p. 235). At the same time, the French tried to raise another issue to put pressure on the Federal Republic. From the very beginning of the negotiations, the latter had taken the position that agreement must be reached on the abolition of the IAR, with all its discriminating regulations concerning West Germany, before the

treaty could be signed. France, however, refused to accept this: abolition of
the IAR could only be discussed *after* the treaty had been signed. It was
not until March 1951 that, with the help of the Americans, a solution was
found to this 'Ruhr problem'. As has been explained above, this problem
had two aspects, of which the first (the decartelization and deconcentration
of the Ruhr industry) was clearly more important than the second (the
abolition of the IAR).

3.3.   The Ruhr Problem: Decartelization and Deconcentration

In order to destroy Germany's war potential, the Allied Powers had
decided that the large conglomerates dominating the Ruhr Basin would
have to be broken up. By 1950, however, little to nothing had come of this
policy. Willis is even of the opinion that '[of] all the objectives of Allied
occupation policy formulated at Potsdam, the one in which least progress
had been made by 1950 was probably the decartelization and deconcentration of German industry' (Willis [1965] 1968, p. 114). In the first
two years after the war, this negligence could be attributed to the fact that
the Ruhr Basin was situated within the British occupation zone and that the
Labour government was in the process of socializing Great Britain's own
coal and steel industries. From the British government's view, a Ruhr
complex in socialist rather than capitalist hands would no longer constitute
a threat to world peace. This was a line of reasoning which the French
found very objectionable (see also Chapter 3, Section 2). Even after the
Bizone had been established, the decartelization and deconcentration policy
did not really get off the ground. In November 1948, the American and
British occupation authorities had enacted a law (Law No. 75) that was
supposed to regulate this issue, but the implementation of this Law had
become bogged down in continuous squabbles between the American and
British occupation authorities. The Americans saw great advantages in it,
because such a policy could improve the competitive strength of the West
German coal and steel industries and thus provide an important stimulus
for the economic recovery of Europe. The British, however, did not feel
any need to help a competitor of their own coal and steel industries re-
establish itself.

Eventually, the Law which was to form the legal basis for the decartelization and deconcentration policy was published on 16 May 1950.
As this happened shortly after the Schuman Plan had been launched, the
Law made a very bad impression in the Federal Republic.[14] Schuman might
be making fair speeches in Paris about a future in which West Germany
would cooperate with the other Western European powers on an equal

footing, but in Bonn present reality was that the High Commission continued to impose unilateral measures that seemed only to reinforce the subordinate position of West Germany. Thus it seemed to be a matter of 'one step forward, two steps back' (cf. Willis [1965] 1968, p. 118).

When Law No. 27 began to be implemented at the end of September, splitting up the large steel conglomerates turned out to meet with the least resistance. There was much more German resistance to the part of the programme that aimed to abolish the so-called *Verbundswirtschaften* by forcing the steel companies to dispose of their own coal-mines. What met with the greatest resistance, however, was the plan to abolish the *Deutsche Kohlenverkauf* (DKV), the central sales organization of coal, which had actually been set up by the British occupation authorities (cf. Schwabe in Schwabe 1988, pp. 233–4).

Despite the problems the implementation of Law No. 27 caused in the Federal Republic, France refused to compromise. The large German steel companies had to be split up and their ties with the coal-mines severed, before the common coal and steel market could begin to operate.[15] Were this not to happen, the French coal and steel industries would soon be wiped out by their German competitors. To the Federal Government, the French position was unacceptable. It could only interpret French adherence to the implementation of the Law as a prior attempt to weaken the competitive position of the West German coal and steel industries on the common market as much as possible. France's implied position that West Germany, in order to join the coal and steel community, apparently had to meet conditions which the other potential participants did not have to meet was completely unacceptable to Chancellor Adenauer from the point of view of *Gleichberechtigung* (cf. Adenauer 1966a, p. 377).

The situation in which France and the Federal Republic found themselves in the winter of 1950–1951 with respect to the establishment of a coal and steel community was much the same as that of states confronted with a 'weak' security dilemma (see Chapter 2, Section 3). Successful completion of the conference on the Schuman Plan was the outcome that both France and the Federal Republic most wanted (for the sake of clarity, the resistance to the whole enterprise, which certainly existed in both countries, will not be discussed here). To France, the great attraction of the plan was that it would gain some control over the West German coal and steel industries, and to the Federal Republic, its merit was that it constituted a decisive first step towards *Westbindung* and a reconciliation with France. At the same time, however, neither of the two powers wanted to be the only one to make concessions, and actually preferred the

Schuman Plan to fail because of their unwillingness to compromise (for France, this meant clinging to decartelization and deconcentration; for the Federal Republic, it meant continuing its resistance to this policy). The worst that might happen as far as France was concerned was that the Schuman Plan would finally fail while the West German conglomerates were still intact. For the Federal Republic, the worst outcome would be that the plan failed after these conglomerates had been broken up.

This 'weak' security dilemma could have been resolved by convincing each other of their good intentions and reliability, but this was of course too much to ask of two arch-enemies that had been at war just a few years before. The conclusion is that, if France and the Federal Republic had been left to their own devices, they would not have come to an agreement and the conference would have been a failure. However, the United States actively intervened in the Franco-German conflict over decartelization and deconcentration, and was able to find a way out of the impasse in early March 1951 thanks to its dominant position as the major occupying power.[16]

As already noted at the beginning of Section 3, in May 1950 Monnet considered the possibility of using the services of an arbitrator to overcome possible deadlocks in the second round of negotiations, which would commence after the participating powers had reached agreement on the main outlines. At a meeting with the American ambassador in Paris on 18 December, Monnet asked him earnestly to encourage the United States to take on this role, as he feared that the Schuman Plan negotiations would otherwise come to nothing. The United States had no objections to this. American policy-makers were in any case averse to the American demand for a West German contribution to the defence of Western Europe being used by the Federal Republic to improve its own position. McCloy's warning to Adenauer at the end of September 1950 that West German participation in a European army must under no circumstances be allowed to become the subject of a deal, illustrates this quite clearly (see Chapter 5, Section 4). Characteristic is Eisenhower's observation, in a conversation with the American Under-Secretary of Defense in December, that the first thing the Germans 'should get over [is] the feeling that they were in command in a trading position' (Department of State 1977, p. 579).

At a meeting of the foreign ministers of the occupying powers in February 1951, devoted to the 'small revision' of the Occupation Statute (see Chapter 3, Section 5), Acheson, Schuman and Bevin soon agreed that 'Adenauer must stop procrastinating over the decartelization program and complete it by Spring' (Acheson 1969, p. 617). It is, of course, easy to say that something has to stop; what really counts is making sure that it actually does. This task was taken on by High Commissioner McCloy, who – after weeks of negotiating in the Federal Republic with all those involved – submitted a non-negotiable solution to Adenauer in early March. Adenauer's objections based on *Gleichberechtigung* would be met and various points of the decartelization and deconcentration programme would be toned down. On the other hand, this programme would be implemented without further ado and the Federal Republic must accept the text of the two anti-trust articles in the draft treaty (cf. Adenauer 1966a, p. 378, and Gillingham in Schwabe 1988, p. 432). Decartelization and deconcentration were no longer conditions for West German participation in the coal and steel community. Instead, the emergence of the Community would create conditions, which – given the powers that the High Authority would have to take action against cartels and price-fixing – should make it possible to opt out of the programme's full implementation. Furthermore, the abolition of the *Deutsche Kohlenverkauf* would be postponed until the autumn of 1952 (incidentally, the Federal Republic would still try to prevent the abolition of the DKV in the course of that year) (cf. Schwabe in Schwabe 1988, p. 238). On 14 March 1951, Adenauer agreed to the proposal as formulated by McCloy.[17]

3.4. The Ruhr Problem: the International Authority for the Ruhr

As has already been explained in Chapter 3, the IAR was one of the results of the London Conference on Germany in 1948 and was a poor substitute for the original French ambition to place the Ruhr Basin under international authority. The IAR's task was to supervise the division of Ruhr coal, coke and steel between domestic and export markets. France, Great Britain and the United States were represented in this body (each having three seats), as were the Benelux countries (each having one seat). In anticipation of the official establishment of the Federal Republic, the three western occupation zones were provisionally represented by the occupation authorities (each zone was also given one seat).

After the foundation of the Federal Republic in September 1949, its representatives were supposed to occupy these seats in the IAR. The Federal Government refused, however, to appoint these three representatives and sent only an observer. This refusal was a protest, not so much against the IAR itself (the official German standpoint was that the IAR might contain the germs of a European federation; see Section 1), but rather against the ongoing dismantlement of West German industry in connection with reparation payments (cf. Milward 1984, p. 384, and

Lademacher in Foschepoth 1985, p. 251). At the beginning of November, Adenauer sent a private message, unsigned and unaddressed, to the French High Commissioner François-Poncet, in which he made the proposal that 'in order to create the necessary preconditions among the French as well as among the German people for a final and lasting settlement of the Franco-German problem', the representatives of the Federal Republic would take part in IAR activities provided that there would be 'an announcement of a deceleration of dismantlings already begun and of a renunciation of new dismantlings' (Adenauer 1966a, p. 202; see also Willis [1965] 1968, p. 66). On 22 November 1949, a few days after they had reached agreement on which factories no longer needed to be dismantled, the High Commissioners and the Chancellor spent the entire day drawing up the definitive text of the agreement and the communiqué in which it would be made public.[18] According to Adenauer, the value of this so-called *Petersberger Abkommen* ('Petersberg Protocol') lay mainly in the sphere of *Gleichberechtigung*. What the Chancellor valued most was that the agreement was also signed by a representative of the Federal Republic, in this case himself, and not imposed unilaterally by the occupying powers, as had been usual up to then. In his memoirs, Adenauer also treated the Petersberg Protocol from this perspective: 'Not all German wishes and proposals had been met; nonetheless, the Petersberg Agreement represented a very great success. For the first time since the collapse we were officially recognized as equal and for the first time we re-entered the international sphere' (Adenauer 1966a, pp. 220–1).[19]

The entry of the West German representatives did not alter the fact that there was considerable dissatisfaction in the Federal Republic about the way in which the IAR operated. As has been mentioned previously (see Chapter 3, Section 3), decisions in the IAR were reached by a majority vote. As a result, the West German delegation was quite often outvoted. In the first six months of 1951, in fact, the West German representatives constituted a minority of three in each vote concerning the distribution of Ruhr coal (cf. Milward 1984, p. 412). The decisions made by the IAR in this period compelled the Federal Republic to supply France with coal it desperately needed for itself. As a result, shortages in the Federal Republic could only be made up by buying American and British coal on the world market at a price considerably higher than France needed to pay for West German coal.

The discrimination against the Federal Republic on which the IAR was based was evidently inconsistent with the whole tenor of the Schuman Plan. This is why, in the first phase of the negotiations, there was no opposition to the West German condition that the countries participating in the conference should agree to the abolition of the IAR before the Federal Republic would sign the treaty. However, no specific steps were taken to comply with West German wishes in this respect. In the autumn of 1950, complications surrounding the decartelization and deconcentration of Ruhr industry and the draft texts of the two anti-trust articles in the treaty made France begin to see matters in a wholly new light.

Adenauer met François-Poncet in Bonn at the beginning of November in order to discuss the state of affairs regarding the Schuman Plan. The Chancellor was pleased that 'the Schuman Plan negotiations were making good progress in general', but also expressed his concern that 'the question of abolishing the Ruhr Authority and certain other restrictions that were incompatible with the Schuman Plan had not yet been cleared up' (Adenauer 1966a, p. 297). Two weeks later, when Hallstein spoke to Monnet about this question, Adenauer's concern proved to be justified. Monnet's standpoint on the IAR was in fact the reverse of the chancellor's position on the decartelization and deconcentration of German conglomerates. Adenauer had declared it unacceptable that the Federal Republic would only be allowed to sign the treaty on the coal and steel community after it had met additional conditions, whereas Monnet declared it unacceptable that West Germany would only sign the treaty after the other participants had met additional conditions. Not a single decision about the IAR could be made before the end of the negotiations concerning the coal and steel community (cf. Gillingham in Schwabe 1988, p. 425).

After weeks of deliberation, France and the Federal Republic finally reached agreement in February 1951 and came up with the following formula: when signing the treaty, France would state that, in its opinion, the IAR must cease its activities once the High Authority was installed and that it would otherwise do its best to bring about the abolition of the IAR (cf. Milward 1984 and Willis [1965] 1968). This last commitment was certainly not an empty gesture, as Great Britain had considerable difficulties in accepting this abolition of the IAR. It was not until October 1951 that the British government was prepared to do so (cf. Lister 1960, p. 150).

In March 1951, with the compromise over the implementation of Law No. 27 and the French government's promise that it would help to abolish the IAR, nothing now stood in the way of the treaty being signed. It was finally initialled on 19 March. The fact that the powers involved eventually managed to find a solution to both aspects of the Ruhr problem within the framework of the Schuman Plan proves that Monnet's original conception was correct. At the same time, the text of the treaty made clear that having a correct 'political' view was no guarantee of having the right perception of how such a view would be translated politically. Unlike the clear framework treaty that Monnet and his staff had had in mind one year earlier, the definitive Treaty establishing the European Coal and Steel Community, signed in Paris on 18 April, was very dense and involved and comprised no fewer than 100 articles.

One last obstacle that had to be removed before the High Authority could actually start its activities was the question of where it should have its seat. Negotiations on this issue dragged on until it was finally settled at a meeting of the foreign ministers on 25 July 1952. At first the ministers tried to postpone the decision even longer, but when this proved impossible for legal reasons, they began to seek a solution. Emotions subsequently ran high during this meeting, which lasted until 5 o'clock the next morning. When the negotiations were about to end in a deadlock, Joseph Bech, the Luxembourg foreign minister – 'a very wise man', according to Adenauer (Adenauer 1966a, p. 340) – proposed establishing a 'provisional' seat in the city of Luxembourg. For want of a better solution, the ministers decided to accept this offer, but only after it had been recorded, at the request of the Belgian delegation, that the whole question 'should be "re-examined" at subsequent meetings of the ministers' (cf. Duchêne 1994, pp. 222–3). As it happened, Bech's 'gesture' put the Luxembourg authorities in rather a tight corner. Where could they possibly find suitable office space and accommodation for the High Authority and its officials in just two weeks?

4. A 'Nature Reserve' for European Integration?

After the European Coal and Steel Community (ECSC) had become operative on 10 August 1952, it was soon clear that it had a less significant role to play on the European stage than its supporters had hoped and its opponents had feared. This was somewhat surprising, as the economic situation was improving and there were no crises in the coal or steel sector requiring drastic reorganizations (cf. Milward 1984, p. 420). Marjolin has attributed the ECSC's limited success to three factors. In his view, the first was that, with the increasing use of oil, coal was becoming less and less important as an energy source. The second factor he identified was the dramatic failure in August 1954 of the European Defence Community Treaty, which had evolved out of the Pleven Plan (see Chapter 7). The third factor was by far the most important one. Practically every decision the High Authority wished to take would have repercussions outside the coal and steel sectors (cf. Marjolin 1989, p. 274). Owing to the Dutch formula, this led to a situation in which it was dependent, for almost all its decisions, on the cooperation of the Council of Ministers. In the case of the ECSC, the 'expansive logic of sector integration' predicted by Haas in his theory of neo-functionalism actually worked in exactly the opposite direction (cf. Haas [1958] 1968, p. 283; see also Chapter 2, Section 6). It seemed that a totally different expansive logic was applicable, namely some form of Gresham's Law, which states that bad money will drive out good (assuming, of course, that supranationality is considered to be 'good').[20] The supranational elements of the ECSC were reduced in favour of the national element. It simply proved impossible for the High Authority to take far-reaching decisions without the prior consent of the member states' governments (cf. Jansen and De Vree [1985] 1988, pp. 115–17). Although the High Authority possessed what was considered the ultimate hallmark of supranationality – the treaty stipulated that it would take decisions by a majority vote – under its first chairman, Monnet, it was already common practice that no important decision was taken until those most directly involved had given their consent (cf. Monnet 1978, p. 388).[21]

During the negotiations on the treaty, Monnet and his staff apparently suffered from a certain naive optimism in this matter. In my view, they finally had to pay for their technocratic approach to the question of the High Authority's position. This proves once again that a correct 'political' view does not necessarily imply a correct view of politics. Zijlstra, who was appointed Minister of Economic Affairs in the Netherlands three weeks after the treaty had come into force, takes the opposite view:

> It was, however, not at all intended that these two branches of industry should continue as a kind of nature reserve for European integration. The creators of this partial integration were very well aware of this. They saw this new community as a dynamic operation, as a tool to break open the existing situation, not as a goal in itself but as a means of achieving the actual goal, i.e. European unification. (Zijlstra 1992, p. 55)

In his defence of the spiritual fathers of the Treaty of Paris, however, Zijlstra ignores the true function of the ECSC in respect of the future development of 'Europe'. In my view, Milward is quite right when he concludes that the main value of the ECSC was not so much that it changed the face of things to come in Europe, but that it laid the foundation for the solution of a problem from the past, i.e. the traditional Franco-German enmity: 'its most lasting attribute, one which shows no substantial signs of weakening, has been its solution to a past problem and not its importance for the future' (Milward 1984, p. 407).[22]

It is no doubt very tempting to lump the Treaty of Paris and the Treaty of Dunkirk together as documents whose authors had shown more interest in the past than in the future. One should not, however, yield to this temptation. The Treaty of Dunkirk was nothing more than a routine confirmation of the existing state practice in those days. The lack of results led at most to a sense of resignation, as 'that is the way things go' in international politics. The Treaty of Paris, on the other hand, opened up new avenues. The fact that these led to such disappointing results was of great concern to those involved in the implementation of the treaty, and it encouraged them to find better ways of dealing with things. If the ECSC was a tool to break open the existing situation, it must have been so in this sense. Its relative impotence made clear to all those involved – with the one important exception of Monnet – that sector integration, as first applied in the ECSC, was a dead end and that, if they wanted to continue along the line of supranational cooperation, a different approach would be required. According to Küsters, several members of the High Authority, such as Spierenburg and Etzel, the West German Vice-Chairman, but also a high ECSC official such as the Frenchman Uri, had already come to this conclusion in 1955 (cf. Küsters 1982, p. 265). This conclusion was clearly reflected in the proposals for an economic community that were formulated in the Spaak Report in the spring of 1956. This report was approved by the foreign ministers of the Six at a meeting in Venice and subsequently formed the basis for the negotiations leading to the Treaty establishing the European Economic Community (see also Chapter 8).

Notes

1. A few weeks later, an interview with Adenauer was published in *Die Zeit*, in which he stated that he did not consider the IAR as a yoke but as the 'first step towards controlling the whole European heavy industry' (Foschepoth 1988, p. 128).
2. 'Technocratic' in the meaning attributed to it in Chapter 1, Section 2: it is possible to find an institutional solution to a problem by referring purely to the nature of the problem (the 'technical side of the matter'), purged of all obfuscating elements, particularly vested interests (see also Section 2).
3. Monnet wrote in his memoirs: 'I asked for this passage in our text to be underlined, because it described at one and the same time the method, the means and the objective, which henceforth were indissolubly linked' (Monnet 1978, p. 298).

4. Monnet had explained the plan at a meeting of the High Commission earlier that day. One of the decisions taken in this meeting was that the High Commission would not attend the coming negotiations concerning the plan (cf. Department of State 1977, p. 708).

5. The fact that, despite Monnet's request but in line with his own ideas about French participation in West German industry (see Section 1), Adenauer wanted to appoint a prominent industrialist as leader of the West German delegation to the negotiations, showed that even Adenauer was not yet fully alive to the plan's political nature and Monnet's technocratic interpretation of it. At Monnet's request, Adenauer dropped this candidate in favour of Hallstein, who was Professor of Law at the University of Frankfurt. In the first years after World War II, he had also been rector of this university. In his autobiography, Monnet paid Hallstein the greatest compliment that he could by saying that Hallstein 'was not a politician, but he had political vision' (Monnet 1978, p. 320; cf. Duchêne 1994, p. 207).

6. With respect to the establishment of a United States of Europe, Churchill said in this speech: 'in all this urgent work, France and Germany must take the lead together. Great Britain, the British Commonwealth of Nations, mighty America, and I trust Soviet Russia – for then indeed all would be well – must be the friends and sponsors of the new Europe and must champion its right to live and shine'. Jansen and De Vree continue: 'the last sentence clearly indicated that Churchill wanted to keep Britain out of the European Union, a fact generally overlooked at that time' (Jansen and De Vree [1985] 1988, p. 55).

7. The Netherlands had joined the negotiations after considerable hesitation. According to Kersten, the Dutch delegation's instructions revealed little willingness in the Netherlands to give the plan the benefit of the doubt. At the suggestion of delegation leader Spierenburg and Dutch foreign minister Stikker, the Dutch cabinet decided to make the reservation that 'it did not regard itself as being tied to the principles of the Schuman Plan if a workable system proved unattainable. The Schuman Plan was so important to Stikker that he refrained from consulting the French regarding the publication of the Dutch reservation' (Kersten in Schwabe 1988, pp. 288–9).

8. In a note written at the end of July, in which Great Britain was informed about the state of the Schuman Plan negotiations, Clappier summarized the relationship between the High Authority and the Council of Ministers as follows: 'it is impossible to separate in an absolute manner the problems of coal and steel from other problems. It is thus indispensable to harmonize action of the High Authority with that of governments which are responsible for the general policies of the states. To this end mutual consultations are provided for between the High Authority and the special Council of Ministers' (Department of State 1977, p. 743).

9. At the end of June, High Commissioner McCloy notified Acheson that 'Adenauer is throwing all his authority behind the plan, stating to the

industrialists that this has such tremendous political significance that they must conform' (Department of State 1977, p. 739).

10. In his memoirs Monnet made fun of Erhard, who in his eyes was a 'dogmatic liberal economist'. When the negotiators proposed a code of conduct, Erhard scented *dirigisme,* and when they tried to give shape to European solidarity, he suspected protectionist aims. Monnet felt sorry for Hallstein, who, in order to satisfy Erhard, felt obliged to pay lip-service to the latter's economic principles during the negotiations (cf. Monnet 1978, pp. 329–30). Apparently, Erhard was not entirely wrong to be suspicious of the talks in Paris. In his own country, too, Monnet was seen as the great market interventionist. Willis quotes former Prime Minister Flandin, who described Monnet as follows: 'this Gray Eminence of all the successive governments of the Fourth Republic represents the continuity of state intervention that characterizes the regime. Having exhausted the advantages of the system at home, it is natural for him to work to extend it on the international level' (Willis [1965] 1968, p. 96).

11. The 'Common Assembly' was originally envisaged as a kind of stockholders meeting, which would convene once a year to discuss results (cf. Duchêne 1994, pp. 210–11).

12. The texts in question were French drafts that, in their definitive form, were included in the treaty as Articles 65 and 66.

13. According to Milward, it is 'impossible to find in the papers of the Belgian delegation the slightest hint of any aspirations to "make Europe"' (quoted in Duchêne 1994, p. 211).

14. Promulgating Law No. 27 at such an inopportune moment seems to be a classic example of how standing operating procedures (SOPs, see Chapter 2, Section 2) can thwart policy drawn up at a higher level. The Law was passed by the High Commission on 13 April 1950. Because the French High Commissioner François-Poncet voted against the Law, its implementation was automatically suspended for a month. This period could subsequently be extended only if two of the three high commissioners considered it appropriate. As the French government did not take any further steps to prevent implementation, the suspension period ended in May and the Law was published a few days later (cf. Willis [1965] 1968, p. 118).

15. The French had fewer problems with the DKV. Similar organizations for the purchase and sale of coal existed in France. It was the Americans who did not want anything to do with the DKV (cf. Duchêne 1994, pp. 216–17, and Milward 1984, p. 410).

16. Duchêne notes in this respect that 'perhaps the most extraordinary feature of the Schuman conference was the enormous, almost internal, role the Americans played. Without them, the conference would have failed and the foundations of the European Community never been laid. This proved that, while France might be able to give a lead, it could not, even in 1950, set the terms of a relationship with Germany' (Duchêne 1994, p. 224).

17. In reply to Adenauer's letter, High Commissioner François-Poncet again

confirmed more than two weeks later that the High Commission 'is of the opinion that the existence of the Schuman Plan makes possible the treatment of these problems in a wider perspective than was otherwise possible. On the assumption that the Schuman Plan will enter into force, the High Commission considers liberal solutions justified' (Willis [1965] 1968, p. 120).

18. The meeting between the High Commissioners and the Chancellor took no less than eleven hours, from 9 a.m. to 10 p.m. with a two-hour break. Although this might lead one to suspect otherwise, the mood of the meeting was actually quite good, if we may believe the diary notes of Adenauer's assistant Blankenhorn (cf. Blankenhorn 1980).

19. Adenauer's great adversary Schumacher held an entirely different opinion. In his view, the agreement was a needless concession to the occupation authorities. In the *Bundestag* debate on this agreement in the night of 24 to 25 November 1949, Schumacher accused Adenauer of having prejudiced the interests of the Federal Republic to such an extent that he deserved to be called 'the Chancellor of the Allies'. He refused to withdraw this accusation and was subsequently suspended for twenty days (cf. Adenauer 1966a, pp. 227–30).

20. Sir Thomas Gresham was governor of Virginia in the sixteenth century. In a letter to Queen Elizabeth I, he described how the coexistence of cotton and gold as means of payment in the colony had led to a situation in which gold was practically no longer used as such. Everyone tried to pay with perishable cotton. He therefore concluded that 'bad money drives out the good'.

21. Gillingham comes to the conclusion that 'as President of the High Authority Monnet could act decisively only outside the framework of the Paris Treaty, his most important personal accomplishment having been to secure an American loan on extremely favorable terms which, being too large for the investment needs of the coal-steel pool, turned the ECSC into an important international lender' (Gillingham in Schwabe 1988, p. 435).

22. Even from an economic perspective, the ECSC has accomplished very little. This is more or less due to Monnet and his staff having failed to enlist the help of experts from the coal and steel industries in drafting the plan. According to Lister, 'the coal and steel industries [were] not the most tractable ones with which to start the experiment of freeing trade and prices' (Lister 1960, p. 403). In his study of how the ECSC functioned during the first six years of its existence, he came to the conclusion that in both the coal and steel industry very little had come of the objective laid down in Article 2 of the Treaty: 'to create those circumstances which ensure the most rational division of the production on the highest level possible' (cf. Lister 1960, pp. 403–4). In his view, the two anti-trust articles in the Treaty had remained a dead letter. Almost from the moment that the Community came into being, concentrations of companies emerged in France, Belgium and the Federal Republic: 'the threat of competition, as usual, stimulated combination' (Lister 1960, p. 168). None of these take-overs or mergers was prohibited by the High Authority.

7. *Westbindung*: from Pleven Plan to WEU

1. Introduction

As has already been explained in Chapter 5, the Pleven Plan was a reaction to the American one package proposal of September 1950. The gist of this proposal was that the United States would satisfy France's ardent wish for American divisions and an integrated command on the condition that an immediate start was made on setting up West German army units for the defence of Western Europe. However, France refused to comply with this condition. The only compromise France was willing to make at the NATO Council meeting in September 1950 was that it would not be opposed to a discussion 'from a technical perspective' within NATO on how the Federal Republic might contribute to the defence of Western Europe. At the end of October, in response to American pressure, France opted for a '*fuite en avant* by drawing up its own proposal' (Wielenga 1989, p. 98). The aim of this plan, named after Prime Minister Pleven, was to establish a European army in which West German troops would ultimately also take part.

Just like the Schuman Plan, this initiative caused quite a sensation and had likewise not appeared out of the blue. In the autumn of 1949, Adenauer had repeatedly shown he was in favour of a West German contingent taking part in a European army under European supreme command (cf. Baring 1969, p. 71). In an interview with the *Cleveland Plain Dealer* in December 1949, which attracted considerable attention, he proclaimed he was against rearmament. If the Allied Powers insisted on a West German contribution to the defence of Western Europe, however, he considered it impossible that this would involve forming a West German army. Such a contribution would only be possible if West German units were integrated into a European armed force (cf. Richardson 1966, p. 17, and Adenauer 1966a, p. 267).

At a Council of Europe meeting in August 1950, at which the events in Korea were, of course, one of the main items on the agenda, several prominent French politicians advocated the formation of an army of united Europe (in which West German soldiers would also take part), to be financed by European taxation (cf. Willis [1965] 1968, p. 132). On 11

August 1950, a large majority of the Council of Europe voted for a motion tabled by Winston Churchill, which proposed 'the immediate creation of a united European army under the authority of a European Minister for Defense, subject to proper democratic European control, and acting in full cooperation with the United States and Canada' (Osgood 1962, p. 73). Less than a week later, at a meeting with the High Commissioners, Adenauer announced that he supported Churchill's motion and was willing to work for West German participation in this European armed force (Baring 1969, p. 86; cf. Adenauer 1966a, p. 277).

An important consequence of the North Korean invasion of South Korea was the United States' conclusion that it was no longer possible to ignore the generally accepted view that West German rearmament was militarily inevitable (see Chapter 5, Section 4). For this reason the war in Korea was also 'the great turning-point in West German post-war history, an unexpected stroke of luck and the beginning of the rise of the Federal Republic in matters of foreign policy' (Baring 1969, p. 81). In relation to the United States, the Federal Republic, once a party which could only hope for favours, now became a party which also had something to offer – something of great value to the Americans (cf. Hanrieder 1989, p. 39). As a result of the Korean war, West Germany had more room to negotiate and soon began to take advantage of this. It was prepared to put up with the United States' indignation at the fact that 'the Germans', barely five years after their unconditional surrender, thought they could impose conditions for their cooperation in rearmament (see also Chapters 5 and 6).

In preparation of the negotiations, Adenauer secretly asked former general Speidel to work out some details of West German participation in a European army. On 8 August 1950, the very same day on which French delegates advocated the formation of a European army in the Council of Europe, Speidel's memorandum 'Thoughts on the Question of the External Security of the German Federal Republic' was sent to the Chancellor through informal channels. In Speidel's view, West Germany could only take part in a European army on the basis of *Gleichberechtigung*. This, in his opinion, necessarily implied that West Germans soldiers would form West German divisions, that integration would only take place at army corps level, and that West German officers would not be excluded from positions of command in the European army (cf. Baring 1969, p. 83).[1]

2. The Launch of the Pleven Plan

Most of the preparations for the Pleven Plan were made by Monnet and his team in the margin of the Schuman Plan conference (cf. Monnet 1978, pp. 344–5). Their main objective was to prevent the question of West German rearmament from wrecking this conference. They wanted to formulate at short notice a proposal which 'simultaneously [could be] represented to the United States and to Great Britain as permitting German rearmament, and to the National Assembly and the French people as preventing just that' (Furniss 1960, p. 65). This plan was prepared quite differently from the Schuman Plan. It was not prepared in the seclusion of the *Commissariat au Plan* – a high *Quai d'Orsay* official was soon added to the team – and Monnet kept in touch with the members of the French cabinet, particularly with Prime Minister Pleven, on an almost daily basis (cf. Monnet 1978, p. 345). The cabinet discussed the draft text on 22 and 23 October. After considerable deliberation (they did not want another proposal by Monnet to be sprung on them), the cabinet ministers approved the new initiative.[2] On 24 October, Pleven made the plan public in a speech to the National Assembly.

Pleven emphasized that France would rather have postponed the discussion on West German involvement in the collective defence of Western Europe until the coal and steel pool was functioning successfully, but that world events had prevented this. Consequently, the French government proposed settling the matter by the same methods and in the same spirit as had characterized the negotiations for the Schuman Plan. This arrangement, which 'took into account the cruel lessons from the past', implied that Western Europe would not be defended by a European army under American supreme command and consisting of American, Canadian and Western European divisions – including some West German ones – as envisaged in the American one package proposal, but by an armed force under American supreme command, which, in addition to American and Canadian divisions, would incorporate a European army consisting of international divisions. In terms of personnel and equipment, this European army would be fully integrated and have its own budget. The European minister of defence, to be appointed by the participating nations, would have the same authority over this European army as a national minister of defence had over a national army.

Although Pleven made it appear otherwise, two crucial points in his plan were completely inconsistent with the spirit of the Schuman Plan. In my view, this explains to some extent why Monnet, in his memoirs, so easily distanced himself from the Plan. The first point was that the Pleven Plan lacked that very element which Spierenburg would have liked to see removed from the Schuman Plan (see Chapter 6, Section 3), namely the creation of a supranational authority with powers of its own, operating independently of national governments. A European Minister of Defence would only be implementing the general guidelines from the Council of Ministers. The second point was that, under the Schuman Plan, France had been prepared to place its entire coal and steel industry under the authority of the proposed supranational body, whereas under the Pleven Plan it refused to put its entire armed forces at the disposal of the European army on the grounds that it also had colonial obligations to fulfil (cf. Monnet 1978, pp. 347–8).

In comparison to the Schuman Plan, the Pleven Plan had seriously weakened the aspect of 'self-binding'. As the Pleven Plan did stipulate that all West German army units would have to be integrated into the European army, this last point was also incompatible with the basic principle of the Schuman Plan that all nations would participate on an equal footing. While the other member states would have their own army, of which certain parts would be at the disposal of the European army, the Pleven Plan proposed that the Federal Republic should not have its own army (since the French objected to a West German minister of defence, the European minister of defence was to assume this role). Unlike the other member states, West Germany did not therefore need its own general staff; as the West German units were to be integrated into the international divisions, such a body would be totally superfluous anyway. This integration would take place 'at the level of the smallest unit possible' (as explained in Chapter 5, Section 4, the French government considered a battalion to be the smallest unit). All in all, this is quite a remarkable interpretation of the spirit of the Schuman Plan: France would have its own divisions, whereas the Federal Republic would not have so much as a battalion of its own!

Finally, Pleven announced that the French government intended to invite Great Britain and 'the free countries of the European continent' to talks on how a European army might be formed in accordance with the principles it had outlined. These talks could commence – and this is what Monnet really had in mind – as soon as the treaty establishing the coal and steel community had been signed (cf. Van Ooijen *et al.* 1996, pp. 65–6).

In Chapter 5, Section 4, it has already been seen that the United States was strongly opposed to the Pleven Plan. It was generally considered as 'a politically impossible and militarily unfeasible subterfuge for preventing German rearmament' (Osgood 1962, p. 85). Acheson said that the plan was 'designed for infinite delay' (Acheson 1969, p. 457). American suspicions were merely increased by the fact that the plan was a complete failure from a military point of view. Monnet and his team had followed the same procedure when drawing up the Schuman Plan, and had tried to find a 'political' solution to the problem of West German rearmament without the help of military experts (in the case of the Schuman Plan, they had likewise refused to consult coal and steel experts) (cf. Monnet 1978, p. 345).[3] This time, however, American policy-makers did not appreciate such an approach. Particularly in the weeks after the failure of the Defence Committee meeting in October, they told anyone who would listen that French military leaders themselves also considered the plan militarily unsound.

When Hallstein informed Adenauer about the plan the day after Pleven had made his speech to the National Assembly, the Chancellor's first instinct was also to reject it. He felt annoyed about exactly the same things as the Americans. Firstly, 'the close link between this plan and the Schuman Plan negotiations' would only mean postponing West German rearmament indefinitely. Secondly, the proposed integration into the European army 'at the level of the smallest unit possible' would only make 'the defensive power of such a mixed army totally insufficient'. He was also of the opinion that this part of the plan 'discriminated against the German contingent' (Blankenhorn 1980, p. 116).

Another complication which the Chancellor had to take into account was that the mass of the West German people were against rearmament. Neither the French nor the Americans had ever given a moment's thought to whether the West Germans would actually be willing to rearm. The fact remained, however, that the whole idea of rearmament was 'very unpopular' in the Federal Republic (Adenauer 1966a, p. 202). Despite all the connections made with the Soviet threat (see Chapter 5, Section 4), the North Korean invasion of South Korea did not produce any change in this attitude. The NATO countries would have to defend the Federal Republic on their own (cf. Willis [1965] 1968, p. 147). At the beginning of November, the *New York Times* therefore came to the conclusion that 'the French aversion to arming the Germans appears to be matched only by the German aversion to being rearmed' (McGeehan 1971, p. 68).

Nonetheless, the Chancellor eventually approved the plan at the beginning of November and expressed his willingness to defy West German public opinion regarding rearmament. Adenauer realized that all the points on which West Germany was discriminated against were also starting points for bringing about Franco-German reconciliation and improving the *Westbindung*. Once the West German delegation was seated at the conference table, it could attain *Gleichberechtigung*. What carried even more weight as far as Adenauer was concerned was that West

Germany 'should take advantage of the nervousness the Korean War had caused in the Western camp and thus further its own military and political interests, as it remained uncertain how long this situation would last' (Baring 1969, p. 105). On 7 November, Adenauer notified François-Poncet that he was favourably disposed towards the Pleven Plan 'despite its many shortcomings' (Adenauer 1966a, p. 298). At a press conference the following day, he stated that the French High Commissioner had assured him that 'Germany within the Pleven Plan will be on fully equal terms and on an equal footing with other partners'. He also remarked with a touch of irony that 'we Germans are glad that certain terms that aroused astonishment amongst us are thus made clear' (*Documents on International Affairs* 1958, p. 344).

3. The Petersberg and Paris Conferences

Both the American one package proposal and the French Pleven Plan contained elements that, from the point of view of *Gleichberechtigung*, were unacceptable to the Federal Republic. It is therefore no surprise that the American-French compromise over West German rearmament, as laid down in the Spofford Plan (see Chapter 5, Section 4), contained provisions that for the same reason were also unacceptable to West Germany. The two restrictions that were most objectionable were that (i) West Germany was not allowed to have its own general staff, and (ii) the West German units would not be allowed the same heavy military equipment (e.g. tanks) as the other units in the European army (cf. McGeehan 1971, p. 85). This was the reason why Adenauer rejected the Spofford Plan. In one of his interviews, he stated that he had no intention of placing West German troops under an American Commander-in-Chief unless 'the Western Allies accepted the principle of complete equality for the German military forces, especially with regard to arms and command authority' (Adenauer 1966a, p. 307).

The NATO Council meeting at the end of December 1950 gave the go-ahead for three types of negotiations: firstly, concerning the military aspects of West German contribution to the defence of Western Europe; secondly, concerning the necessary adaptation of the Occupation Statute in the light of this West German contribution; and thirdly, concerning the Pleven Plan. The negotiations on the first two issues would be conducted on the Petersberg near Bonn; those on the Pleven Plan in Paris.

Negotiations on the military aspects proceeded very smoothly. They began on 6 January 1951 and ended six months later. They resulted in the so-called Petersberg Plan, in which the West German desire for *Gleich-berechtigung* was amply satisfied. The Petersberg Plan therefore contained various elements that were out of tune with the Spofford Plan. These successful negotiations showed once again that West German rearmament was undisputed among military leaders, the French included (cf. McGeehan 1971, p. 125). However, it was out of the question that the Federal Republic could settle such a sensitive issue as *Gleichberechtigung* indirectly through talks between military experts. Thus the results of the Petersberg negotiations were doomed to prove irrelevant. As Baring concluded, this West German attempt 'to push *Gleichberechtigung* through was pointless from the very beginning. The talks failed before they had even started' (Baring 1969, p. 101).

Negotiations on the Occupation Statute proceeded less smoothly. Although Adenauer had talked with the High Commissioners immediately after the NATO Council meeting, it was not until 10 May 1951 that the negotiations actually started. At the meeting in December, the occupying powers and the Federal Republic proved to hold diametrically opposed points of view as to what implications West German participation in the defence of Western Europe would have for their mutual relations. François-Poncet stated that the High Commission took the same position as in September (see Chapter 5, Section 4), namely that the fundamental principles of the occupation and the resulting rights remained non-negotiable.[4] In the High Commission's view, the only negotiable issue was the way in which these rights were being exercised. It was therefore prepared to take West German proposals on that subject into consideration. Adenauer, however, expected that sovereignty would be restored as a *quid pro quo* for West German rearmament. The Chancellor was 'aghast' at the High Commission's attitude (Adenauer 1966a, p. 313). He saw one ray of hope, however, for François-Poncet had mentioned in his explanation that the nature of the occupation could not be changed 'at this moment'. He hoped the High Commissioners would understand him if he 'considered this "at this moment" as short a period of time as possible' (Adenauer 1966a, p. 312; cf. Baring 1969, p. 126).

As has already been mentioned, the actual talks started on 10 May and lasted until the beginning of August. Partly due to the discord between the occupying powers, these talks did not produce any concrete results. The negotiators got more or less bogged down in exploring all the problems to be solved (cf. Baring 1969, p. 127). Nonetheless these negotiations did produce one result which was very important to the Federal Republic, though not very concrete 'at this moment'. The occupying powers agreed that future negotiations on this matter would focus on laying a new foundation for their relationship with the Federal Republic (cf. Grewe in Blumenwitz *et al.* 1976, p. 702).

The Pleven Plan conference started on 15 February 1951. Schuman concluded his opening speech with words that could hardly be reconciled with the origins of the plan:[5] France was trying to find a lasting solution that would express the idea of the European community and that would not be an 'improvisation imposed on us by immediate necessity' (Adenauer 1966a, p. 350). The conference was attended not only by France and the Federal Republic, but also by Italy, Belgium and Luxembourg. Great Britain and the Netherlands sent observers. The Dutch decision not to take part was rather remarkable. After all, the Netherlands was one of the participants in the ECSC negotiations and the Pleven Plan did meet the proposal which the Dutch had put forward in these negotiations, namely that the Council of Ministers would have primacy (see Chapter 6, Section 3). Nevertheless Dutch foreign minister Stikker was of the opinion that the Pleven Plan still contained too many supranational elements. In his view, the Atlantic security pact was 'infinitely more preferable'. Stikker also feared the French initiative would only lead to estrangement between the United States and Europe, which could only have an adverse effect on the Netherlands (cf. Wielenga 1989, pp. 100–1).

During the negotiations on the Pleven Plan, the West German delegation led by Hallstein[6] resorted to its old familiar tactics of delaying the proceedings. The Germans focused entirely on the Petersberg negotiations (cf. Baring 1969, pp. 100–1). The very complicated nature of the matters discussed also slowed down the negotiations for what was soon to be called the European Defence Community (EDC). In his memoirs, Acheson wrote there were only two Americans who dared say they knew what was going on at the conference: 'Ambassador David Bruce and a Treasury attaché named Tomlinson who had forsaken foreign exchange problems to become a passionate supporter of and expert on the Community. Neither of them could impart understanding of the negotiations to the rest of us; indeed, Bruce would not try' (Acheson 1969, p. 557).[7] A final factor that had also caused considerable delay in the first months of the negotiations was that the participants did not really want to make any decisions before knowing the results of the French National Assembly elections, scheduled for mid-June (cf. Duchêne 1994, p. 231).

4. An American Summer Offensive

Shortly after the French elections, the United States suddenly changed its attitude and was no longer opposed to the Pleven Plan. During a lunch arranged by McCloy, Monnet had been able to convince NATO Commander-in-Chief Eisenhower that West German rearmament would come to nothing unless it were to take place in the context of a European army. In his view, the Americans had been wrong to ignore the symbolic value of a European army in which French as well as German soldiers would wear the same uniforms. What the United States had failed to recognize was that German rearmament was in the first instance a human problem rather than a military one. In his *Memoirs* Monnet described how Eisenhower rebuked General Gruenther, his Chief of Staff, who had argued that it was all very well to exchange such generalities but that it all eventually came down to how many divisions would be set up and how many soldiers these would comprise. Admittedly, Eisenhower did this by making a rather Monnet-like remark:

> You're a typical technician: you only see the part you're interested in – you don't look at the problem as a whole. The strength of the divisions is one aspect of things, but the real problem's a human one. What Monnet's proposing is to organize relations between people, and I'm all for it. (Monnet 1978, p. 359)[8]

As a result of Monnet's intervention, the Americans began to see that 'the caterpillar of German rearmament' could emerge as 'the butterfly of supra-national European unification' (McGeehan 1971, p. 33).

Somewhat later Monnet also persuaded France, in response to the American change of policy, to give up its resistance to the American view that German troops should be integrated into the European army at army corps level (cf. Osgood 1962, p. 382, and Duchêne 1994, p. 232).

The first time that this American change of policy was clearly demonstrated was in a speech by Eisenhower in London on 3 July 1951, in which he commented favourably on the European army (cf. McGeehan 1971, p. 127). On the same day, McCloy – who had just returned from the United States – informed Adenauer, much to the latter's surprise, that the time had now come for the Federal Republic to take the Paris negotiations seriously (cf. Baring 1969, p. 108).[9] The Chancellor realized there was very little room for manoeuvre left for West Germany now that the United States and France had come to terms on the European army. Consequently, the negotiations in Paris now made more progress. Within three weeks the delegations reached agreement on the formation of a defence community that would have its own funding and an army of twenty divisions. This result was laid down in the so-called Alphand Report, which, at the specific request of the West German delegation, also mentioned the issues that had not yet been agreed on. There turned out to be many problems that still had to be resolved (Baring 1969, p. 110). For example, the delegations were still divided over whether they should appoint a European minister of defence or a Commission on which the participating countries would be represented. The report furthermore revealed that there was disagreement as to the division of votes in the Council of Ministers and the Assembly, the scope of the military contribution of the participating countries (the French stated that the West German contribution could never become larger than their own), and how the member states' financial contributions would be regulated. According to Blankenhorn, these were 'all very difficult problems which would lead to many more lengthy negotiations' (Blankenhorn 1980, p. 124).

Now that the negotiations on the European army had regained their momentum and the moment of actual West German involvement in the defence of Western Europe was near, the occupying powers could no longer avoid seeking a satisfactory settlement regarding their relationship with the Federal Republic under international law (in anticipation of a definitive peace treaty). At a conference in Washington in mid-September, the ministers of foreign affairs agreed that the West German contribution to the EDC should take place on an equal footing. They also accepted the implication that the West German contribution to the EDC was incompatible with maintaining the Occupation Statute. Once the West German contribution to the European army was definitely settled, the Occupation Statute could be abandoned (cf. Baring 1969, p. 112). This would be replaced by new terms for mutual relations to be laid down in treaties with the Federal Republic. At the same time, however, the ministers decided, in the public interest, that the occupying powers would retain certain rights. This meant the occupying powers still did not think that 'a normal relationship with the Federal Republic under international law' was possible (Grewe in Blumenwitz *et al.* 1976, p. 704).

Although Adenauer greeted the results of the conference in Washington with great approval, Willis has pointed out – in my opinion, rightly so – that they actually meant that France had Germany in a stranglehold. As long as West German rearmament within the framework of the EDC had not been regulated to the satisfaction of France (and also, of course, the United States and Great Britain, but these countries had hardly any problems with the rearmament of the Federal Republic), the position of the

Federal Republic under international law would remain that of an occupied power (cf. Willis [1965] 1968, p. 135).

5.   The Bonn and Paris Conferences

The negotiations on the treaties in which relations between the Federal Republic and the occupying powers would be laid down started a few days after the ministers of foreign affairs had reached agreement on this issue in Washington. As a token of the changed relations, the meetings were no longer held on the Petersberg, where the High Commission had its seat, but in the headquarters of the High Commissioners and occasionally in the Chancellor's residence. The first meeting between the High Commissioners and the Chancellor proceeded in much the same way as their meeting immediately after the NATO Council meeting in Brussels at the end of December (see Section 3). The two parties proved to hold completely opposing views as to what had to be done. While the High Commission was in favour of paring the Occupation Statute down to the bone, the Federal Government wanted to conclude treaties on a reciprocal basis. Both parties immediately rejected the draft texts prepared by the other as being 'totally unsuitable for discussion' (Baring 1969, p. 130).[10] This time, however, the result was not a long-lasting impasse. Within three weeks, the Chancellor and the High Commission had reached agreement on the main outlines and decided that further details could be left to the experts.

They had found the following solution. On the one hand, the parties to the treaty – the three powers and the Federal Republic – acknowledged that the Occupation Statute was incompatible with the aim of integrating the Federal Republic into Europe (which was clearly not the same as being incompatible with the sovereign status of the Federal Republic). On the other hand, the parties accepted that, given the specific international situation in Germany, the *three* powers would only retain those rights which served the common interest of the *four* signatories.

At the end of November, in Paris, the Convention on the Relations between the Three Powers and the Federal Republic was initialled. The text of this convention was not made public in anticipation of the successful completion of the negotiations on the other conventions concerning the end of the occupation, the foreign troops to be stationed on the Federal Republic's territory, and the size of the Federal Republic's financial contribution to these foreign troops and the EDC. It would still take six months to settle these 'technical' issues, but the Bonn Conventions were then finally signed by the four ministers of foreign affairs.

A new round of military discussions also led to a basic agreement in November. Its most important features were that (i) divisions would be the basic units of the European army (although they were not called 'divisions' but *groupements*, consisting of 12,000–13,000 men); (ii) West German officers were also eligible for command of an army corps or the European army; (iii) the member states with territories overseas were allowed to have national troops for the defence of these territories (in the case of France, these amounted to a total of six divisions), and (iv) the defence community was to be responsible for the lines of communication of the European army (cf. McGeehan 1971, p. 156).

Compared with what had been stipulated in the Pleven Plan one year earlier, this agreement clearly showed that the West Germans had achieved success. This was exactly what annoyed Jules Moch, France's former Minister of Defence, when he was informed of the contents of the agreement. This result was completely unacceptable to him. The Pleven Plan, which he had helped to draw up, had aimed to create a European framework which would render the formation of West German army units superfluous, whereas this agreement 'made so many concessions to Germany that [the EDC] had become merely a blind behind which the *Wehrmacht* would be reconstituted'. Moreover, if the French attempt to 'rearm the West Germans without rearming West Germany' now proved to have failed,[11] why should France still impose restrictions on itself in the context of a European Defence Community (cf. Furniss 1960, p. 73)? Moch's angry response clearly illustrated once again that the intention of the Pleven Plan was not at all to treat the Federal Republic on an equal footing in the military sphere, but, on the contrary, to keep the Federal Republic under control. If the EDC was to be organized in such a way that the Federal Republic would truly participate on an equal footing with France, what French interest would be served by France's participation? Participation in a supranational defence community only made sense to France if this would result in lasting military subordination of the Federal Republic to France. In his memoirs, Acheson may have complained about the French policy of keeping 'Germany hedged about by restrictions and limitations on rearmament wholly inconsistent with the position of a self-respecting ally' (Acheson 1969, p. 611), but it was not at all France's intention to help the Federal Republic attain that position. For the same reason, when Adenauer told the ministers of foreign affairs of the three powers that the negotiations on the defence community were being conducted in rather a strange way, his words fell on deaf ears as far as Schuman was concerned:

> We are being asked to promise this or that three or four times as proof of our good intentions. Please do not misunderstand me if I say that it must be a strange partner who on entering the partnership has to declare three times running that he is a decent fellow and has nothing but honest intentions. Surely everybody must be aware that declarations and agreements mean nothing where there is no good will. But if you keep on asking one of the partners for proofs of his good will, it makes a very bad impression. (Adenauer 1966a, p. 410; cf. Department of State 1983, p. 68)

The same went for Acheson's earlier admonition at this same meeting that 'they all keep the great objective in mind' (Department of State 1983, p. 63), i.e. that the Federal Republic was to become a partner in the collective defence of Western Europe. To France, however, the 'great objective' of the defence community was not that the Federal Republic should become a partner, but to subject West Germany to conditions and restrictions, which would in any case not apply to France.

A nice example of French policy in this matter was an issue that dominated the Pleven Plan conference in the winter of 1951–1952 (this conference had been reopened in October 1951).[12] This concerned the so-called 'security controls'. The French delegation proposed incorporating a clause in the treaty prescribing that certain types of weapons such as nuclear, chemical and bacteriological weapons, aircraft, warships and guided missiles could not be produced in 'strategically exposed areas'. It was argued that production lines for such weapons might otherwise fall too easily into the hands of an advancing Soviet army. There was, however, only one strategically exposed area: the Federal Republic. For this reason the French proposal was unacceptable to the West German delegation. The same went for another closely related stipulation originating in the Spofford Plan (see Section 3), namely that the Federal Republic would be the only member state without armoured units.

A solution was finally found during the talks between Acheson, Schuman, Adenauer and the new British foreign minister, Eden, in London in mid-February 1952. (The ministers were in London for King George VI's funeral; Adenauer had to wait two days before the other three would allow him to join the talks.) These talks were held in a rather tense atmosphere – Schuman just managed to avoid saying that Adenauer was the only German he trusted (cf. Department of State 1983, p. 70). The solution was based on an arrangement on which the three powers had reached agreement earlier in London, and to which the Chancellor resigned himself. It proves just how far Adenauer was prepared to go to wrest himself from France's stranglehold. From the point of view of

Gleichberechtigung, West Germany could, of course, no longer accept limitations being imposed on it. However, this view also implied – and this was a discovery – that nothing prevented the Federal Republic from accepting certain limitations of its own free will. Consequently, the Chancellor made the statement that 'in view of the international tension and Germany's geographical position', the Federal Republic 'would not regard it as discriminatory' if certain weapons were not produced in the Federal Republic; which weapons this meant remained the subject of further negotiations. The three powers in turn declared that the West German units would be given all the weapons necessary to execute the tasks assigned to them (Department of State 1983, pp. 69 and 75; cf. Kelleher 1975, p. 20).

Partly thanks to such cunning manoeuvres, France and the Federal Republic were able, under the watchful eyes of the United States and Great Britain, to reach gradual agreement on a defence community which 'internally' did not discriminate between member states, as confirmed by the treaty's preamble (cf. Van Ooijen *et al.* 1996, p. 82), but which 'externally' set the seal on the military subordination of the Federal Republic. Whether all the agreements, promises and declarations outside the framework of the defence community would provide sufficient guarantees for the continuation of this subordination was a matter of continuous concern to the French.

Acheson, Eden and Schuman subsequently flew from London to Lisbon for a NATO Council meeting. The Council agreed to a West German contribution of twelve divisions within the European army. The United States, Great Britain and the other NATO countries that did not participate in the EDC would assume the same obligations towards the EDC as they had previously done towards the NATO member states (cf. Osgood, 1962, p. 87).

On 10 March 1952, the Soviet Union tried to intervene in the negotiation process. In a note sent to the other three occupying powers, it proposed starting talks on a German peace treaty on the basis of a united and neutral Germany that would also acquire an army of its own, though limited in size (cf. Baring 1969, p. 146, and Wielenga 1989, p. 137). This note was the first 'shot' in what Eden called 'the battle of the notes' (Acheson 1969, p. 631).[13] The West generally considered this Soviet note and the three that were to follow as an attempt by the Soviet Union to undermine Adenauer's position in the Federal Republic by making the West Germans believe that the much desired reunification was possible without having to pay the dreaded price of rearmament (see Section 2), and thus to ensure that the negotiations on the EDC and the Bonn Conventions would fail.[14] Each Soviet note was therefore resolutely rejected, the main argument being that negotiations on the peace treaty could only be conducted after free elections had been held in the whole of Germany. The Soviet Union refused to discuss this demand (cf. Wielenga 1989, pp. 162–70).

Of much more importance to the prospects of the defence community and the 'contractual agreements' was that two Americans who had played a prominent part in European politics and had been responsible to a large degree for the dynamics in the European integration process had announced their resignation. These were High Commissioner McCloy, who had managed to resolve the Franco-German deadlock over decartelization and deconcentration of the Ruhr industry, and NATO Commander-in-Chief Eisenhower, whose support had saved the Pleven Plan negotiations. McCloy stated that he would return to the United States on 15 July in order to resume his business career. Eisenhower announced in mid-April that he hoped to be nominated for the presidency by the Republican Party and asked President Truman to relieve him of his duties as of 1 June. His request was granted the following day.

The American President had himself already made clear in March that he did not wish to stay on for another term. Truman's decision also did not bode well for the future of the defence community and the Bonn Conventions, as he was now no longer in a position to develop new initiatives or exert pressure on the European powers. His Secretary of State, Acheson, now merely played the role of arbitrator lacking the power to resolve deadlocks (cf. Chapter 6, Section 3). In any case, until the inauguration of the new president in January 1953, the Six as well as Great Britain would have to fend for themselves as far as 'Europe' was concerned.

The French remained doubtful about the whole enterprise. A new concern of theirs was that no arrangements had been made for the situation that would arise if the Federal Republic decided to secede from the defence community (for example, after the West German army units had been brought up to full strength). France therefore demanded a guarantee from the United States and Great Britain that they would never tolerate such a development. This demand epitomized in Acheson's eyes 'the accumulation of all the French Government's neuroses' (Acheson 1969, p. 640). The United States was for the time being not prepared to go beyond confirming that it would be 'seriously concerned' if this unlikely situation were to occur. It also refused to state what the consequences would be of its serious concern (cf. McGeehan 1971, p. 204). Of course, the United States did not get off the hook so easily. When Acheson left for Europe at the end of May to sign the Conventions in Bonn and the EDC Treaty in Paris, he knew that France would not sign unless it had been satisfied on this matter – and many others (cf. Acheson 1969, p. 644). Eventually the United States and Great Britain signed a declaration in Paris stating that they would both consider any act that threatened the integrity of the defence community as a threat to their own security, and that they were determined 'to station such forces on the continent of Europe, including the Federal Republic of Germany, as they deem necessary and appropriate to contribute to the joint defense of the North Atlantic Treaty area' (Osgood 1962, p. 92).

One day after the Convention on the Relations between the Three Powers and the Federal Republic, and all the other related conventions, had been signed in Bonn, the EDC Treaty and corresponding protocols were signed in Paris, together with some other treaties and agreements that regulated the EDC's relations with Great Britain (in its capacity as a member of the Brussels Pact) and NATO.

The first article of the Convention stipulated the price the three powers had to pay for West German participation in the joint defence of Western Europe: 'The Federal Republic shall have full authority [which is not the same as 'supreme authority'; see Chapter 3, Section 4] over its internal and external affairs, except as provided in the present Convention'. The exceptions laid down in Article 2 concerned: '(a) the stationing of armed forces in Germany (b) Berlin, and (c) Germany as a whole, including the unification of Germany' (Van Ooijen *et al.* 1996, p. 39).[15]

The institutional structure of the EDC was rather similar to that of the ECSC, be it that the position of the Council of Ministers *vis-à-vis* the Commissariat (which had eventually replaced the European minister of defence) had indeed been reinforced, although not as much as proposed in the Pleven Plan. The Commissariat consisted of nine members and was responsible for the formation, recruitment, exercising and equipping of the 'basic units' (the word 'division' was still taboo) of the European army. The basic units would be placed under the authority of a European Commander-in-Chief who in turn would take orders from the NATO Commander-in-Chief. The Council of Ministers not only coordinated the policies of the Commissariat and member states, but could also give directions to the Commissariat.[16] The Assembly of the EDC was the same as that of the ECSC. At meetings concerning the EDC, it would have nine additional representatives: three from the Federal Republic, three from France and three from Italy. The Court of Justice of the ECSC would also function as Court of Justice of the EDC.

Finally, all the treaties, conventions, protocols and agreements concluded in Bonn and Paris on 26 and 27 May, with the obvious exception of the EDC Treaty, stipulated that they would only come into effect after the EDC had become operative. In anticipation of this situation, the High Commissioners organized most of their activities as if the Bonn Conventions had already taken effect (cf. Hanrieder 1989, p. 234, and Wielenga 1989, p. 141).

Adenauer was extremely satisfied with the result of the negotiations. As he stated at a meeting of the parliamentary CDU party in mid-June, the Germans 'were once again the subject of politics and strategy, whereas until now we had only been the object' (Foschepoth 1988, pp. 131–2). A few days before the treaties were signed, at a meeting of the West German cabinet, the Chancellor said he expected the Federal Republic would play first fiddle in the EDC and 'despite the fact that it had a population of only 50 million, would become a controlling factor in Europe' (Baring 1969, p. 122).

Although France had signed everything it had been requested to sign, it was rather dissatisfied with the whole state of affairs.[17] In a memorandum written on the day the EDC Treaty was signed, the *Quai d'Orsay* came to the conclusion that the supranational aspects of the EDC would have an adverse effect on France. In the view of the French Ministry of Foreign Affairs, the Germans were the better negotiators and were supported by the United States. In the ECSC France might be dominant, but in the EDC it would be subordinate to Germany (cf. Wall 1991, p. 265).

6.   Ratification of the EDC Treaty

After the EDC Treaty had been signed, the decision-making process concerning the EDC came to a standstill. The whole idea of West German rearmament within a defence community in which the Federal Republic would probably play a dominant role was completely unacceptable to France. However, refusing to ratify the Treaty and openly admitting that a serious mistake had been made was no option. After all, the EDC Treaty was the result of a French initiative to take the lead in solving the issue of West German rearmament, and France did eventually sign the Treaty. Its reputation as the leading Western European power and a reliable partner was at stake. France therefore postponed the ratification for as long as possible. It was not until August 1954 that the ratification of the Treaty was discussed in the National Assembly. France was hoping that developments in international politics would make ratification of the Treaty no longer necessary, so that France could get out of it without losing face. For example, after the death of Stalin in March 1953 and the truce in Korea four months later, France tried to convince the United States and Great Britain that, given the reduced Soviet threat, West German rearmament and therefore also the EDC Treaty had in fact become superfluous. Attempts at a *rapprochement* with the Soviet Union should take precedence over the formation of a European army. As such a 'happy coincidence' might well not occur, with the result that the dreaded decision on whether or not to ratify the Treaty could no longer be postponed, France also constantly tried to bind the United States and Great Britain more closely to the EDC. By means of additional protocols, it also tried to eliminate the restrictions that would be imposed on it within the defence community.

It was not the Pinay government (March–December 1952), responsible for the signing of it, but the Mayer government (January–May 1953) that submitted the Treaty to the National Assembly for ratification. However, the Mayer government also stated that the treaties should only be ratified after a number of French wishes had been met by additional protocols. These protocols were discussed by the ECSC ministers of foreign affairs at a conference in Rome at the end of February.[18] Schuman's successor, Bidault, explained that the protocols were only meant to inform the other signatories to the EDC Treaty about the French interpretation of certain provisions in the Treaty. Adenauer, however, refused to except this and strongly criticized the contents of the protocols. The ambiguous final communiqué could hardly conceal the major differences of opinion (cf. Willis [1965] 1968, p. 164, and Poidevin in Volkmann and Schwengler 1985, p. 123).[19]

At the beginning of May, in line with an earlier appeal from President Eisenhower to the new Soviet leaders to end the Cold War, Churchill proposed in the House of Commons that a conference be convened of the 'Big Four' to discuss a possible peace treaty with Germany and Austria. At a meeting of the ministers of foreign affairs of the Western 'Big Three' in July, it became clear that Churchill had not really appreciated the import of Eisenhower's appeal. The United States was not very happy with this initiative. France, however, fully supported it. As French ratification of the EDC Treaty would be a needless burden on the preparations for such a conference with the Soviet Union, Bidault assured his counterparts that, for the time being, there would not be a majority in the French National Assembly for ratification (cf. Wall 1991, p. 270, and Willis [1965] 1968, p.

166).[20]

By the end of June 1953, the Laniel government was in power in France. In November 1953, Prime Minister Laniel announced that he would not ask the National Assembly to ratify the Treaty as long as a number of unresolved issues had not been settled to France's satisfaction and the United States and Great Britain had not reaffirmed their intention to keep their troops stationed on the European continent. In April 1954, agreement was reached in this respect. Great Britain would send a representative to the EDC's Council of Ministers meetings and also agreed to permanent representation on the Commissariat. Moreover, Great Britain promised, after the United States had also done so, that it would not withdraw its troops stationed on the European continent as long as the security of the area was under threat (cf. McGeehan 1971, p. 219).

The Mendès-France cabinet was formed a few days after the Laniel government collapsed on 12 June 1954. The new French Prime Minister, who was also foreign minister, carried the French conditions for ratification of the Treaty to extremes, if not to the point of absurdity. On 13 August the French cabinet approved a protocol drawn up by Mendès-France, including a whole shopping list of additional conditions (three ministers resigned in protest against the cabinet's decision, because they thought the protocol did not go far enough). The additional conditions were specifically meant to undermine further the supranational aspects of the defence community, and to give France as much freedom of action as possible once the defence community became operative.[21] The protocol was subsequently sent to Paul-Henri Spaak, the Belgian foreign minister, with a request to convene a conference to discuss it (at the end of June, the Benelux countries had already pressed for a conference on the state of affairs concerning the EDC).

To American policy-makers, all this was a source of great concern. French resistance to the EDC was not only holding up West Germany's rearmament and rehabilitation, but was also undermining the foundations of American policy with respect to Western Europe, which was to encourage Western European unification. As early as December 1953, Secretary of State Dulles, who had succeeded Acheson at the beginning of that year, had warned the other parties at a NATO Council meeting that 'if the European Defense Community should not become effective; if France and Germany remain apart so that they would again be potential enemies. This would compel an agonizing reappraisal of basic United States policy' (Osgood 1962, pp. 94–5). Fully and openly supported by President Eisenhower, he repeated this warning several days later in a speech to the

National Press Club (cf. McGeehan 1971, p. 229).

The United States was, however, confronted with the problem that it had no effective sanctions to make France realize that it would also be in its own interest to join the supranational defence community. Unlike the Federal Republic, France was not an occupied power trying to regain its sovereignty. The only concrete sanction the United States could impose if France refused to join the EDC was to postpone or even end military assistance programmes concerning France within NATO. However, such a sanction would have had no deterrent effect whatsoever, because France would rather have done without this assistance than accept the defence community (compare the situation with respect to Marshall Aid in 1947 as sketched in Chapter 4, Section 3). The only remaining option for the United States was to warn France once again of the risk of American anger if it caused the EDC project to fail, and to encourage the other five signatories not to give in to France's demands and to cling to the supranational aspects of the defence community.

At the conference on the French protocol, which started in Brussels on 19 August 1954, Mendès-France tried to convince the other parties that their approval of the protocol was absolutely vital in getting the French National Assembly to accept the EDC Treaty. His position was that of an 'honest broker' who was doing his utmost to find an arrangement which would leave enough of the EDC intact to give the supporters of the project what they wanted, but in which the EDC was whittled down to such extent that a majority of the French parliament would be willing to accept it (cf. *L'Année politique* 1955, p. 422). The other five parties at the conference were very distrustful. Faure, one of the ministers in the French delegation, had told a Belgian negotiator during lunch on the opening day: 'let Brussels fail and let the Americans arm the Germans so we can forget this EDC nonsense' (Department of State 1983, p. 1054). This had certainly done Mendès-France's credibility no good, but what had mainly made the Five doubt the French Prime Minister's sincerity was his demand that the French protocol should be submitted for approval to the national parliaments. Apart from the fact that the text of the protocol was by no means certain to be accepted by the parliaments, this procedure also meant that it would take another year and a half to complete the ratification procedure for the Treaty. In their view, Mendès-France was after one thing only: sabotaging the EDC. As the other parties almost openly doubted his sincerity, there were several occasions during the conference when the French Prime Minister exploded with fury and in fits of emotions criticized the others for not understanding the predicament in which he and his government found themselves. At the conference and outside it – particularly to the large number of American observers who were present in Brussels – he loudly complained that the other parties, despite all his efforts to oblige them, were not prepared to make any concessions (cf. Department of State 1983, pp. 1052–68). He thus entirely misrepresented what actually was taking place at the conference, as the other delegations were quite prepared to make various concessions which, in Spaak's view, were very substantial (cf. Spaak 1971, pp. 170–1). Indeed, in a personal interview on the second-last day of the conference, it was Mendès-France himself who confided to Spaak that such concessions would be of very little use anyway. As far as he was concerned, the aim was not to reach any form of agreement. He told Spaak: 'I do not want to assume responsibility for a premature rupture, but I can tell you here and now that I have decided to say no' (Spaak 1971, p. 169).

The conference dragged on until the early morning of 22 August, as no substantial progress could be made. After Spaak had proposed ending the conference, Mendès-France proceeded to read a statement. According to Spaak, there was every indication that this statement 'had been carefully prepared. This was not an improvised statement by someone forced to make a snap decision at the end of a debate. This was a declaration carefully weighed up in every detail and drawn up to serve as a brief in any subsequent discussion'. The French Prime Minister announced that he would now submit the EDC Treaty to the National Assembly. However, he was afraid that, as he 'was returning to Paris empty-handed there was not the slightest chance of the French Parliament ratifying the EDC Treaty' (Spaak 1971, p. 170; cf. Beyen 1968, p. 233).

The debate in the French National Assembly on the EDC Treaty started on 28 August with the committees that had examined the Treaty reporting their findings orally. All these committees proved to have objections of one kind or another. The Foreign Affairs Committee also stated that, in its view, rejecting the EDC Treaty would also mean that the Bonn Conventions could not take effect. On the following day, Mendès-France delivered a speech in which he gave an account of his experiences in Brussels. He gave the members of parliament the impression that France's reasonableness had foundered on the uncompromising attitude of the other parties. Further negotiations were therefore pointless. In any case, the time had come to decide. As far as the French cabinet was concerned, it was an open question. Mendès-France told the representatives that the cabinet had decided not to ask for a vote of confidence as the Treaty had sown too much discord among the French themselves. As far as he himself was concerned, he did not care whether the Treaty was accepted or rejected (cf. *L'Année politique* 1955, pp. 429–30).

The supporters of the EDC Treaty in the National Assembly tried to postpone further discussions on the Treaty to enable Mendès-France to examine whether agreement could still be reached with the other EDC participants on the basis of the protocol. However, the Prime Minister did not feel any need to do so.[22] When the supporters nevertheless wanted to put a motion to that effect to the meeting on 30 August, their opponents resorted to posing the *question préalable* ('prior question'). Under the National Assembly's rules of procedure, such a *question préalable* took precedence over a motion. To end discussions on a certain issue, supporters and opponents were allowed to make one more speech on the issue before the *question préalable* was put to the vote. If this was passed, the issue in question could no longer be discussed. In this case, this would mean rejection of the EDC Treaty. After two speeches, in which Herriot made an all-out effort on behalf of the opponents and Pineau spoke on behalf of the supporters, the *question préalable* was passed by 319 votes to 264. Thus the EDC Treaty was rejected (cf. *L'Année politique* 1955, pp. 429–32, and Department of State 1983, pp. 1104–9).[23]

7. The Paris Agreements

Referring to the events in the National Assembly, in their introduction to *France Defeats the EDC*, editors Lerner and Aron observed: 'so an idea born in France died in France' (Lerner and Aron 1957, p. x). However neatly formulated, this conclusion does not entirely take into account the reason why the National Assembly rejected the Treaty. For it was precisely this 'idea born in France' – preventing West German rearmament by means of a European structure – which the EDC Treaty in its definitive form failed to do full justice to. What died in France was a supranational organization that would have made West German rearmament possible, and in which the Federal Republic would also have played a dominant part. If West German rearmament was necessary, it might better take place outside the framework of the EDC.

Well before the Brussels Conference, Mendès-France had sounded out the United States and Great Britain about an alternative framework that might allow West German rearmament. Both powers, however, adopted a rather reserved attitude. This was not only because they were clinging to their official standpoint that the EDC was a worthwhile enterprise, or because they were not inclined to let France continue to play a leading role in this matter after the charade of the EDC negotiations, but mainly because they did not know exactly what this alternative framework would be (cf. Department of State 1983, p. 1056 ff.). Fortunately, a few days after France had rejected the EDC, Anthony Eden, the British foreign secretary, had a brainwave, as he said 'while taking a bath' (cf. Eden 1960, p. 151). Eden's flash of inspiration was that, if the Brussels Pact were also to include the Federal Republic and Italy, it would provide exactly the framework that might solve France's problem. Compared with the EDC, such a Western European Union (WEU) would give France two great advantages. Firstly, the WEU, which was to succeed the Brussels Treaty Organization (BTO), would be an *intergovernmental* organization. Secondly, France would no longer have to deal with the Federal Republic on its own, but might form a counterweight to it together with Great Britain. In exchange, France would have to accept that the Federal Republic would join NATO and that the Bonn Conventions would be reviewed to bring them more into line with the Federal Republic's position as an equal member of the WEU and NATO.

Eden visited a number of Western European capitals to explain his proposal. It was greeted with approval everywhere. According to Eden, the aspect of his proposal that pleased the German Chancellor most was that as a member of the WEU the Federal Republic would no longer only be dealing with France, but also with Great Britain. Mendès-France accepted Eden's solution, provided that the security controls envisaged in the EDC were also realized in some form or other in the WEU. The British initiative still nearly foundered on American resistance, because, as Dulles told Eden, 'the Brussels Pact [had] no supranational features'. Without first consulting Eden, Dulles travelled to Bonn and London – pointedly by-passing Paris – in a last attempt to save 'Europe'. In a personal interview with his British counterpart, however, he had to admit that he did not know how the problem could otherwise be solved. After having impressed on Eden the significance 'of keeping alive the idea of real integration in Europe', he gave his full support to the plan (Eden 1960, pp. 162 and 164).

It took two conferences to work out the details of Eden's idea. The first started on 28 September 1954 in London. The second took place in Paris at the end of October on the eve of a NATO Council meeting where the Federal Republic's entry had already been placed on the agenda. At the London Conference, the United States, Canada, Great Britain and the EDC countries reached an agreement in principle. Subsequently, the experts had two and a half weeks to settle the differences as far as the details were concerned and draw up the texts of the treaties, protocols and other agreements.

France's concerns were met by the United States and Great Britain in various ways. The United States made clear that the failure of the EDC would not have any influence on its firm intention, which it had expressed twice before (see Sections 5 and 6), to keep its troops stationed in Europe, including the Federal Republic, as long as it deemed this necessary for the defence of the NATO treaty area. For its part, Great Britain promised to keep four divisions and part of its air force stationed in West Germany until 1998, the year in which the Brussels Pact was to end, and not to withdraw these troops against the wishes of the majority of Brussels Pact countries.[24] Together with France, both powers also declared that:

> they will regard as a threat to their own peace and safety any recourse to force which, in violation of the principles of the United Nations Charter, threatens the integrity and unity of the Atlantic Alliance or its defensive purposes. In the event of any such action, the three governments, for their part, will consider the offending government as having forfeited its rights to any guarantee and any military assistance provided for in the North Atlantic Treaty and its protocols. They will act in accordance with Article 4 of the North Atlantic Treaty with a view to taking other measures which may be appropriate. (Furniss 1960, p. 104)

When the negotiations in London had almost come to a standstill, the German Chancellor for his part repeated his promise – 'the only really "lonely decision" I made while being Chancellor, as I did not consult the cabinet or my party' (Adenauer 1966b, p. 347)[25] – that the Federal Republic would not produce any atomic, bacteriological or chemical weapons (so-called ABC weapons), or any other heavy weapons 'such as rockets, warships and aircraft.[26] Adenauer was also prepared to allow inspectors to enter the Federal Republic. These would check whether this promise was actually being kept.

The future WEU member states agreed also to establish a WEU body that would control weapon stocks and arms production on the European continent.[27] Moreover, they agreed that their maximum contribution to NATO would be laid down in a separate agreement and that this maximum contribution could only be increased after all the member states had given their consent (cf. Ruhm von Oppen 1955, p. 602). The Federal Republic finally accepted France's demand that it must first become a member of the WEU before it could join NATO.

France had lost face on the question of West German rearmament, since the Federal Republic was now going to participate as an equal partner in the joint defence of Western Europe. The main aim of all the statements and provisions was therefore to make things reasonably bearable for France. The revised text of the Convention on the Relations between the Three Powers and the Federal Republic made West Germany's new status quite clear. It was no longer a convention signed by the three powers on the one hand and the Federal Republic on the other, but a convention signed by four equal powers (cf. Wielenga 1989, p. 142). In the original convention's preamble the three powers and the Federal Republic had listed the reasons why the Occupation Statute could be abolished (see also Section 5). In Article 1, the three powers now briefly stated that they 'will terminate the Occupation Régime in the Federal Republic, revoke the Occupation Statute and abolish the Allied High Commission' (Van Ooijen *et al.* 1996, p. 39). Pending the ratification of the Paris Agreements by the national parliaments and settlement of all affairs concerning the termination of the occupation, they also ordered the High Commissioners to act henceforth as if the Federal Republic had already regained its full authority (as actually happened on 5 May 1955).

Mendès-France submitted the Paris Agreements to the French National Assembly for ratification as early as mid-December. Again, it was uncertain whether the National Assembly would give its approval. Discussions on the Agreements proceeded with great difficulty and there was even a brief panic in Washington, London and Bonn when, on the early morning of 24 December, the National Assembly rejected that part of the Agreements referring to the establishment of the WEU and the Federal Republic's entry into NATO (cf. Eden 1960, pp. 170–1). This panic was somewhat subdued when it became clear that this rejection was primarily an act of revenge by the supporters of the EDC against Mendès-France (cf. Department of State 1983, p. 1519). After the French Prime Minister had asked for a vote of confidence, the Paris Agreements were finally ratified by the National Assembly on 30 December.

After a struggle lasting more than four years, France resigned itself to a future in which West German soldiers would wear West German uniforms, even though, as Blankenhorn wrote in his diary on 30 December, 'the numerous speeches of the representatives in the National Assembly' made clear that 'the anxiety over German divisions remained undiminished' (Blankenhorn 1980, p. 203). Thus it was not on 30 August 1954, when the EDC Treaty was rejected, that 'an idea born in France died in France', as Lerner and Aron thought, but on 30 December 1954, when the Paris Agreements were ratified.

8. The European Political Community

At the end of December 1951, the foreign ministers of the ECSC accepted the plan of their Italian colleague De Gasperi, proposing that the Assembly provided for in the draft treaty of the EDC should develop proposals for a federal structure into which the EDC and ECSC could be integrated (cf. Lipgens in Volkmann and Schwengler 1985, p. 27). At the end of May 1952, a few days after the EDC Treaty had been signed, the Council of Europe rejected Spaak's plan proposing that the ECSC Assembly should draw up a treaty for a European Political Community of the Six, which the other members of the Council of Europe might join at a later stage. Pinay and Schuman, however, greeted Spaak's proposal with approval. After Schuman had consulted De Gasperi, it was submitted to the foreign ministers of the Six at the beginning of September 1952. The ministers decided to instruct the ECSC Assembly, which was also to include the nine EDC representatives, to draw up a treaty for a European Political Community (cf. Willis [1965] 1968, p. 159). Only a few days later, the Assembly was transformed into an Ad Hoc Assembly, which began its work with great zeal and completed its task in less than six months. At the beginning of March, the draft treaty was carried by fifty votes. There were only five abstentions and no opposing votes. However, no fewer than thirty-two members of the Ad Hoc Assembly did not take part in the vote.

The Draft Treaty Containing the Statute of the European Community provided for a Parliament with two chambers, a Senate with eighty-seven members (the same amount as in the Ad Hoc Assembly) to be elected by the national parliaments, and a Peoples' Chamber with 288 members to be elected directly. The size of the delegations from the member states was roughly proportionate to the size of their population. France was given some extra seats in the People's Chamber for representatives from its overseas territories. A European Executive Council that would be entrusted with the administration of the Community was also provided for. The Senate would elect the chairman of this Council by an absolute majority of votes. The Council could be dissolved by the Senate or the Peoples' Chamber by a motion of no confidence. Furthermore the draft treaty provided for a Federal Court, an Economic and Social Council, and a Council of National Ministers that was responsible for harmonizing the policies of the European Executive Council with those of the governments of the participating states (cf. Van Ooijen *et al.* 1996, pp. 96–105).

After the Ad Hoc Assembly had adopted the draft text, its chairman, Spaak, said it had just completed 'one of the greatest works in history'

(Jansen and De Vree [1985] 1988, p. 130). Unfortunately for him, the complications surrounding the EDC and the fact that Schuman was no longer foreign minister had finally turned the tide in France as far as 'Europe' was concerned. According to one of the legal advisers to the *Quai d'Orsay*, the draft treaty was outrageous. 'If this notion of the extension of powers were adopted,' he wrote, 'we would have to ask ourselves if future historians would not ask with incredulity how France herself opened up the question of her own succession'. Many officials at the *Quai d'Orsay* were of the same opinion and argued that France should refrain from undertaking new supranational ventures and instead continue along the trusted line of intergovernmental cooperation (Bossuat in Deighton 1995, p. 27).

Eventually, the draft text was discussed by the foreign ministers of the Six at a conference in Baden-Baden at the beginning of August 1953. At this conference, 'the French tenaciously resisted anything which as much as hinted at a supranational solution. No substantial progress was made. Further discussions were postponed to future conferences' (Blankenhorn 1980, p. 164). In the meantime a Committee of Deputies would have to study this question. This committee produced a report that made quite clear that the differences of opinion were rather great.

One of the subjects which seriously divided the Six in Baden-Baden concerned the Dutch plan to combine the establishment of the EPC with the implementation of a common market. At the conference in September 1952, Johan Beyen, the Dutch foreign minister, who had been appointed only a few days before, managed to ensure with the support of Hallstein that a passage was included in the resolution instructing the Assembly to draw up a draft treaty. In this passage, 'the institution of a European Political Community with a federal or confederal structure was linked to the creation of a common basis for economic development of the Member States and to a fusion of their most essential interests' (Beyen 1968, p. 208).

In December, Beyen subsequently sent a plan to his counterparts that aimed at gradually establishing a 'customs union'. In this customs union, the tariff walls between the participating countries would be abolished and a common tariff would be applied in trade with countries outside it. If the implementation of the customs union created difficulties for the participating states, it might grant these states temporary exemption.

Beyen's proposal was discussed at the foreign ministers' conference in Rome at the end of February 1953 (see also Section 6). These deliberations did not produce any specific result, but neither did they lead to a rejection of the proposal. Undaunted by the lukewarm response to his ideas, Beyen began to work on a plan that had even more far-reaching implications. In this plan, which he sent to his colleagues in May 1953, the customs union was only a first step towards a common market. It also went much further in another respect. To make the transition to a common market as smooth as possible, it provided not only for a community body that could grant member states temporary exemptions, but also for a community fund that would give financial support to member states facing problems. The plan also proposed implementing the customs union in prearranged phases (cf. Beyen 1968, pp. 228–9).

At the follow-up to the Baden-Baden conference, which took place in The Hague at the end of October 1953, it once again proved impossible to reach agreement on the EPC. It became clear that France wanted nothing to do with any attempt to link the EPC to the creation of a common market. The ministers decided to establish a permanent study commission on the EPC. The report of this study commission, which again was mainly a review of the existing differences of opinion, was completed at the beginning of March 1954. It was not discussed, however, because the ministers had decided that this would be pointless as long as France did not ratify the EDC Treaty. They did ask the study commission to continue its activities, but these were nevertheless suspended in June 1954. This was the pitiful state of 'one of the greatest works in history' when it was finally put paid to by the French National Assembly's rejection of the EDC Treaty.

Notes

1. If Speidel's interpretation of *Gleichberechtigung* in the context of the European army is compared with the American position on West German rearmament (see Chapter 5, Section 4), the first two aspects of his interpretation correspond to the American position, but the last one does not. In the American plans, West German generals would only have command over West German divisions.
2. According to Willis, Schuman would later refer to these discussions in the French cabinet as 'the most serious and the most interesting of my political life' (Willis [1965] 1968, p. 132).
3. For comparison, Young's conclusion was: 'how a motley collection of small units, speaking different languages, was supposed to resist a Soviet onslaught was unimportant to Monnet' (Young 1984, p. 172).
4. At this meeting, McCloy stated that 'it was not possible to agree to a

contractual basis because a contract could be terminated by either side. Thus it was conceivable that the Federal Republic would give notice of termination and the Allies were not willing to expose themselves to that, as it would remove the legal basis for the presence of Allied troops in the Federal Republic' (Adenauer 1966a, p. 313).

5. See also Spaak's view on this in his political autobiography: 'the plan, far from being the fruit of long and careful preparation, was but an emotional reaction to the idea that a German army might re-emerge' (Spaak 1971, p. 155).

6. The diplomat Alphand, who, on behalf of the *Quai d'Orsay*, had helped to draw up the Pleven Plan, was leader of the French delegation. Monnet and his staff were not involved this time.

7. Acheson's observation was undoubtedly inspired by Palmerston's famous remark on the Schleswig-Holstein question, which arose in the 1860s. According to the then British foreign minister, this question was so complicated that only three people had ever understood what it was all about. The first was the Prince Consort, who had died; the second was a German professor who had gone mad, and the third was Palmerston himself, but he had completely forgotten how it all fitted together (cf. Taylor [1977] 1980, p. 70).

8. According to ambassador Bruce 'Monnet rose to great heights in defending something he didn't really believe in' (Duchêne 1994, p. 231).

9. On 9 July 1951, the state of war between the Federal Republic and the United States, Great Britain, France and about forty other countries came to an end.

10. Adenauer wrote in his memoirs that McCloy had said at this meeting, after reading the West German draft text: 'none of the Allied countries would be in a position to sign it' (Adenauer 1966a, p. 374).

11. According to Willis, this phrase was used by Schuman in a debate in the Council of Europe on the Pleven Plan at the end of November 1950 (cf. Willis [1965] 1968, p. 130).

12. After the Franco-American *rapprochement* regarding the European army, there was no longer any reason for the Netherlands not to participate fully in the Pleven Plan conference. At the end of September, Stikker concluded that 'we have no other choice but to take part'. At the beginning of October, the Dutch cabinet therefore decided to do so 'without any enthusiasm and forced by the international situation' (Wielenga 1989, p. 106).

13. The Soviet Union sent a total of four notes on the German peace treaty in the period March–August 1952. The other three occupying powers answered each time by sending separate but identical notes.

14. In retrospect, this assessment of the three powers appears to have been correct. Gaddis mentions in *We Now Know* that 'the east Germans themselves were informed that the purpose of the note was to prevent [West German rearmament] by bringing down the Adenauer government'. When a high Soviet diplomat discussed with Stalin the proposal to send a note, the latter supposedly had asked whether it was certain that 'the Americans would turn

the note down. Only when assured that it was did the Soviet leader give his approval' (Gaddis 1997, p. 127; cf. Mastny 1996, pp. 134–8).

15. According to Baring this last point meant that the Federal Republic could not pursue the reunification of the two Germanies on its own, but needed the support of the three powers in this respect. He quotes Grewe, who did not have a good word to say about the term 'full authority'. 'If the sentence that sovereignty with restrictions cannot exist has any real meaning, it can at least be said with as much justification that "full authority" which is restricted to certain fields is no longer full authority' (Baring 1969, p. 410).

16. The EDC Treaty provided for situations in which the Council could make decisions on the basis of a simple or qualified majority (instructions to the Commissariat had to be carried by a unanimous vote). Roughly speaking, Article 43 laid down that, in the event of a tie, the votes of the member states that together provided at least two-thirds of the total contributions to the Community would be decisive. A 'contribution' was the average of the percentage of the effective financial contribution and the percentage of the effective contribution of troops. It was this supranational provision that France objected to soon after the Treaty had been signed, when it became clear that its own effective contribution would remain far behind that of the Federal Republic due to its weak financial and military position. This conjured up the terrifying vision of a European army that would consist of nothing else but a *Wehrmacht* supplemented by units from other member states (see Willis [1965] 1968, p. 182).

17. 'The note of pain and strain was echoed from the Elysée, where I called at President Auriol's request. What had I done, he asked tragically, mistaking the real danger in Europe and leading Schuman into the dreadful error of rearming Germany? For an hour he reviewed the unchanging menace of Germany' (Acheson 1969, p. 650).

18. The discussions involved the following issues:
    - whether France should be allowed to withdraw troops from the EDC for the defence of the French Union, i.e. France and its overseas territories, without the prior consent of the European Commander-in-Chief (he would only be informed) and without this having consequences for the weight of the French vote;
    - whether the weight of France's vote should equal that of the Federal Republic, irrespective of the size of the French contingent in the European army;
    - whether French troops in the Federal Republic should have the same status as the British and American troops stationed there and therefore not be part of the European army;
    - whether the Commissariat should have no jurisdiction over the production and export of arms within the French Union.

19. One month later, the working group that had to prepare a solution to these problems proposed turning down the greater part of France's wishes. It

recommended that France should only be satisfied with respect to the production and export of arms. As to the proposal that France should be allowed to withdraw troops to defend the French Union, it was agreed that this was an option provided the other members of the defence community did not object.

20. The conference of the four occupation powers eventually took place in Berlin at the end of January 1954. The only result after four weeks was that they agreed to hold the following conference in Geneva; this time the subject would be Indo-China, and China would also be represented.

21. The list was several pages long (in defence of Mendès-France, it may be said that the draft treaty with its 132 articles was also rather extensive). The most important features of the protocol were the following:

    • the member states were free to end their participation in the defence community once the United States and Great Britain withdrew their troops from the European continent or the two Germanies were reunified;

    • integration of troops would remain limited to units stationed in parts of the Federal Republic, Belgium and the Netherlands;

    • within a period of eight years, any member of the Council of Ministers could lodge a complaint against a decision of the Commissariat, invoking the vital interests of his or her country. The Commissariat would then be obliged to reach agreement with the Council of Ministers. The final result would only be accepted after the Council of Ministers had approved it by unanimous vote. During the said period of eight years, the Commissariat was not allowed to appeal to the Court of Justice in the event of a conflict between the Commissariat and the Council of Ministers;

    • all provisions in the Treaty that required a decision by unanimous vote of the Council of Ministers – in short, all the important provisions in the Treaty – would remain inoperative for an indefinite period of time (the so-called 'initial period'). This period could only be terminated with the consent of all the members of the Council.

    The protocol also stipulated that membership of the High Authority was incompatible with membership of the Commissariat and – to top it all – that this would remain the case for a period of five years after membership of one of these institutions had ended (cf. *L'Année politique* 1955, pp. 420–1). 'This shot was, of course, aimed directly at the technician of European unity, Jean Monnet' (Furniss 1960, p. 99).

22. It seems that the worst that could have happened to Mendès-France in Brussels was getting everything he wanted, since then he would have had to defend the EDC, or at least the caricature it would have become, in the French National Assembly. In game theoretical terms, at the Brussels conference, he considered the outcome (C,C) the least satisfactory of the four possible outcomes. This meant that his order of preference as far as these outcomes were concerned was in any case not the same as that of a state faced with a 'strong' or 'weak' security dilemma (cf. Chapter 2, Section 3).

23. The rejection of the EDC Treaty was, of course, a severe blow to Adenauer's *Deutschlandpolitik*. When Hallstein and another member of the Chancellor's staff visited Adenauer at his own request at his holiday address in order to discuss the result of the debate in the French National Assembly, they expected him to be in low spirits. They were rather amazed when this proved not to be the case. The Chancellor teasingly reprimanded his most prominent negotiator by saying: 'Herr Hallstein, what those folks in the parliament in Paris have said is in some respects not so stupid at all'. In any case, the account of the events in the French parliament had made Adenauer study somewhat more closely the text of the Treaty, 'which you [Hallstein] have negotiated in Paris', and, to be honest, 'the Treaty wasn't really as good as you have always maintained' (Weidenfeld in Volkmann and Schwengler 1985, p. 270).

24. According to Osgood, this promise was 'a radical departure from Britain's traditional foreign policy' (Osgood 1962, p. 98). Furniss takes an entirely different view: 'rather than "history-making" the statement was "history-repeating". Britain had already promised to maintain forces on the European continent and in Germany. The present undertaking not to withdraw them was subject to three qualifications adequate to cover every possible contingency' (Furniss 1960, p. 102). The three reservations Furniss refers to all meant that future decisions on the number of British troops on the European continent, for example, following a crisis overseas or an excessive increase in costs, would be taken outside the framework of the WEU (cf. Ruhm von Oppen 1955, pp. 604–5).

25. This statement should probably be taken with a pinch of salt. In any case, McCloy referred in 1951 to 'Adenauer's chronic indisposition to consult with members of his Cabinet and the Bundestag in matters of vital policy' (Department of State 1981, p. 1320).

26. Earlier at the conference, the Benelux countries had also declared they would not produce any ABC weapons.

27. In other words, weapons stocks and arms production in Great Britain, as well as those in the French overseas territories, fell outside the competence of this body. In this respect it is rather significant that France also insisted that 'the agency was empowered to control all ABC weapons stocks only after "effective production" was begun on the Continent' (Kelleher 1975, p. 27). A few weeks later the French cabinet decided to set up a study programme for the development of nuclear weapons (see also Chapter 8, Section 2).

8. *Das Junktim*: the EEC and Euratom

1. A *Relance Européenne*

As far as their last major integration project in the fifties was concerned, the Western European powers had to rely on themselves. The United States was not actively involved in the negotiations that led to the European Economic Community (EEC) and Euratom. In the course of this chapter it will nonetheless become clear that it did indirectly make a very important and possibly decisive contribution. This was at the beginning of November 1956, when the United States unceremoniously forced Great Britain and France to give up their attempt to settle their conflict with Egypt over the Suez Canal by means of military force.

After the EDC fiasco, the Americans seemed to be sick and tired of all the complications and setbacks apparently inherent in the process of European unification. They had always been supporters of a common market, but, after the collapse of the defence community, they were no longer very willing to labour for this cause.

Many people in Western Europe shared the American sense of malaise – the feeling that with the failure of the EDC the European integration process had been damaged beyond repair. As in the spring of 1950, Monnet acknowledged this sense of dejection, realized how threatening it was to the successful development of Western Europe, and refused to resign himself to the situation. A new initiative was required (cf. Monnet 1978, pp. 397–8). On 3 September 1954, just four days after the French National Assembly rejected the EDC Treaty, Monnet had the first of many talks with Spaak on how they might breathe new life into the European integration process (cf. Duchêne 1994, p. 263). In the following months they gradually conceived a plan to add transport and energy to the ECSC's sphere of activity and establish a new community for the peaceful use of nuclear energy. Nuclear energy seemed to lend itself particularly well to a new European initiative to integrate industrial sectors, above all because the peaceful use of nuclear energy appealed strongly to the imagination. The general expectation was that this would lead to a new industrial revolution of which the results would surpass those of the first. In addition, none of the Western European powers on its own was deemed capable of catching up with the United States, which had a large technological advantage in this field. The Western European powers would only be able to do so if they joined forces (cf. Küsters 1982, p. 66).[1]

At the beginning of November 1954, Monnet announced that he did not intend to be the president of the High Authority for a second term. He felt he could lobby more effectively for 'Europe' outside the ECSC. At the beginning of April 1955, the talks between Monnet and Spaak finally resulted in a letter to the ministers of foreign affairs of the Federal Republic, France and Italy, in which Spaak explained his and Monnet's ideas concerning further sectoral integration, and proposed convening a conference to discuss these ideas, with Monnet again as chairman.[2] However, Adenauer and Martino did not want to commit themselves to Spaak and Monnet's initiative. France's Prime Minister Faure, the same person who in August 1954 had wanted to see the EDC 'nonsense' ended as soon as possible (see Chapter 7, Section 6), was even downright hostile to the whole idea. The French ambassador in Brussels told Spaak informally that France had no need whatsoever for a new EDC and that Faure was not inclined to give Monnet even more power than he already had (cf. Duchêne 1994, p. 271).

Spaak had also agreed with Monnet that he would inform his Benelux counterparts Beyen and Bech by word of mouth of their plans to add the transport and energy sectors to the ECSC and establish a new nuclear energy community. At the end of March, the Second Chamber of the Dutch Parliament debated the ratification of the Paris Agreements. In this debate, prompted by various Europe-minded members of parliament, Beyen proposed that the Western European integration process be revived. He thought the best opportunity for doing so would present itself at the next conference of the ministers of foreign affairs of the ECSC (cf. Küsters 1982, p. 95). In preparation for this conference, Beyen almost single-handedly wrote a memorandum, which he sent to his counterparts on 4 April. In it, he rejected further sectoral integration. Beyen's view was that the ultimate goal should be a community for the general economic integration of Western Europe. In fact, he was reintroducing his old plan for the formation of a customs union, which would function as a stepping-stone towards a common market (see Chapter 7, Section 8).

Beyen and Spaak had agreed, at the latter's request, to meet over the weekend of 23 and 24 April to discuss the possibilities of a joint European initiative by the Benelux countries. A few days earlier, on 21 April, Beyen made a speech in which he explained the basic ideas in his memorandum. The content of this speech alarmed Monnet so much that he immediately travelled to Brussels to consult Spaak, as he feared that their European initiative was heading in the wrong direction.

Monnet's concern was not unjustified, because Beyen did not see much in Spaak and Monnet's proposal for further sectoral integration. He advocated his own proposal for an economic community based on a common market. Spaak expected that France would never accept this, as protectionism was still rampant in France. The talks therefore did not produce the desired result. However, the shared desire to launch a new European initiative eventually outweighed any differences of opinion. At the beginning of May, Beyen and Spaak were able to reach a compromise: both routes would be taken. Spaak agreed to support Beyen's view that sectoral integration without general economic integration was a dead end, and Beyen in turn agreed that, if the ambitious plans for an economic community were to fail, he would not cling to his own views but would support the more modest proposals for the expansion of the ECSC and the establishment of a nuclear energy community (cf. Küsters 1982, p. 102, and Duchêne 1994, p. 274).[3]

With a view to the coming Messina conference,[4] the joint memorandum from the Benelux countries based on Beyen's memorandum was sent to the other governments on 18 May. This marked the birth of the *relance européenne*, as the initiative was called in the French press.

The memorandum stated that the governments of the Benelux countries believed the time had come 'to take a new step on the road to European integration'. The development of the ECSC had made clear the need for 'an expansion of the common market in the areas closely connected to the organizations's sphere of activity'. At the same time, the Benelux countries were of the opinion that 'such an expansion would have no chance of success unless general economic integration was undertaken'. Expansion would have to take place in three fields: transport, energy, and peaceful use of nuclear energy, for which a 'common authority' would have to be established. As far as general economic integration was concerned, they advocated the creation of an economic community which 'should be based on a common market to be realized by gradual abolition of quantitative restrictions and customs duties'. Such an economic community 'necessit-ated the establishment of a common authority entrusted with the power necessary to achieve the specified goals'.[5] Just like Beyen's original plan, the memorandum provided for phased implementation of the common market, a system of escape clauses and the creation of a readaptation fund (see Chapter 7, Section 8). The Benelux countries also believed it was essential to harmonize the social legislation of the various countries concerning 'working hours, overtime pay (night work, working on Sundays and holidays), the number of days of holiday and holiday pay'. Finally, the Benelux countries proposed convening a conference to study texts and draw up agreements in order to carry out the tasks referred to. They stated that not only the six ECSC countries should be invited to this conference, but also the countries that had signed an association agreement with the ECSC and the ECSC itself (cf. Van Ooijen *et al.* 1996, p. 115).[6]

The difference of opinion between Spaak and Beyen as to what should have priority in reviving 'Europe' – the new initiative for sectoral integration or the effort to achieve general economic integration – also existed in the Federal Republic. The West German Ministry of Foreign Affairs had come to the conclusion that 'under the present circumstances, Monnet's proposals for sectoral integration that would lead to the creation of a European Atomic Energy Community provided the best opportunities for realizing institutional integration in the long term', whereas the Ministry of Economic Affairs was of the opinion that 'further sectoral integration would eventually only lead to the disintegration of other sectors of the economy' and that the Federal Republic should therefore give priority to promoting general economic integration (Küsters 1982, p. 113). An additional complication was that the West German Minister of Economic Affairs, Erhard, attached little value to the doctrine of *Westbindung*. He felt the Federal Republic should reject both approaches – although, in his view, the common market was clearly the lesser of two evils – and instead promote a global free trade system. Economically speaking, this would prove far more beneficial to the Federal Republic (cf. Duchêne 1994, p. 276).

However, the Benelux memorandum and the scheduled Messina Conference forced the Federal Republic to adopt a unanimous position. At the end of May, supporters of the various viewpoints met in Eischerscheid. This meeting proved a success for the supporters of the common market. The so-called Eischerscheid Decisions were laid down in a memorandum and clearly expressed a preference for an economic community which should 'encompass all those areas that are not regulated by the ECSC' (Küsters 1982, p. 118; cf. Duchêne 1994, pp. 276–7).

In its response to the Benelux memorandum, the Federal Republic adopted a moderately positive attitude and paid particular attention to aspects relating to the implementation of a common market. France's response was completely the opposite. At a press conference, Faure announced that he was favourably inclined towards the idea of increasing sectoral integration, especially in the field of nuclear energy, but he did not say anything about a possible common market.

The Messina Conference took place on 1–2 June. 'The outside world, including the press, did not show much interest. Many people thought it would be "just another failure"' (Beyen 1968, p. 238). After the other five delegations had accepted the French proposal to appoint Mayer as Monnet's successor, they spent the rest of the conference trying to get France to accept the proposal in the Benelux memorandum for convening a conference at which texts would be studied and treaties be drawn up for the various communities proposed.[7] The French, however, thought a conference would put them under too many obligations and were not at all inclined to draw up any treaties of this kind. Eventually, after the talks had continued well into the night, France agreed to the establishment of a Committee of Government Representatives, which would be assisted by experts and chaired by a 'political personality'. This committee would be responsible for preparing the way for a number of conferences on the Benelux proposals (not just one conference as envisaged in the original proposal; this made a link between sectoral integration and general economic integration, which France immediately tried to undo).[8] This decision was laid down in the Messina Resolution – a fairly accurate representation of the text of the Benelux memorandum, which in turn was largely based on the memorandum Beyen had written in April. It was therefore all the more surprising that this resolution no longer contained the observation expressed in the Benelux memorandum that 'such an expansion [of ECSC activities] had no chance of success unless general economic integration was undertaken'. As a member of the WEU and an associate member of the ECSC, Great Britain was invited to participate in the activities of the committee (Van Ooijen *et al.* 1996, pp. 116–17). After a few days of diplomatic consultation, the Six decided to appoint Spaak – who was apparently the appropriate political personality – as chairman of the committee.

After the conference, all options were still open, as in fact nothing substantial had yet been achieved. The resolution also failed to remove the general scepticism about 'Europe'. According to the West German diplomat Carstens, many observers spoke mockingly of the 'excavations at Messina' (Carstens in Blumenwitz *et al.* 1976, p. 591). Had the failure of the EDC not made it abundantly clear that such initiatives were obsolete? For reasons which sound all too familiar, Adenauer was among those who did not really warm to this new initiative. The entire project was economic rather than political in nature, and too much so for his taste. In his memoirs, the Chancellor wrote that he had mixed feelings about the resolution because he feared that 'the economic tasks would distract us from the main task, which is the creation of political union. However, I welcomed the resumption of negotiations, because I hoped that these admittedly weaker links would at least be something and that we would later establish stronger, political links' (Adenauer 1967, p. 30).

In retrospect, the resolution nevertheless led to two very important results that made Messina 'a decisive turning point in the process of Europe's creation' (Marjolin 1989, p. 283). The first evokes associations with the NATO Council meeting in September 1950, where the main result had been that France would not oppose the discussions on a West German contribution to the joint defence of Western Europe. Now, the parties had persuaded France not to oppose the discussions on a common market, which was another very sensitive issue in France. After all, 'in 1955–56 the vast majority of the French, that is the thinking French, were fundamentally opposed to any freedom of trade, even if geographically confined to Europe... *France at that time was essentially protectionist*' (Marjolin 1989, p. 281; emphasis in original). The second important result was that agreement had been reached on the procedure to be followed during the ensuing talks (cf. Beyen 1968, p. 239).

2.   The Spaak Committee

A few days after the Messina Conference, in his capacity as chairman of the ECSC Council of Ministers, Bech invited Great Britain to take part in the activities of the Spaak Committee. In addition, Beyen again travelled to London to explain the Messina Resolution (cf. Beyen 1968, pp. 239–40). On 1 July the British cabinet decided to accept the invitation, although it did so without making any prior commitment and without subscribing to the Messina Resolution. It appointed Bretherton, a high official of the Board of Trade, as the British member of the committee. The constituent meeting of the Spaak Committee took place in Brussels on 9 July. It was decided to create eight technical committees that would operate under the supervision of an Executive Committee (the *Comité Directeur*) consisting of the leaders of the seven delegations, plus Spaak as chairman. The deliberations started on 20 July after this Executive Committee had drawn up guidelines for them.

The key issue at the initial meetings of the Executive Committee was the common market, although the right of the atomic energy community to exist was not contested. For the participants it was not so much a question of *whether* a common market would be established as *how* this would be done – while Spaak gave the issue another twist by saying that this was a political problem rather than a technical one. With the exception of Bretherton, all the parties agreed that a customs union would be the right way to get such a common market off the ground (cf. Küsters 1982, p. 163). The French government – and Monnet too – saw this as an alarming development, since France was in fact only interested in Euratom.

It will probably come as no surprise to the reader that France's interest in a European community for peaceful use of nuclear energy was not based on any underlying European ideal. Once again, France was using 'European' rhetoric to conceal its attempts to manoeuvre itself into an advantageous position *vis-à-vis* the Federal Republic (cf. Weilemann 1983, p. 37). France's interest in an atomic energy community was based on two considerations in particular. The first was that such a community would enable France to gain control over the development of nuclear energy for peaceful purposes in West Germany (cf. Kelleher 1975, p. 27). The second was that the community might be instrumental in strengthening France's position *vis-à-vis* the other three nuclear powers (the United States, the Soviet Union and Great Britain) and thereby indirectly its position *vis-à-vis* the Federal Republic (cf. Furniss 1960, p. 253, and Osgood 1962, p. 219). This might happen in two ways. Firstly, access to the other member states' research on peaceful use of nuclear energy might speed up the development of French nuclear technology. Secondly, the costs of the ambitious French nuclear programme, which were well beyond France's means, might be shared within the framework of the community (cf. Weilemann 1983, pp. 41–2 and p. 113).

At the same time, many French people had considerable doubts about the whole project, particularly those at the *Commissariat à l'Energie Atomique* (CEA), which was responsible for the development of nuclear energy. Of the six states, France was by far the most advanced in developing nuclear energy for peaceful purposes. The CEA was afraid that France's participation in a European atomic energy community would result in the other five – and particularly the Federal Republic – taking advantage of France's achievements. The CEA also considered such a community as a direct threat to its privileged position in France. Its directors were not keen on what they saw as 'a "shotgun wedding" in the nuclear sector' (cf. Weilemann 1983, p. 39).

There was also the complication that, at the end of December 1954, when the ratification of the Paris Agreements was discussed in the National Assembly, the French cabinet had decided to set up a secret study programme for the development of a nuclear weapon and a nuclear submarine. At this cabinet meeting Mendès-France had mentioned that he was fully aware of the gap in international politics between the nuclear powers and the other powers. It was therefore a dire necessity that France should also become a nuclear power – particularly now that the Federal Republic had undertaken in the Paris Agreements not to produce any nuclear weapons. Building up a nuclear force would give France an excellent opportunity to strengthen its position *vis-à-vis* West Germany (cf. Mendl 1970, pp. 29–30, and Soutou 1996, p. 37).[9]

If not unfavourably disposed towards them, the Federal Republic was certainly reluctant to embrace the plans for an atomic energy community. It became even more so when Strauss was appointed Government Commissioner for Nuclear Affairs at the Ministry of Economic Affairs in October 1955. The possible advantages of such a project for France were equal disadvantages for the Federal Republic. In addition, there were many who wondered whether the deficit in the field of peaceful use of nuclear energy could not simply be made up by working together with the United States and Great Britain, which had already stated that they would welcome such cooperation.

The negotiations in the Spaak Committee did not proceed very smoothly. According to the Messina Resolution, the committee was to have completed its activities by 1 October 1955. It did not do so, however. The fact that the Federal Republic and France had serious doubts was already bad enough, but now Great Britain made matters even worse by pursuing a strategy of delay. Consultations in the technical commissions dragged on very slowly. At the end of November, the Nuclear Energy Commission was the only one to have produced a final report. This officially introduced the name Euratom for the community, a name thought up by Armand, the French chairman of the commission. It also advocated that all the raw materials for peaceful use of nuclear energy such as uranium, heavy water and nuclear fuel should become the property of the community, and that the community should purchase these on behalf of the member states (cf. Weilemann 1983, p. 46).

It was around that time that Spaak decided he had had enough of the slow proceedings and began to take matters into his own hands. All the remaining unresolved issues were to be dealt with by the *Comité Directeur* itself. From then on, Spaak was assisted by Uri, one of Monnet's confidants who was working for the ECSC at the time (see Chapter 6, Section 4), and Von der Groeben, a high official of the West German Ministry of Foreign Affairs. These two were assigned the task of drawing up the report required by the Messina Resolution. Spaak also forced Bretherton out by an act that strongly resembled the way in which Monnet and Schuman had got the British government to refrain from joining the conference on the Schuman Plan at the beginning of June 1950 (see Chapter 6, Section 2). At the meeting of the Executive Committee on 7 November, Spaak stated that only those delegations that accepted the idea of a customs union could participate in future meetings (cf. Küsters 1982, p. 211). Four days later, the British government decided to withdraw its delegation. The *Comité Directeur* had however to cease its activities before they were truly under way, as the Faure cabinet collapsed at the end of November and decided to call early elections on 2 January 1956.[10] By the end of January, the socialist Mollet, who had proved to be an advocate of the EDC in the past, managed to form a cabinet that had the support of the National Assembly.

In the meantime, the Spaak Committee had resumed its activities on 15 January. A few days later, the first meeting of the Action Committee for the United States of Europe, set up in October under Monnet's supervision, was opened with great pomp and circumstance. After several months of intensive lobbying, Monnet had persuaded all the political parties from the Six, except the Gaullists, Communists, and so-called Nenni Socialists from Italy, as well as all the trade unions, again except for the Communist ones, to be represented on this Action Committee by their chairmen (with the exception of Mendès-France, the Chairman of the French Radical Party) (cf. Duchêne 1994, p. 287). As I have already made clear, Monnet saw Euratom as *the* project of the future. According to Pascal Fontaine, a close collaborator of Monnet in the last years of the latter's life, an economic community was 'only a hazy image' in his mind (cf. Marjolin 1989, pp. 298–9).[11] The attempts made after the Messina Conference to realize both projects found no favour in his eyes. In his view, those who thought both initiatives were feasible were out of touch with reality. The result could only be that both projects would fail. One of the two projects would therefore have to be abandoned, and to Monnet it was completely clear which it should be (cf. Küsters 1982, p. 229). The Action Committee's meeting was almost exclusively dedicated to Euratom. This initiative was to take priority over that of the common market (Weilemann 1983, p. 74). The Action Committee unanimously accepted a resolution in which they pressed for the establishment as soon as possible of a community for the peaceful use of nuclear energy, after the model of the ECSC. Following the report by the Armand Commission, the Action Committee stipulated that this organization should own all the raw materials necessary for the peaceful use of nuclear energy in the member states, and be the sole agent authorized to purchase them (cf. Monnet 1978, p. 419).

The West German delegation was unpleasantly surprised when Mollet declared at the Action Committee's meeting that 'Euratom [would] not stand in the way of a possible French decision to build nuclear weapons' (Monnet 1978, p. 420). Although France did not feel any need for a new EDC, the nuclear energy community certainly began to resemble it closely, much to the dismay of the Federal Republic. Within Euratom, France was prepared to treat the Federal Republic on an equal footing in exchange for control over its peaceful use of nuclear energy – something which could ultimately be regarded as a concession, given the original French plans for the EDC. Outside Euratom, however, the Federal Republic would still be a subjugated nation, as it did not have the same freedom as France to build up a nuclear force.

In the Federal Republic, the battle between supporters and opponents of further European integration continued unabated. The former were mainly found in the Ministry of Foreign Affairs, the latter in the Ministry of Economic Affairs. According to Erhard and Strauss, both projects were technically speaking nonsense. As always, Erhard emphasized that, given the position of the West German economy, global free trade was far preferable to a Western European trade bloc. What particularly annoyed him was that the envisaged harmonization of social legislation in this trade bloc threatened to undermine the Federal Republic's competitive position, and that the Federal Republic would have to make the largest contribution to the readaptation fund as well. Strauss held on to his view that the Federal Republic would do better to build up a nuclear industry of its own, preferably in collaboration with the United States and Great Britain. According to officials at the Ministry of Foreign Affairs and Deputy Minister Hallstein, however, these considerations ignored the core issue, namely that Western European cooperation was not meant to improve the Federal Republic's economic position or allow it to build up an advanced nuclear industry, but to bring about reconciliation with France through *Westbindung* on the basis of *Gleichberechtigung*. Until the reconciliation with France and the *Westbindung* had been established, no value could be attached to arguments such as those of Erhard and Strauss.

In the light of the previous chapters, it will come as no surprise that Adenauer fully supported this last view. On 19 January 1956, in an attempt to end the ongoing battle between the various ministries, the Chancellor issued a *Richtlinie der Politik* (policy guideline; see Chapter 3, Section 5), drawn up by Hallstein and other supporters of Western European cooperation, in which he unequivocally took sides with the Ministry of Foreign Affairs. In this guideline, the Chancellor stated that the interests of the Federal Republic were best served by implementing the programme laid down in the Messina Resolution. This implied that West German efforts should focus on:

> the promotion of integration of, first of all, the Six with *all* appropriate means, that is to say, both in the area of general (horizontal) integration and of suitable (vertical) sector integration. [...]
>
> The talks on the establishment of a common European market – i.e. a market similar to an internal market – which so far have passed very satisfactorily, must emphatically be brought to a successful conclusion. In this framework, European institutions with discretionary powers must be created in order to secure the functioning of this market and simultaneously further the full development of political integration. [...]
>
> On the other hand, according to world public opinion, the peaceful use of nuclear energy cannot be separated from the possibility of the production of atom bombs. The German attempt to start a nuclear project on a purely national basis would be viewed abroad with the greatest suspicion. More in particular, we cannot reject a common European exploitation of certain raw materials when this is necessary from the point of view of security, provided of course that Germany will not be discriminated against, and German research and industry will have the greatest free scope possible.[12] (Adenauer 1967, p. 255)

The conference of ministers of foreign affairs provided for in the Messina Resolution took place in mid-February 1956. At this conference, the preliminary results of the Spaak Committee's activities were discussed. Once again, there were differences of opinion between the Federal Republic and France. Although the Federal Republic was favourably disposed towards the common market, it continued to have objections to Euratom. Conversely, France was favourably disposed towards Euratom, but only saw problems where the common market was concerned. The Federal Republic refused to accept the discriminatory character of Euratom. Existing relations had, after all, undergone drastic changes as a result of the Paris Agreements and West Germany's entry into NATO. West Germany was, in fact, no longer a power in a subordinate position that, in order to end its subordination as soon as possible, was willing to put up with quite a lot. The Federal Republic proposed that the Euratom member states should refrain from using nuclear fuel for military purposes. This proposal was naturally immediately rejected by France.

In any case, the conference made clear that if one of the two projects was rejected, the other would be too. 'The *Junktim* (the linkage) had been saved' (Weilemann 1983, p. 79). In Spaak's opinion the discussions proceeded quite well, despite the problems surrounding the military use of nuclear energy. He therefore proposed to his counterparts that they order the delegation leaders to draw up a final report. This proposal was accepted. Very soon, Spaak sent Uri and Von der Groeben off to the South of France for a few weeks to write this report in seclusion.

This 135-page report was divided into three parts. The voluminous first part, which made up almost two-thirds of the report, was devoted to the establishment of a common market. The second part concerned Euratom. The third part, which consisted of only a few pages, contained a few final observations devoted to the energy, aviation, postal and telecommunication sectors, in which the necessary work had to be done.[13]

The common market would be implemented in three four-year phases. Protective clauses of limited duration to resolve transitional problems were allowed. Power to determine general economic policy remained with the member states, and a Council of Ministers, which would reach decisions by unanimous vote, was responsible for coordinating this policy. The Council was also the body in which the harmonization with the community would take place. A European Commission, whose chairman and members would be appointed by the governments of the member states and which would reach decisions by a simple majority vote, was entrusted with the execution of the treaty. It would also supervise the development and operation of the common market. The Court would be the same as that of the ECSC. The European Commission would be accountable to the ECSC's Joint Assembly, whose size would be increased and in which the distribution of seats would be altered in favour of the three largest member states (cf. Comité intergouvernemental 1956, pp. 25–6).

The Common Market's Council of Ministers, Court and Assembly would be responsible for carrying out the tasks assigned to Euratom.[14] In addition, a separate European Commission for Atomic Energy was established, which would operate in accordance with principles similar to those of the European Commission for the Common Market (cf. Comité intergouvernemental 1956, pp. 102–3). The Commission would lay down safety standards for the entire community – which would be submitted for approval to the Assembly after they had been accepted by the Council – and would regulate the inspection of nuclear installations. Euratom would be responsible for the purchase and distribution of ores and nuclear fuel within the community (cf. Comité intergouvernemental 1956, pp. 114–15).

The report did not deal with the question of military use of nuclear energy. The delegation leaders were of the opinion that 'the problem of possible use of atomic energy for military purposes by certain states [was] of a political nature that exceeded their competence. They [did] not deem it necessary to offer a solution to this in the present report' (Comité inter-gouvernemental 1956, p. 122).

In the introduction to the report, the delegation leaders emphasized that the results achieved were entirely their responsibility and that the governments were not bound in any way whatsoever. They did unanimously agree, however, that the result of their labour provided the governments with a basis for negotiations on the treaties (Comité intergouvernemental 1956, p. 10). By means of this wording, Spaak managed to ensure that none of the delegation leaders would insist on including a formal objection to any part of the final report. He convinced them that this would not be necessary. If they had any objections, the coming negotiations would provide ample opportunity to remove them. At the end of April, the delegation leaders decided to accept the text of the final report after some minor changes had been made.

The governments of France and West Germany both came to the conclusion that the report by the Spaak Committee provided a sound basis for further negotiations between the governments of 'the Six'. In Bonn, the Ministry of Economic Affairs still refused to accept both projects and the Ministry of Agriculture, too, began to have doubts about the economic community. They were, however, no match for the Ministry of Foreign Affairs and the Chancellor. Adenauer 'wanted integration, even if, for the time being, it would only involve the economic sphere' (Küsters 1982, p. 267). The fact that the French government did not reject the proposals for an economic community out of hand was primarily the achievement of a small group of leading French officials, who managed to convince Mollet and foreign minister Pineau that the French economy would actually benefit from competition in the common market (cf. Marjolin 1989, pp. 282–6, Küsters 1982, p. 267, and Duchêne 1994, pp. 290–1).[15]

The conference of the Six on the report by the Spaak Committee took place in Venice at the end of May. According to Beyen, the delegations 'did not have much to do' given the results already achieved by the Spaak Committee (Beyen 1968, p. 243).[16] The ministers of foreign affairs accepted the report and agreed to government negotiations on the treaties for the economic community and Euratom. These negotiations would again be led by Spaak as chairman. France still made a feeble attempt to break up the *Junktim*, as the link between the two communities was now called by almost everyone (cf. Duchêne 1994, p. 290), but the other five powers stood their ground, since Euratom could only succeed within the context of a common market. The five powers were more favourably inclined towards the French proposal that its overseas territories be included in the economic community (cf. Küsters 1982, p. 256). As far as the military use of nuclear energy was concerned, there was total deadlock. The final communiqué laconically stated that the ministers still had to express their views on this issue (cf. Weilemann 1983, p.101).

3. Indissolubly Bound Together

3.1. The First Phase of the Negotiations: June–October 1956

The first round of negotiations took place in Brussels at the end of June 1956. To facilitate the process, the negotiators divided themselves up into four groups: a Delegation Leaders' Committee, a Working Group on the Economic Community, a Working Group on Euratom, and an Editorial Group.

With the exception of the tricky problem of the military use of nuclear energy, the negotiations in the Euratom Group proceeded very smoothly – so smoothly that, in September, the *Junktim* was under serious threat. The West German participants in the working group therefore proposed a two-week break to bring the negotiations on the two communities back into line. The greatest concern of the West German delegation was that the French negotiators might try to create a situation in which the Euratom Treaty would have been worked out in detail while the negotiations on the economic community still had a long way to go. It would then be very tempting to sign just the Euratom Treaty, in which case nothing would come of the negotiations on the economic community (cf. Weilemann 1983, pp. 117–18).

By the middle of September, with the consent of the French government, Monnet began to intervene in the negotiation process (cf. Marjolin 1989, p. 296). Monnet pleaded with Adenauer and Etzel, the vice-chairman of the High Authority, to break the link between Euratom and the Common Market. Both Adenauer and Etzel proved susceptible to Monnet's arguments. The Chancellor promised that he would no longer link the progress of the negotiations on Euratom to the progress of those on the Common Market (cf. Duchêne 1994, p. 297). Monnet's assistant Kohnstamm tried to induce the West German chairman of the Working Group on the Economic Community, Von der Groeben, to delay the negotiations on the Common Market. He was, however, less successful than his boss in convincing the person in question. Indeed, he achieved quite the opposite, because Von der Groeben, alarmed by Kohnstamm's efforts, contacted Etzel and managed to convince him that the *Junktim* should remain intact (cf. Weilemann 1983, p. 119). With the help of

Hallstein, Etzel subsequently also managed to get Adenauer to support the *Junktim* once more by using the argument that 'the concept of sectoral integration will eventually fail for political reasons if the two projects under negotiation become separated'. For his part, Uri talked to Monnet and tried to make clear to his former superior that his efforts to separate Euratom from the Common Market would be to no avail, as the two projects were indissolubly bound together. Monnet was not, however, very receptive to Uri's arguments. He clung to his own preference for Euratom. A few days later, at his instigation, the Action Committee for the United States of Europe passed a motion calling for rapid completion of the negotiations on the Euratom Treaty, without even mentioning the economic community (cf. Küsters 1982, p. 311).

At a meeting of the Delegation Leaders' Committee at the end of September, the negotiations on Euratom nonetheless reached a deadlock over the question of the military use of nuclear energy. The Federal Republic once again insisted that the Euratom member states should follow its example by stating unilaterally that they would refrain from using nuclear energy for military purposes. France refused even to discuss this demand, as it did not wish to make any concessions with regard to its military programme. In response to this, the Federal Republic proposed that the use of nuclear energy for peaceful and military purposes by Euratom member states should be subject to the same rules and controls. As far as France was concerned, this was not an option either (cf. Weilemann, 1983, p. 126). In the end, the delegation leaders decided that this problem should be dealt with at the conference of ministers of foreign affairs, to be held in Paris on 20 and 21 October. In any case, the ministers could no longer evade the question of military use of nuclear energy.

Negotiations on the Common Market were entirely focused on the 'endless list' (cf. Marjolin 1989, p. 288) of demands and guarantees that France wished to see satisfied and realized before it was willing to agree to such an enterprise. France tried at all costs to prevent the French welfare state being harmed when the French economy was exposed to competition from the other member states. The other member states would therefore have to adapt their social policy to that of France. This would mean, among other things, the introduction of a forty-hour working week, equal pay for women and men, and three weeks' paid holiday (cf. Küsters 1982, p. 300). France was also looking for all kinds of arrangements that would postpone as long as possible the moment when French entrepreneurs had to compete with their counterparts in the other five member states. Prime Minister Drees of the Netherlands sneeringly remarked at a Dutch cabinet meeting that France was obviously only prepared 'to sign a treaty as long as it did not apply to France for the time being' (Dimmendaal 1987, p. 45). In France's view, the transition from the first to the second phase of the customs union should by no means be automatic. Spaak's compromise proposal, which implied that the other member states would make a concession to France's susceptibilities in this matter if France in turn was willing to adopt a more compliant attitude towards the question of social legislation, found no favour in the eyes of the French (cf. Küsters 1982, p. 313). By the middle of October, the negotiations on the Common Market had therefore also reached a deadlock. Once again, the delegation leaders decided that the forthcoming conference of ministers of foreign affairs would have to provide the solution.

At this conference some progress was made as far as Euratom was concerned, but the negotiations on the economic community came to a complete standstill. After the French delegation, as a concession, had dropped its demand for the right to veto the transition from the first to the second phase of the customs union, the West German delegation became isolated over the harmonization both of the forty-hour working week and of overtime pay (it was willing to commit itself to the principle of harmonization, but not to the point in time when it would be realized.) This was because the other four delegations felt it was now time for West Germany to make a concession. As the West German delegation was not prepared to do so, the French delegation withdrew its own concession. Consequently, the conference was a total failure (cf. Weilemann 1983, p. 129 and Milward 1992, pp. 213–14). Carstens has described how the six ministers, at an informal gathering on the last day of the negotiations, were overcome by 'a profound feeling of dejection. Some of them thought this great project was about to fail' (Carstens in Blumenwitz *et al.* 1976, p. 594).

3.2. The Adenauer–Mollet Agreement

In response to the failure of the Paris Conference, the West German Ministry of Foreign Affairs wrote a note to the Chancellor, indicating that the limited room the West German delegation had had to negotiate on the harmonization both of the forty-hour working week and of overtime pay was believed to be the cause of this failure. In the Ministry's opinion, this should never have happened: no matter how important 'the harmonization of social legislation is, it is only a sector. Failure of the European integration project as a result of this sector could not be justified' (Carstens in Blumenwitz *et al.* 1976, p. 595). In the note, the Ministry of Foreign

Affairs also urged Adenauer to place the issue of harmonization on the agenda of his meeting with Mollet, which had been scheduled for 6 November. After consulting all those involved on the West German side, Adenauer agreed to do so. He announced that he would personally take up the matter with Mollet. In the light of the tense world situation, 'disintegration of Europe was not justifiable' in his view (Carstens in Blumenwitz *et al.* 1976, p. 595).

The international situation was indeed very tense. On the night of 23 October, the Hungarian people rose in revolt against the Communist regime. A few days later, after fierce fighting in practically every part of the country, a government came to power that also included representatives from the old democratic parties. At first, it looked as if the Soviet Union had resigned itself to the new situation; the Red Army had already begun to pull out of Budapest. However, when the new Hungarian government announced that it intended to leave the Warsaw Pact, the Soviet leadership decided to put a stop to it. On 4 November, the Red Army attacked Budapest, and by the night of 5 November, when Adenauer left for Paris, it was already clear that the Soviet Union was winning.

What caused even greater tension in Paris and Bonn was the Suez Crisis. In July 1956, Egypt nationalized the Anglo-French-controlled Suez Canal Company, which had been granted the concession to run the canal. It also announced that it would pay compensation to the owners. Great Britain and France protested fiercely against this measure and demanded that the canal should be placed under international control. There were several rounds of talks between the parties involved, but these did not lead to the desired agreement. The United States supported the Anglo-French demand for internationalization of the Suez Canal, but rejected the use of force. France and Great Britain nevertheless concluded a secret agreement with Israel in which they promised Israel military support if it decided to resolve its conflict with Egypt over the Straits of Tiran by force of arms. Israel's attack would allow Great Britain and France to send troops to Egypt under the terms of a clause in the treaty with Egypt that Great Britain had signed in 1954 when transferring the canal zone to Egypt. Israel invaded Egypt on 29 October. The following day, France and Great Britain vetoed a resolution drawn up by the United States, in which the Security Council of the United Nations condemned Israel's act of aggression. That same day, France and Great Britain themselves delivered an ultimatum to the contending parties. They demanded that hostilities should cease within twelve hours and that Egypt and Israel should agree to the evacuation of a ten-mile-wide zone on either side of the canal – a zone where not a single Israeli soldier was to be found! – and to the occupation of the towns of Suez, Port Said and Ismailiya by France and Great Britain. Egypt rejected this ultimatum. One day later, British and French ships and airplanes bombarded Egyptian targets. On 2 November, the General Assembly of the United Nations accepted a resolution drawn up by the United States demanding that the contending parties should cease hostilities and that Israel should withdraw its forces from Egypt. Three days later, French and British paratroops were dropped in Egypt. That same day, the Prime Minister of the Soviet Union, Bulganin, wrote a letter to his French and British counterparts asking them how they would feel if they were attacked 'by stronger states, possessing all types of modern destructive weapons? And such countries could, at the present time, refrain from sending naval or air forces to the shores of Britain and use other means – for instance, rocket weapons?' In addition, he assured them that the Soviet Union was determined 'to crush the aggressors by the use of force and to restore peace in the East' (Kissinger 1994, pp. 542–3; cf. Gaddis 1997, pp. 235–6). Bulganin's letter arrived in London and Paris on the night of 5 to 6 November. On the morning of 6 November, British and French troops landed near Port Said. However, during the night of 6 to 7 November, Great Britain and France decided, at Great Britain's instigation, to declare a cease-fire. Israel and Egypt followed suit. Much against the wishes of France, Great Britain had decided to end its military operations in Egypt, because the consequences of the United States withholding its support had meanwhile become very clear. As the United States refused to help Great Britain in any way in the armed conflict with Egypt, it was very likely that this would cause a run on the pound sterling and an acute shortage of oil.

In Germany, voices were heard in the opposition party SPD, the coalition party FDP, and also in Adenauer's own CDU, saying that the Chancellor would be wise to cancel his trip to Paris (cf. Küsters 1982, p. 327). It would certainly do the reputation of the Federal Republic no good if it were associated with the Anglo-French colonial adventure. Adenauer, on the contrary, thought that such a gesture towards France would be of great value in the context of Western European cooperation. He was probably right in this respect, because his French hosts were highly pleased with his visit.

In such a crisis situation, overtime pay was clearly a less important issue. According to Carstens, 'in the light of the tragic events in Hungary and the threatening attitude the Soviet Union had adopted towards Britain and France, it would have been absurd if European integration had foundered on the question of overtime pay' (Carstens in Blumenwitz *et al.*

1976, p. 601). Two small delegations, led by Marjolin and Carstens respectively, were instructed to find a solution to the outstanding problems surrounding the economic community, while Mollet and Adenauer discussed the real problems. The compromise the negotiators managed to achieve was that the harmonization of social legislation would no longer be a prerequisite for the implementation of the second phase of the transitional period, but that instead the member states would be obliged to do what they could to bring about such harmonization. They also reached agreement on a special regime for France throughout the entire transitional period concerning import and export levies as well as on the conditions under which this regime would be terminated. This compromise was accepted by Adenauer and Mollet without further ado (cf. Carstens in Blumenwitz *et al.* 1976, p. 599, and Weilemann 1983, pp. 131–2).

Thus the European integration process was saved. All things considered, the agreement boiled down to a French concession for the sake of good relations with the Federal Republic in time of need. However, as far as their views on the economic community were concerned, they had not come any closer (cf. Küsters 1982, p. 328).

3.3. The Second Phase of the Negotiations: November 1956–March 1957

The events in Hungary and Egypt had made clear that the Western European powers were of little account compared with the two superpowers. France had been painfully reminded of how dependent it still was on the United States. To Adenauer it seemed as if his terrifying vision of the superpowers striking a bargain at the expense of the Federal Republic might become a reality at any moment (see Chapter 3, Section 5). The importance of further Western European integration was thus brought clearly into perspective. Adenauer and Mollet were now determined to bring the negotiations concerning the economic community and Euratom to a successful completion, no matter how great the outstanding problems (Küsters 1982, pp. 331–2, and Bossuat in Deighton 1995, p. 30).

Once again, France interpreted its new adherence to the European ideal in a very peculiar way: together with Belgium, it introduced the *Eurafrique* concept into the negotiations. The most important features of this plan were the following. First of all, it proposed that the overseas territories of a member state should be open to the other member states of the economic community. Secondly, the economic community should give preference to certain agricultural products from overseas. Thirdly, it provided for an investment fund to which the member states, with the exception of France and Belgium, would annually contribute 1 billion ECU (cf. Küsters 1982, p. 334). The plan was in fact the umpteenth expression of 'the poverty of France'. It wanted so much, but could do so very little. Without the support of third parties, it could not even maintain its *mission civilisatrice* in the world. At the meeting of delegation leaders on 16 November, at which they accepted the Adenauer–Mollet agreement, Marjolin informed the others that, as far as France was concerned, the acceptance of the Eurafrique concept was a *sine qua non*. If the other powers rejected it, France would not agree to the economic community.

In the Federal Republic practically everybody rejected the idea. Erhard was once again up in arms. The last thing he needed was to become involved in France's colonial activities in Africa, which the Federal Republic would no doubt have to pay for as well. Only Adenauer and the Ministry of Foreign Affairs could bring themselves to be sympathetic to French wishes in this matter, although even they found it hard.

As far as the negotiations on Euratom were concerned, the Federal Republic eventually dropped its demand that the member states of this community should refrain from using nuclear energy for military purposes and accepted the provision in the treaty stating that none of the member states would suffer discrimination in the inspection of installations and raw materials (cf. Weilemann 1983, p. 138). This concession can only be understood in the light of the great political value that the Federal Republic attached to progress in the European integration process. In this case, the *Junktim* thwarted the Federal Republic's plans. If France was not allowed a free hand in the production of nuclear weapons, this would lead to the failure of Euratom, of the economic community and, consequently, of 'Europe'. This was the last thing the Federal Republic wanted in the current international situation. Furthermore, there was the fact that West Germany had once before accepted such a dual arrangement of 'internal' equality and 'external' subordination, namely with respect to the defence community (see Chapter 7, Section 5).

At the end of January 1957, the French National Assembly discussed the economic community. The vote at the end of the debate proved that a large but not very enthusiastic majority was in favour. A few days later, a conference of the ministers of foreign affairs was convened. They accepted the principles of the association of overseas territories and of an investment fund. However, they did not manage to reach agreement on how these principles should be worked out in actual practice. In mid-February, the ministers met once again, but they still could not find a solution. The government leaders, who were to meet in Paris two days later, would therefore have to reach a decision, which they did. They agreed that the investment fund would initially be set up for a period of five years, after which the whole exercise would be re-examined. France and Belgium would also contribute to the fund. The European Commission would be responsible for managing the fund.

Adenauer and the West German Ministry of Foreign Affairs defended the West German contribution to the investment fund in the old familiar way. Politics – in this case Western European integration – should take precedence over economics. Küsters has pointed out that to Adenauer 'the question of association and the consequent economic burdens were only side issues that should not stand in the way of the real goal, i.e. the political unification of Europe' (Küsters 1982, p. 392). In an interview with *Der Spiegel*, foreign minister Brentano said that the essence of the agreement reached in Paris was 'the political aspect prevailing over economic interests' (Weilemann, 1983, p. 141).

The way towards signing the treaties on the European Economic Community and Euratom finally lay open. The details could now be left to the experts. However, there were still so many things that needed to be settled and put into the correct legal wording that, when the organization of the Western European cooperation took definite shape with the solemn signing of the two treaties in Rome on 25 March 1957, the final texts of the treaties were not yet ready.

France and the Federal Republic had managed to solve the problems on their own. This was quite an achievement, particularly as there was much opposition to the two treaties in both countries. It is not true that France attached such great value to Euratom that it was willing to put up with the drawbacks of the economic community. In France the CEA would in any case have preferred to go on independently, and accordingly, the powers of Euratom were reduced to the absolute minimum. To France, Euratom was only important as an instrument for controlling the West German nuclear industry (through the joint ownership of the necessary raw materials and the right to inspect nuclear installations) and as a means of facilitating the acquisition of funds for the ambitious French civil nuclear programme. Nor is it true that the Federal Republic attached so much value to the economic community that it was willing to put up with Euratom and all its discriminatory aspects. The possible economic advantages of the common market for the Federal Republic were too controversial for that. What was decisive was that, in the autumn of 1956, both countries began to realize how disastrous it would be for Western Europe's position in the world – and consequently the positions of France and the Federal Republic – if these two European initiatives were to fail. The Federal Republic was more aware of this than France and therefore made the most concessions in the final stage of the negotiations. To paraphrase Zijlstra, the Chancellor and the West German Ministry of Foreign Affairs were determined to take 'a fundamentally political stand, which would set the course for further developments' (see Chapter 1, Section 2). It is one of history's ironies that these two initiatives, which were clearly the least politically motivated of the four, were eventually only realized on the basis of purely political considerations.

Notes

1. As Duchêne has observed: 'it was easy to see nuclear power as God's gift to integrators' (Duchêne 1994, p. 265).
2. In that case Monnet would have also been prepared to remain president of the High Authority. Since the beginning of February, when his term ended, he had been waiting for the appointment of his successor.
3. The Dutch cabinet was, incidentally, rather sceptical about Beyen's initiative and the Benelux memorandum, but it ultimately did not oppose them (see, for example, Duchêne 1994, p. 273).
4. This conference was originally scheduled for 10 February 1955, but was postponed because of the collapse of the Mendès-France government on 5 February. After the formation of the Faure cabinet, 26 April was the new date on which the ministers were to meet. As they subsequently came to the conclusion that it would be better not to develop any new initiatives concerning Europe before the Federal Republic's official entry into NATO, which was to take place at the beginning of May, the conference was again postponed, this time to the end of May. However, at the beginning of May, they decided to postpone the conference even further, to 1 and 2 June. As a gesture to Italian foreign minister Martino, and with a view to the regional parliamentary elections in Sicily, they decided to hold the conference in Messina.
5. Referring to this passage, Beyen wrote in his memoirs: 'to bring about this economic integration, we wanted a new "community" (not an intergovernmental organization such as the OEEC), with an Executive Body that would have responsibilities of its own *vis-à-vis* a common Parliament. But for the time being we only expressed this as our conviction and avoided the term "supranational"' (cf. Beyen 1968, p. 238).
6. On the same day that the Benelux countries sent their memorandum, Faure proposed to the French cabinet that Mayer be appointed as Monnet's successor. A week later, this proposal was accepted. As Monnet was not chosen for a second term as president of the High Authority, he no longer had any chance

to lead the proposed conference.

7. In Beyen's words: 'Bech presided over the meetings. Spaak and I defended the proposal. Antoine Pinay was well-disposed towards us despite the disapproving looks of the *Quai d'Orsay* officials and Branly Hallstein had to speak in German – which I had never heard him do before – because the officials of the West German Ministry of Economic Affairs could otherwise not check sufficiently whether he was not being too "European"' (Beyen 1968, p. 238). Hallstein led the West German delegation instead of Adenauer, who – if we may believe Duchêne – preferred not to be witness to the expected failure (cf. Duchêne 1994, p. 281). A more plausible reason would be that he did not feel the need to attend another exhausting conference, as he was to resign as Minister of Foreign Affairs just a few days later. On 6 June, Brentano was appointed as his successor.

8. It was Spaak who finally managed to win over his French counterpart Pinay on the early morning of 3 June. This led to the balcony scene which is too famous not to be mentioned here. This is the version told to Duchêne by a member of the Belgian delegation, De Staercke: 'When Spaak finally returned to his room it was early morning, with the sun coming up, and he was so pleased he ordered a bottle of champagne. Then he began to face the dawn [on the balcony] and [to] sing "O Sole Mio". Pinay occupied the room above. He opened the shutters and said: "Look here, Spaak. You have been pestering me all night, can't you give me a chance to sleep?"' (Duchêne 1994, pp. 281–2).

9. In July 1955, during the first round of negotiations in the Spaak Committee, the French government secretly decided to build nuclear submarines (cf. Mendl 1970, p. 30).

10. As a result of this decision to call early elections, Faure was expelled from the Radical Party on a proposal of party chairman Mendès-France.

11. Monnet wrote in his memoirs that it was not he who had no clear idea of the economic community, but the majority of the French: 'For the majority of French people an atomic energy Community was a clear and distinct idea – while that of an economic Community remained nebulous' (Monnet 1978, p. 419).

12. Küsters has some doubts about the guideline's effectiveness. 'As a means of disciplining certain cabinet ministers, however, the guideline ultimately had no effect. It did not resolve the conflict on methods, nor did it prevent Erhard and Strauss from continuing their attacks on the Euratom and Common Market project' (Küsters 1982, p. 226).

13. The part on the Common Market contained a separate chapter on agriculture. This special attention was justified by the argument that, although agriculture was one of the sectors that would benefit the most from the establishment of a Common Market, it had such a special structure, partly because it was exposed to a high degree of government intervention, that free exchange of agricultural products could not be ensured. A separate regime within the Common Market would therefore have to be established on the basis of various stabilization

mechanisms, supplemented by additional buying-up regulations and guaranteed prices. The European Commission was allocated the task of establishing this separate regime (cf. Comité intergouvernemental 1956, pp. 44–52).

14. Perhaps this is the right place to recall the struggle between Monnet and Spierenburg over the relationship between the High Authority and the Council of Ministers in the summer of 1950. It is clear that the authors of the Spaak report tried to subordinate the supranational element to the intergovernmental element as far as possible, in Euratom even more than in the economic community. This is illustrated by the order in which the Council and the two European Commissions were discussed in the text. In both cases, the authors first paid attention to the Council and then to the Commission. In the Treaty of Paris, it was exactly the other way round.

15. Marjolin, Pineau's chief of staff, was one of the leading officials who supported the economic community. The fact that he started his account of this period in his memoirs with the heading 'The Battle of Paris' makes clear how fierce resistance to this proposal actually was (Marjolin 1989, p. 284).

16. 'The weather was fine, it was not too hot. Luckily, the meeting did not last very long, so there still was some time for sightseeing' (Beyen 1968, p. 243). Baron Snoy et d'Oppuers, Secretary-General of the Belgian Ministry of Economic Affairs, called it the 'miraculous conference'. 'Never before had agreement on questions of such importance been reached so swiftly' (Spaak 1971, p. 240). According to Snoy, the Venice Conference was the shortest he had ever attended in his long career. On the two days reserved for the conference, the parties conferred for only seventy-five minutes (cf. Küsters 1982, p. 261).

9. The Continuing Struggle

1. Recapitulation

Looking back on the history of the struggle for the organization of Europe in the period 1947–1957, one of the first things that catches the eye is that it was actually only for a very short time that France saw the creation of supranational European institutions (in which it would participate on an equal footing with the Federal Republic) as a means of securing its position *vis-à-vis* that same Federal Republic. With the launching of the Schuman Plan in the spring of 1950, supranationality came to the forefront in quite a spectacular way; but hardly five months later, during the preparations for the Pleven Plan, traditional thinking in intergovernmental terms prevailed once again. In the Pleven Plan, the supranational aspect had been subordinated to the intergovernmental aspect. Moreover, this Plan contained many parts that discriminated against the Federal Republic, which immediately raised doubts as to France's good intentions. When one year later negotiations concerning the defence community took an un-favourable turn for France – in the sense that the supranational aspect was enhanced and the discrimination against the Federal Republic diminished – supranational solutions fell completely into disfavour with the French. In the eyes of the French, 'Europe' was no longer a means of controlling the Federal Republic. It was not 'self-binding', but the largest possible freedom of action that might be expected to protect France from West German domination. The political struggle waged between opponents and supporters of the EDC Treaty in the French National Assembly from 1952 to 1954 was not a struggle between opponents and supporters of supranational solutions. It was a struggle between those who thought France's international position would be *harmed* and those who thought France's position would *improve* if the treaty was not ratified. While the former tried to make the most of a very unsatisfactory situation by obtaining American guarantees and whittling down the supranational provisions in the treaty, the latter expected more good to come from throwing the supranational ballast overboard.

This also clearly illustrates how controversial Monnet's initiative had actually been in France and how dependent he had been on Schuman's protection in the eleven months between the launching of the Schuman Plan and the signing of the ECSC Treaty. It would have been practically impossible for Monnet to succeed without Schuman's protection. Schuman is quite rightly considered to be one of the founding fathers of 'Europe'. If he had not decided to give Monnet a chance, the struggle for the organization of Europe would almost certainly have ended in failure.

The fact that the French cabinet was taken by surprise on 9 May 1950 also appears to have been crucial. Before the French cabinet knew what plan it had accepted, it had already been made public. However effective this action may have been, from then on the French ministers followed all of Monnet's activities with great suspicion, as they considered him to be the man behind this *fait accompli* policy. Although some of them had great difficulty with it, the ministers reconciled themselves with the situation as it had evolved, and accepted that it was best to let Monnet finish the job. It was, however, out of the question that he would get a new one. The French cabinet gratefully acknowledged Monnet's services as far as the formulation of the Pleven Plan was concerned, but they did not want his involvement in this plan to go any further. In July 1951, they once again required his services to save the conference on the Pleven Plan. In September 1956, the French government also accepted Monnet's offer to help the proposed economic community to an untimely end. It seems the inevitable conclusion must be that Monnet was already sidetracked in the French struggle for power in the autumn of 1950. His departure to the High Authority in 1952 was a reward for services rendered as well as a confirmation of the fact that he no longer played a significant role in France's centre of power.

The French cabinet called in Monnet's help in the spring of 1951, because it wished to make use of his good contacts with prominent American policy-makers to persuade them to save the conference on the Pleven Plan. This request aptly illustrates how much France depended on the support of the United States for its European 'German policy' to succeed. Without the intervention of the United States, the European coal and steel community would have foundered on the question of decartelization and deconcentration of the West German industrial conglomerates, and the impasse at the conference on the Pleven Plan would not have been overcome.

In the first phase of the organization of Western Europe, the United States not only played a crucial role as saviour of the French initiatives. As a great power engaged in a struggle for power with the Soviet Union, trying to prevent the latter from gaining hegemony over Europe, it also played the role of initiator. In early 1948, after having been invited to do so by Great Britain, the United States took on the role of leader of the North Atlantic security community. The United States demanded in return that the Western European powers would jointly concentrate all their efforts on making the greatest possible contribution to the defence of Western Europe. In this context the United States argued in favour of West German participation in the defence of Western Europe. Initially, the United States merely wanted Germany to supply raw materials to the defence industries of the other Western European powers and produce certain light weapons, but when the Korean war broke out, it also insisted on a military contribution from the Federal Republic. No matter what the form, the American endeavours to involve the Federal Republic actively in the defence of Western Europe implied the rapid recovery of West Germany and, as such, formed a serious threat to the position of France *vis-à-vis* its arch-enemy. It was this threat that induced France to develop two European initiatives in 1950. It thereby hoped to steal a march on the United States and secure its position *vis-à-vis* the Federal Republic.

The North Korean invasion of South Korea greatly affected the struggle for the organization of Western European cooperation. This act of Communist aggression convinced the United States that the American military contribution to the collective defence of Western Europe had to be increased. In return, the United States demanded that the Western European powers also stepped up their defence efforts. From the American point of view, this would have to be done by setting up a large number of West German divisions within the framework of a European defence force, which would also include American and Canadian divisions. The fact that the Americans insisted on the rearmament of West Germany led to a drastic change in the power relations between France, the Federal Republic and the United States. When Schuman launched his plan at the beginning of May 1950, the Federal Republic was completely dependent on the good-will of the occupation authorities and therefore welcomed any initiative that might reduce its subordination. In September 1950, as a result of the American 'one package proposal', a situation had evolved in which the Federal Republic could afford to be particular as far as these types of initiative were concerned and set conditions for its cooperation. Initially, the United States had great difficulty accepting the more assertive attitude of the Federal Republic, as hardly five years had passed since Germany's total defeat in World War II. Its aversion to West Germany's increased self-confidence almost made it blind to the fact that the Federal Republic was not using its improved international position to brush aside the reconciliation with France and *Westbindung* as artefacts of its subordinate position. Supranational initiatives had lost none of their attraction for the Federal Republic. It was simply that after September 1950 the Federal Republic was no longer prepared to take things for granted in the context of the reconciliation with France and *Westbindung*, and insisted on more equal treatment. One year later, the United States had fully accepted this attitude.

The position of West Germany as an occupied power was of decisive importance in making the first step towards the organization of Europe a success. Knowing that, if need be, the occupying powers could, unilaterally, carry through the complete programme of decartelization and deconcentration of the Ruhr industry against its wishes, the Federal Republic decided in March 1951 to accept the compromise in this matter as formulated by the American High Commissioner McCloy, even though the Federal Republic believed this to be detrimental to its own coal and steel industry. It was this compromise that cleared the way for the signing of the ECSC Treaty.

It was precisely because its collaboration was not required that the Federal Republic decided to collaborate in the decartelization and deconcentration of the Ruhr industry. A similar situation arose in the case of the defence of Western Europe within the framework of a North Atlantic security community. It was precisely because this defence could be organized without the cooperation of France that France decided to cooperate. The situation concerning the EDC was the complete opposite. The cooperation of France was essential for the defence community to be established. France could therefore afford the luxury of not cooperating.

The question remains how the Six nevertheless managed to make a success of the *relance européenne*, which the Benelux countries initiated in the spring of 1955. After all, it looks as if the factors that had worked in favour of the ECSC had lost their potency, whereas the ones that had had a negative effect on the EDC had not. The Federal Republic no longer found itself in the subordinate position of an occupied power. In France, Schuman and Monnet had had to abandon the field to others. (Monnet did not even have any scruples about influencing the game from the sideline and tried to thwart the plans for an economic community.) What remained was the French distrust of supranational institutions, which had not diminished. What had also remained undiminished was the fact that the United States could not impose 'European' solutions on France nor on any other sovereign Western European power. Fortunately, there was a third factor that had remained constant; one that had a beneficial influence on the organization of Western Europe and had been of decisive importance for the success of the *relance européenne*. This factor concerned the West German ambition to bring about a reconciliation with France and strengthen the *Westbindung*. Apparently, the Federal Republic had lost sight of both objectives in the course of the negotiations as a result of having to deal with such enervating questions as overtime pay, the number of holidays and length of the working week. They even seemed to have definitely dropped out of sight when the conference of foreign ministers completely failed at the end of October 1956. The Hungarian uprising and the Suez Canal crisis suddenly brought 'Europe' back into the limelight, which also made clear how little had been achieved as far as the Franco-German reconciliation and *Westbindung* were concerned. The Federal Republic's rediscovered willingness to take the next step in the organization of Western Europe was not sufficient to actually do so. For this, the Federal Republic required the cooperation of France. France decided to cooperate, first of all, because the Federal Republic had been willing to make concessions to France in the last phase of the negotiations, and secondly, because there were just about enough influential people in France at the beginning of 1957 who had become convinced that it was desirable for the French economy to be exposed to competition within the context of a common internal market.

2. From Rome to Maastricht

With General de Gaulle coming to power in France at the end of May 1958, the European integration process lost its momentum. In de Gaulle's 'Europe of the Fatherlands', there was no need for intricate institutional arrangements to regulate Franco-German relations. In de Gaulle's view, the Franco-German treaty of friendship of 1963, which provided for regular consultations between both countries, offered sufficient possibilities for doing so. At the same time, the general was among those who thought that participation in the common market would have a beneficial effect on the French economy. Aside from this, he saw the EEC mainly as a source of finance for the French agricultural sector.

The French aversion to the provisions in the EEC Treaty that would give the Council of Ministers the power to take decisions by a qualified majority led to a crisis between France and the other member states in 1965–1966. The solution to this crisis was found in the Luxembourg Compromise. The member states agreed that, in situations where 'very important interests of one or more partners are at stake' the Members of the Council 'will endeavour, within a reasonable time, to reach solutions which can be adopted by all the Members of the Council', even if the Treaty of Rome provided for taking decisions by a qualified majority. Furthermore the member states recorded that 'the French delegation considers that, where very important issues are at stake, the discussion must be continued until unanimous agreement is reached', and, although the other member states did not share this view, they were nevertheless of the opinion that 'this divergence of views does not prevent the Community's work being resumed in accordance with the normal procedure' (cf. Van Ooijen *et al.* 1996, p. 195).

By the end of the 1960s, France had rediscovered the value of 'Europe' as a means to check the threat of West German dominance. However, this rediscovery did not lead to a new supranational initiative, but to the introduction of the traditional policy of the balance of power within the existing European framework. In 1969, after having blocked Great Britain's entry to the European Economic Community on two previous occasions, France finally agreed to Great Britain becoming a member. However, France's hope that, together with Great Britain, it might form a counterweight to the Federal Republic evaporated almost immediately after Great Britain's entry in 1973. It turned out that Great Britain still showed no interest whatsoever in the political dimension of 'Europe'.

The common agricultural policy of the EEC formulated in the course of the 1960s forced the member states to coordinate their exchange rates when the old system of fixed exchange rates based on the American dollar collapsed in 1971. It was in this context that West Germany's Chancellor Schmidt and France's President Giscard d'Estaing developed an initiative for a European Monetary System (EMS) in the spring of 1978. After the EMS had been implemented in March 1979, it soon became apparent that the system largely functioned as a D-Mark zone. This was because the Bundesbank, the independent West German central bank, refused to subordinate its task of maintaining price stability in the Federal Republic to the EMS's objective of stabilizing the exchange-rate ratios between the participating countries. The monetary policies of the states participating in the EMS were not entirely subject to the decisions taken by the Bundesbank, because of the restrictions on capital transactions still in force in the participating countries, particularly in France and Italy. In the spring of 1986, however, the member states of the European Community signed the Single European Act. In this document, they declared their intention to complete before 1 January 1993 something which, according to the EEC Treaty, they should already have completed twenty years earlier: an internal market for free movement of goods, persons, services and capital (cf. Van Ooijen *et al.* 1996, p. 239). Within the framework of this project, called Europe '92, they agreed to abolish the existing restrictions on capital transactions as of 1 July 1990. This meant that the last defence line against West German monetary dominance over Europe would disappear.

In the light of this threat, supranational solutions exerted a new attraction. In January 1988, Édouard Balladur, the French Minister of Finance, distributed a memorandum among his European counterparts in which he expressed the French objections to the way in which the EMS was functioning. He proposed that they should together investigate the possibilities of replacing the EMS by a central European bank. France had had enough of sitting on 'the folding chair next to the command post in the European economy', as *Le Monde Diplomatique* put it (cf. Ludlow 1982, p. 199). It wished to exchange it for a seat in that command post. Giuliano Amato, Italy's Minister of Finance, applauded Balladur's idea. In his response, he proved to be even more critical of the effects of the EMS than Balladur. He ended his note with a statement which might just as easily have flowed from Monnet's pen. As far as Amato was concerned, a self-imposed loss of autonomy in favour of a European bank in which all participants would have a say was preferable to the unilateral loss of autonomy which Germany imposed on its partners in the EMS (cf. Colchester and Buchan 1990, p. 167).

Balladur and Amato's ideas were received favourably by the European Commission and the majority of the member states. True to tradition, there was a divergence of views in the Federal Republic. The West German Ministry of Finance and the Bundesbank rejected the ideas on economic grounds, whereas the Ministry of Foreign Affairs regarded them positively, given the political importance of further integration. Foreign minister Genscher expressed his willingness to investigate whether a European bank could be realized, provided of course that it was modelled on the Bundesbank.

At the European summit meeting in Hanover in June 1988, the member states decided to set up a committee to study the concrete steps involved and make proposals for the establishment of an Economic and Monetary Union (EMU). The composition of the study committee provided a clear indication of the framework in which the Federal Republic and France were going to play the game in the years to come. The West German demand for monetary solidity was met by appointing the presidents of the national banks as members of the study committee. French supranational ambitions were recognized by entrusting the chairmanship of the study committee to Jacques Delors, the French Chairman of the European Commission.

The Delors Report issued in the spring of 1989 recognized the desirability of an Economic and Monetary Union (EMU), but also stated that the creation of such a union was going to be a long-term affair given the considerable differences between the economic policies of the member states. Only if a sufficient degree of economic convergence could be achieved would EMU have a chance of success. The report therefore proposed the establishment of EMU in three stages. Furthermore, it advised against fixing the transition from Stage I (which was to commence on 1 July 1990 when the capital markets of the community would be liberalized) to Stage II, or that from Stage II to Stage III (cf. Van Ooijen *et al.* 1996, pp. 251–2).

In the Delors Committee, political urgency had had to make way for monetary prudence. The Franco-Italian attack on the Bundesbank appeared to have been thwarted. In the spring of 1989, everything seemed to indicate that EMU would be postponed indefinitely. However, at the beginning of November 1989 something happened that no one could have predicted six months earlier, lending new weight to the political arguments in favour of EMU. This concerned the decision of the East German leaders to terminate the German Democratic Republic's isolation from the West by opening up the Berlin Wall. This decision heralded the end of the Communist regime in the GDR. That the opening up the frontiers would also lead to the rapid downfall of the GDR itself was less evident in these hectic times.

In the GDR the outcry for a monetary union with the Federal Republic soon gathered strength. At the beginning of February 1990 Chancellor Kohl proposed starting discussions on a German monetary union as soon as possible. This proposal was made following emergency talks with the leaders of the East German CDU who feared an exodus from the GDR if the D-Mark was not introduced soon. Kohl had not consulted the Bundesbank about his proposal. Worse still, the president of the Bundesbank had stated to the press only a few hours earlier that it was premature to be thinking of a German monetary union, given the large differences between the two economies. Two months later the Bundesbank was bypassed again. This time it had been asked for advice, but the federal government decided not to follow it. Although the Bundesbank had proposed to set the rate of conversion of the East Mark into D-Mark at 2:1, the cabinet decided to set it at 1:1 (cf. Marsh [1992] 1993, pp. 209–16).

Kohl's unification policy was a faithful copy of Adenauer's European integration policy. No matter how great the economic and monetary problems resulting from the unification of East and West Germany, they should never prevent the realization of the political goal. In *Ich wollte Deutschlands Einheit* ('I wanted Germany's unity'), the book Kohl wrote about his experiences at the time, he stated he had been fully aware that an exchange rate of 1:1 'was a very unusual offer, which you would not find in any textbook of economics', but that he had not seen any alternative. An economically sound offer was 'practically impossible for political reasons' (Kohl 1996, p. 262).

Moreover, the situation called for drastic measures. The possibility of a unified Germany still aroused so much suspicion among neighbouring countries that they would never provide the Federal Republic with anything which the latter had not already obtained through a *fait accompli* policy. This naturally also applied to France, which, as one of the occupying powers, would have to agree explicitly to the unification in a peace treaty. At the same time, Kohl realized fully that a *fait accompli* policy was not exactly the most obvious way of removing the suspicions. The best way to achieve this was by confirming and strengthening the *Westbindung*. By doing so, Kohl proved once again that he was a true successor of Adenauer. Is there a better way to remove the fear of German dominance than by relinquishing the power over a domain where the Federal Republic has practically achieved this dominance anyway? At the European summit meeting in Strasbourg in December 1989, Kohl agreed to an inter-governmental conference (IGC) to be convened by the end of 1990. At this conference, the members would make preparations for the treaty changes needed to implement EMU.

In September 1990, at the preparatory talks for the IGC, Spain proposed implementing the second stage of EMU as of January 1994. The Bundes-bank and the German finance ministry were against this proposal. They clung to the view that fixing a commencing date for the second stage made little sense if the required convergence had not been achieved. A few days after the official German unification on 3 October 1990, Kohl brushed aside the objections of the Bundesbank and the finance ministry. On French television (!) he announced that he agreed to the proposal to implement the second stage in January 1994. He also restated the German standpoint that a European Central Bank (ECB) should be independent just like the Bundesbank and that it should be given the exclusive task of maintaining price stability (cf. Story and De Cecco in Story 1993, p. 349).

At the ICG, it turned out that the delegations could not reach agreement on the role of the Council of Ministers in EMU and the way in which the transition to the third stage of EMU would have to take place. France was in favour of an ECB with extensive powers, but subordinate to the Council of Ministers. This proposal was completely unacceptable to the Federal Republic. It clung to the independence of the ECB. Regarding the way in which the transition to the third stage should take place, the negotiators did agree that the participants in EMU would have to meet strict convergence criteria, but they failed to reach agreement on questions such as how exactly these criteria should be formulated, how to determine whether a member state had met the criteria, and how many countries should meet those criteria before EMU could become operational (cf. Story and De Cecco in Story 1993, p. 350). These problems would have to be solved at the ICG in Maastricht.

The compromise which Kohl and President Mitterrand of France eventually managed to reach in a private conversation at the Maastricht Conference ensured that the Federal Republic would get what it wanted with regard to the ECB, the policy the ECB was to pursue, and the convergence criteria. In return, France obtained the crucial concession that the third stage of EMU would be irrevocably implemented on 1 January 1999 for all the member states that met the convergence criteria. This meant that the Bundesbank would not be able to prevent the implementation of the third stage of EMU using the failing monetary policies of Greece and Italy as an argument. It was now up to France itself whether or not it would get a seat in the command post of the European economy on 1 January 1999.

3. The Continuing Struggle

In Maastricht neither Mitterrand nor Kohl reckoned with the possibility that, when it was to be decided, in the spring of 1998, which member states of the European Union had qualified for the third phase of EMU, the Federal Republic itself might not be able to meet the convergence criteria – specifically, the criterion that the government's budget deficit should not exceed three per cent of GDP. If Germany did not qualify, the whole point of their agreement would be lost. However, in the course of 1997, the financial situation of the Federal Republic had deteriorated to such an extent that, if it insisted on a strict application of the convergence criteria to its own finances, it could still prevent the other member states from taking up their seats in the command post of the European economy. Another thing that Kohl and Mitterrand failed to see at Maastricht was that France, notwithstanding the enormous benefits participation in EMU would bring, might at the last moment spurn its seat in the command post by deliberately exceeding the three per cent norm in pursuance of its own socio-economic policies.

Throughout 1997 speculation abounded that Germany and France might reconsider their position and decide not to go ahead with the third phase of EMU. In this context it might be as well to emphasize once again (see also Chapter 2, Section 6) that there was nothing inevitable about the French and German decision in the spring of 1998 to take another step in the organization of Europe. It is emphatically not the case that economic developments in Europe (the completion of the common market) or in the world left both powers no option but to let the third phase of EMU start on 1 January 1999. They always had the power to postpone this third phase, and would certainly have used it had they deemed this desirable from the point of view of political logic – no matter how large the sums of money that banks (including the central banks), insurance companies, pension funds and corporations, both national and multinational, would already have spent preparing for the arrival of EMU and Euro. Similarly, they still have the power to tear down the European construction they have built so laboriously in the course of the past fifty years, should they decide that this would better suit their interests. It must be said, however, that this is a very remote possibility considering the great benefits both powers still derive from participating in the common market.

As far as EMU is concerned, France would certainly have liked to see the ECB having more objectives than that of solely maintaining price stability. At the same time, it still holds that French participation in the common market without EMU would have meant France either submitting to a monetary policy strictly tailored to the needs of the German economy, or, if it wished to avoid this situation, adopting an even stricter monetary stance than the Bundesbank (in order to gain the necessary credibility). For this reason France is far better off with the ECB, in which it helps to take decisions on Europe's monetary policy on an equal footing with the Federal Republic. In the terms used above (see also Chapter 2, Section 5), if the collective good of monetary stability is to be provided one way or the other, then it is only in France's interest to make sure it has a say in forming the conditions under which this provision will take place.

In his analysis of the relations between France and Great Britain in the 1840s, Schroeder observes that 'the government of Guizot and Louis-Philippe was more ready than any French government had ever been before to accept Britain's superiority in power; its goal was equality in status, rank, honour and satisfactions' (Schroeder [1994] 1996, p. 773). It seems to me that, substituting 'Mitterrand' for 'Guizot and Louis-Philippe', and

'Germany's' for 'Britain's', Schroeder's observation describes perfectly the position Mitterrand adopted *vis-à-vis* the Federal Republic, when in the winter of 1989–1990, he came to the conclusion – after first having spent several months in yet another futile attempt 'to escape from history' (cf. Chapter 3, Section 2) – that German unification could no longer be prevented (cf. Ziebura [1970] 1997, pp. 364–9 and Kohl 1996, pp. 232–6). Mitterrand acquiesced in France's role as the Federal Republic's junior partner, provided that France's status remained unimpaired, a demand Kohl was prepared to satisfy in the most generous terms. Clearly, Mitterrand's Gaullist successor Chirac has great difficulty in adopting the same attitude. Chirac's open defiance of German wishes, in nominating a French candidate for the first presidency of the ECB, is a clear example of this. Lionel Jospin, his socialist Prime Minister, who came to power in June 1997 after the general election Chirac had called with a view to strengthening the position of his right-wing government in fact returned a left-wing majority, appears to be more prepared to face up to the German ascendancy. Notwithstanding some initial professions of socialist sentiment, he seems to have convinced himself of the necessity of France meeting the Maastricht criteria, and, at the decisive Brussels conference in early May 1998, he ostentatiously let Chirac fight the battle for the presidency alone.

Mitterrand and Kohl succeeded in reaching agreement in Maastricht, because it was the chancellor's firm conviction that the destruction of the organization of Europe's original foundation, the division of Germany, had to be compensated by strengthening this organization. The Federal Republic's entanglement in 'Europe' had brought it so many advantages that Kohl was prepared to pay a high price for the continued successful functioning of 'Europe'. With the approach of the third phase of EMU, many in Germany began to wonder whether the price paid by the chancellor had not been too high after all in terms of German self-interest. Not only because they feared for the stability of the currency when the Euro was substituted for the D-Mark, but also because the costs of German unification continued to be a very heavy burden for the German economy. Why should Germany go on being the paymaster of 'Europe'? Would it not be far better to spend this money on the reconstruction of East Germany and the preservation of the German welfare state? Why should the Federal Republic continue to treat a second-rate power like France on an equal footing? Had the time not come to make clear to France how relations between the two countries really stood?

However, those who argue in favour of a more independent German policy and a more assertive attitude towards the other member states of the

European Union (EU), particularly France, risk forgetting that, although the division of Germany has been ended, with the exception of monetary matters the Federal Republic is in no position to manage things unilaterally in the European Union, let alone in Europe as whole. While in the 1970s and 1980s, the Soviet Union was 'the incomplete superpower' (cf. Dibbs [1986] 1988), nowadays the Federal Republic is 'the incomplete great power'. Germany can decide to throw off the supranational ballast, but this would only harm its position in the European states system. As the most important power in the European states system, the Federal Republic feels responsible for the way things go in this system, but it is not powerful enough to organize it according to its wishes. When it tries to find solutions for the many problems facing the European states system, Germany is still dependent on the cooperation of other European powers. In this respect the Federal Republic and the other European powers find themselves in the same situation as the states facing a 'weak' security dilemma (cf. Chapter 2, Section 3). A German decision to pay less regard to the interests of the other EU member states in the future would increase these states' suspicion of the Federal Republic, and would therefore only result in Germany having more difficulty persuading those states that it is also in their interest to extend this cooperation.

Adenauer never lost sight of the fact, and Kohl is also very much aware that German participation in 'Europe' has always had the function of removing its neighbours' suspicions of Germany and German initiatives. As such, 'Europe' has brought the Federal Republic countless advantages. For this reason it was merely sound politics that the Kohl government should have refrained from insisting on a strict interpretation of the convergence criteria. Had it done so, Germany would certainly not have been able to fulfil these criteria, which would likely have meant the indefinite postponement of the third phase of EMU. Thus, France was at last allowed to take up its seat in the command post of the European economy. The fact that France was unable to do so graciously, with Chirac turning the Brussels conference into a public relations disaster for 'Europe' as a result of the row over the presidency of the ECB, must surely be attributed to France's fully understanding that, although it is better off with EMU than without it, this holds good even more for Germany. Those in Germany who are worried by the idea that, from 1 January 1999, the Bundesbank will no longer be 'the bank that rules Europe' (cf. Marsh [1992] 1993), should find comfort in the realization that from a power politics point of view 'Europe' has brought Germany nothing but success.

Bibliography

Acheson, D. (1969), *Present at the Creation. My Years in the State Department*, New York: Norton

Adenauer, K. (1966a), *Memoirs 1945–53*, London: Weidenfeld and Nicholson

Adenauer, K. (1966b), *Erinnerungen 1953–1955*, Stuttgart: Deutsche Verlags-Anstalt

Adenauer, K. (1967), *Erinnerungen 1955–1959*, Stuttgart: Deutsche Verlags-Anstalt

Allison, G.T. (1971), *Essence of Decision. Explaining the Cuban Missile Crisis*, Boston: Little, Brown and Co.

Baring, A. (1969), *Aussenpolitik in Adenauers Kanzlerdemokratie. Bonns Beitrag zur Europäischen Verteidigungsgemeinschaft*, Munich and Vienna: Oldenbourg

Barnes, J. (1990) (ed.), *A History of the World in 10½ Chapters*, London: Picador

Beyen, J.W. (1968), *Het Spel en de Knikkers. Een Kroniek van Vijftig Jaren*, Rotterdam: Donker

Blankenhorn, H. (1980), *Verständnis und Verständigung. Blätter eines politischen Tagebuchs 1949 bis 1979*, Frankfurt: Propyläen

Blumenwitz, D. *et al.* (eds) (1976), *Konrad Adenauer und Seine Zeit. Politik und Persönlichkeit des Ersten Bundeskanzler*, I, Stuttgart: Deutsche Verlags-Anstalt

Botti, T. (1987), *The Long Wait. The Forging of the Anglo-American Nuclear Alliance, 1945–1958*, New York: Greenwood Press

Bull, H. (1977), *The Anarchical Society. A Study of Order in World Politics*, London and Basingstoke: Macmillan

Burley, A.-M. and W. Mattli (1993), 'Europe before the Court: a Political Theory of Legal Integration', in: *International Organization*, 47, 41–76

Buzan, B. (1982), *People, States and Fear. An Agenda for International Security Studies in the Post-Cold War Era* (1991), New York: Harvester Wheatsheaf

Buzan, B., C. Jones and R. Little (1993), *The Logic of Anarchy. Neorealism to Structural Realism*, New York: Columbia University Press

Carr, E.H. (1939), *The Twenty Years' Crisis, 1919–1939. An Introduction to the Study of International Relations* (1964), London: Harper & Row

Claude, I.L. (1956), *Swords into Plowshares* (1964), New York: Random House

Clausewitz, C. von (1832), *Vom Kriege* (1980), Bonn: Ferd. Dümmler

Clausewitz, C. von (1976), *On War* (1989), Princeton: Princeton University Press

Colchester, N. and D. Buchan (1990), *Europe Relaunched. Truths and Illusions on the Way to 1992*, London: Hutchinson

Collingwood, R.G. (1946), *The Idea of History* (1957), New York: Oxford University Press

Comité intergouvernemental créé par la conférence de Messine (1956), *Rapport des Chefs de Délégation aux Ministres des Affaires Etrangères*, Brussels

Davies, N. (1996), *Europe. A History*, Oxford and New York: Oxford University Press

Dedman, M.J. (1996), *The Origins and Development of the European Union 1945– 1995. A History of European Integration*, London and New York: Routledge

Deighton, A. (ed.) (1995), *Building Postwar Europe. National Decision-Makers and European Institutions, 1948–63*, Basingstoke and London: Macmillan

De Jasay, A. (1989), *Social Contract, Free Ride. A Study of the Public Goods Problem*, Oxford: Oxford University Press

Department of State (1970), *Treaties and Other International Agreements of the United States of America 1776–1949*, I, Washington: United States Government Printing Office

Department of State (1973), *Foreign Relations of the United States 1948, Germany and Austria*, Washington: United States Government Printing Office

Department of State (1974), *Foreign Relations of the United States 1948, Western Europe*, Washington: United States Government Printing Office

Department of State (1975), *Foreign Relations of the United States 1949, Western Europe*, Washington: United States Government Printing Office

Department of State (1977), *Foreign Relations of the United States 1950, Western Europe*, Washington: United States Government Printing Office

Department of State (1981), *Foreign Relations of the United States 1951, European Security and the German Question*, Washington: United States Government Printing Office

Department of State (1983), *Foreign Relations of the United States 1952–1954, Western European Security*, Washington: United States Government Printing Office

DePorte, A.W. (1978), *Europe between the Superpowers. The Enduring Balance* (1986), New Haven and London: Yale University Press

Deutsch, K.W. (1968), *The Analysis of International Relations*, Englewood Cliffs, New Jersey: Prentice-Hall

De Wilde, J. (1991), *Saved from Oblivion: Interdependence Theory in the First Half of the 20th Century. A Study on the Causality Between War and Complex Interdependence*, Aldershot: Dartmouth

Dibbs, P. (1986), *The Soviet Union. The Incomplete Superpower* (1988), Basingstoke and London: Macmillan

Dimmendaal, F. (1987), 'Uiterlijk een Behoorlijke Geste. Nederland en de Onder- handelingen voor het EEG-Verdrag 1955–1957', Enschede: mimeo

Documents on International Affairs 1949–1953 (1958), London: Oxford University Press

Duchêne, F. (1994), *Jean Monnet. The First Statesman of Interdependence*, New York and London: W.W. Norton

Easton, D. (1965), *A Systems Analysis of Political Life*, New York: Wiley

Eden, A. (1960), *Full Circle*, London: Cassell

Ellwood, D.W. (ed.) (1988), *The Marshall Plan Forty Years After: Lessons for the International System Today*, Bologna

Ellwood, D.W. (1992), *Rebuilding Europe. Western Europe, America and Postwar Reconstruction*, London and New York: Longman

Ferguson, A. (1773) (ed.), *An Essay on the History of Civil Society*, London: Caddell

Foschepoth, J. (ed.) (1985), *Kalter Krieg und Deutsche Frage. Deutschland im Widerstreit der Mächte 1945–1952*, Göttingen and Zürich: Vandenhoeck & Ruprecht

Foschepoth, J. (ed.) (1988), *Adenauer und die Deutsche Frage*, Göttingen: Vandenhoeck & Ruprecht

Furniss, E.S. (1960), *France, Troubled Ally. De Gaulle's Heritage and Prospects*, New York: Praeger

Gaddis, J.L. (1997), *We Now Know. Rethinking Cold War History*, Oxford: Clarendon Press

Gimbel, J. (1972), 'Byrnes' Stuttgarter Rede und die amerikanische Nachkriegspolitik in Deutschland', in: *Vierteljahresheft für Zeitgeschichte*, 20, 39–62

Goldstein, J.S. (1996), *International Relations*, New York: Harper Collins

Greenwood, S. (1983), 'Return to Dunkirk: the Origins of the Anglo-French Treaty of March 1947', in: *Journal of Strategic Studies*, 6, 49–65

Haas, E.B. (1958), *The Uniting of Europe. Political, Social and Economic Forces 1950–1957* (1968), Stanford: Stanford University Press

Haffner, S. (1987), *Von Bismarck zu Hitler. Ein Rückblick* (1989), München: Kindler

Hanrieder, W.F. (1989), *Germany, America, Europe. Forty Years of German Foreign Policy*, New Haven and London: Yale University Press

Henkin, L. (1968), *How Nations Behave. Law and Foreign Policy* (1979), New York: Columbia University Press

Hobbes, T. (1651), *Leviathan or the Matter, Forme and Power of a Commonwealth Ecclesiastical and Civil* (1947), New York: Macmillan

Hogan, M.J. (1982), 'The Search for a "Creative Peace": the United States, European Unity, and the Origins of the Marshall Plan', in: *Diplomatic History*, 6, 267–85

Huberts, L.W.J.C. and J. Kleinnijenhuis (eds) (1994), *Methoden van Invloedsanalyse*, Amsterdam and Meppel: Boom

Hume, D. (1985) (ed.), *Essays. Moral, Political and Literary*, Indianapolis: Liberty Press

Ireland, T.P. (1981), *Creating the Entangling Alliance. The Origins of the North Atlantic Treaty Organization*, Westport: Greenwood Press

Jachtenfuchs, M. and B. Kohler-Koch (1996), *Europäische Integration*, Opladen: Leske und Budrich

Janis, I. (1972), *Groupthink. Psychological Studies of Policy Decisions and Fiascoes* (1982), Boston: Houghton Mifflin

Jansen, M. and J.K. De Vree (1985), *The Ordeal of Unity. The Politics of European Integration since 1945* (1988), Bilthoven: Prime Press

Kant, I. (1795), *Perpetual Peace. A Philosophical Essay* (1903), London and New York: George Allen & Unwin

Kelleher, C.M. (1975), *Germany & the Politics of Nuclear Weapons*, New York and London: Columbia University Press

Kennan, G.F. (1951), *American Diplomacy, 1900–1950* (1952), London: Secker & Warburg

Kennedy-Pipe, C. (1995), *Stalin's Cold War. Soviet Strategies in Europe, 1943 to 1956*, Manchester and New York: Manchester University Press

Keohane, R.O. (1984), *After Hegemony. Cooperation and Discord in the World Political Economy*, Princeton: Princeton University Press

Keohane, R.O. (ed.) (1986), *Neo-Realism and Its Critics*, New York: Columbia University Press

Kissinger, H. (1994), *Diplomacy*, New York: Simon and Schuster

Knutsen, T.L. (1992), *A History of International Relations Theory*, Manchester and New York: Manchester University Press

Kohl, H. (1996), *Ich Wollte Deutschlands Einheit*, Berlin: Propyläen

Kossmann, E.H. (1987), *Politieke Theorie en Geschiedenis. Verspreide Opstellen en Voordrachten*, Amsterdam: Bert Bakker

Krieger, W. (1987), *General Lucius Clay und die amerikanische Deutschlandpolitik, 1945–1949*, Stuttgart: Klett-Cotta

Küsters, H.J. (1982), *Die Gründung der Europäischen Wirtschaftsgemeinschaft*, Baden-Baden: Nomos

Kuypers, G. (1973), *Grondbegrippen van Politiek*, Antwerpen and Utrecht: Het Spectrum

L'Année politique 1954 (1955), Paris: Presses Universitaires de France

Lasswell, H. (1936), *Politics: Who Gets What, When, How*, New York: Smith

Leffler, M.V. (1984), 'The American Conception of National Security and the Beginnings of the Cold War', in: *American Historical Review*, 89, 346–81

Lerner, D. and R. Aron (eds) (1957), *France Defeats the EDC*, New York: Praeger

Lieshout, R.H. (1995), *Between Anarchy and Hierarchy. A Theory of International Politics and Foreign Policy*, Aldershot and Brookfield: Edward Elgar

Lieshout, R.H. (1996), *Een Waarlijk Politiek Instrument. Frankrijk, Duitsland en de Integratie van Europa*, Bussum: Coutinho

Lister, L. (1960), *Europe's Coal and Steel Community. An Experiment in Economic Union*, New York: Twentieth Century Fund

Ludlow, P. (1982), *The Making of the European Monetary System. A Case Study of the Politics of the European Community*, London: Butterworths

Lynch, F.M.B. (1984), 'Resolving the Paradox of the Monnet Plan: National and International Planning in French reconstruction', in: *Economic History Review*, xxxvii, 229–243

Macridis, R.C. (ed.) (1958), *Foreign Policy in World Politics* (1989), Englewood Cliffs: Prentice-Hall

Marjolin, R. (1989), *Architect of European Unity: Memoirs 1911–1986*, London: Weidenfeld and Nicolson

Marsh, D. (1992), *The Bundesbank: The Bank that Rules Europe* (1993), London: Mandarin

Mastny, V. (1996), *The Cold War and Soviet Insecurity. The Stalin Years*, New York and Oxford: Oxford University Press

McGeehan, R. (1971), *The German Rearmament Question. American Diplomacy and European Defense after World War II*, Urbana: University of Illinois Press

Mendl, W. (1970), *Deterrence and Persuasion. French Nuclear Armament in the Context of National Policy, 1945–1969*, London: Faber & Faber

Miller, J.D.B. (1962), *The Nature of Politics*, (1965), Harmondsworth: Penguin Books

Milward, A. S. (1984), *The Reconstruction of Western Europe 1945–1951*, London: Methuen

Milward, A.S. (1992), *The European Rescue of the Nation-State*, London: Routledge

Monnet, J. (1978), *Memoirs*, Garden City, New York: Doubleday

Morgenthau, H. (1948), *Politics among Nations. The Struggle for Power and Peace* (1978), New York: Albert Knopf

Niedhart, G. (1986), 'Konrad Adenauer und die außenpolitischen Anfänge der Bundesrepublik Deutschland im Lichte neuer Quellen', in: *Neue Politische Literatur*, XXXI, 165–74

Official Gazette of the Allied High Commission for Germany (1950), Bonn-Petersberg

Ohmae, K. (1993), 'The Rise of the Region State', in: *Foreign Affairs*, 72, 78–87

Osgood, R. E. (1962), *NATO. The Entangling Alliance*, Chicago: Chicago University Press

Peterson, J. (1995), 'Decision-making in the European Union: towards a framework for analysis', in: *Journal of European Public Policy*, 2, 69–93

Polybius (1922), *The Histories* (1954), London and Cambridge (Mass.): William Heineman

Popper, K.R. (1982), *The Open Universe. An Argument for Indeterminism*, London: Hutchinson

Richardson, J.J. (ed.) (1996), *European Union. Power and Policy-Making*, London and New York: Routledge

Richardson, J.L. (1966), *Germany and the Atlantic Alliance. The Interaction of Strategy and Politics*, Cambridge (Mass.): Harvard University Press

Richardson, J.L. (1972), 'Cold-War Revisionism: a critique', in: *World Politics*, 24, 579–612

Risse-Kappen, T. (1996), 'Exploring the Nature of the Beast: International Relations Theory and Comparative Policy Analysis Meet the European Union', in: *Journal of Common Market Studies*, 34, 53–80

Rousseau, J.-J. (1755), *Discourse on the Origin of Inequality* (1994), Oxford: Oxford University Press

Ruggie, J.G. (1998), *Constructing the World Polity. Essays on International Organization*, London and New York: Routledge

Ruhm von Oppen, B. (ed.) (1955), *Documents on Germany under Occupation 1945–1954*, London: Oxford University Press

Russett, B. and H. Starr (1981), *World Politics. The Menu for Choice* (1996), New York: W.H. Freedman

Scharf C. and H.-J. Schröder (eds) (1979), *Die Deutschlandpolitik Grossbrittaniens und die Britische Zone 1945–1949*, Wiesbaden: Steiner

Schelling, T. (1960), *The Strategy of Conflict* (1980), Cambridge (Mass.) and London: Harvard University Press

Schroeder, P. (1994), 'Historical Reality vs. Neo-Realist Theory', in: *International Security*, 19, 108–48

Schroeder, P.W. (1994), *The Transformation of European Politics 1763–1848*, (1996), Oxford: Oxford University Press

Schwabe, K. (ed.) (1988), *Die Anfänge des Schuman-Plans 1950/51; The Beginnings of the Schuman-Plan*, Baden-Baden: Nomos

Senate Committee on Foreign Relations (1950), *A Decade of American Foreign Policy. Basic Documents, 1941–49*, Washington: United States Government Printing Office

Soutou, G.-H. (1996), *L'Alliance Incertaine. Les Rapports Politico-Stratégiques Franco-Allemands, 1954–1996*, Paris: Fayard

Spaak, P.-H. (1971), *The Continuing Battle. Memoirs of a European 1936–1966*, London: Weidenfeld and Nicolson

Spruyt, H. (1994), *The Sovereign State and its Competitors. An Analysis of Systems Change*, Princeton: Princeton University Press

Story, J. (ed.) (1993), *The New Europe. Politics, Government and Economy since 1945*, Oxford and Cambridge (Mass.): Blackwell

Stuurman, S. (1995), *Staatsvorming en Politieke Theorie. Drie Essays over Europa*, Amsterdam: Bert Bakker

Taylor, A.J.P. (1977), *How Wars Begin* (1980), London: Futura

Thucydides (1954) (ed.), *History of the Peloponnesian War*, Harmondsworth: Penguin Books

Van Deth, J.W. (ed.) (1993), *Handboek Politicologie*, Assen: Van Gorcum

Van Ooijen, M., I.F. Dekker, R.H. Lieshout and J.M. van der Vleuten (eds) (1996), 'Bouwen aan Europa. Het Europese Integratieproces in Documenten', Nijmegen: Faculty of Policy Sciences

Vattel, E. de (1758), *The Law of Nations or the Principles of Natural Law. Applied to the Conduct and to the Affairs of Nations and Sovereigns* (1916), Washington: Carnegie Institution of Washington

Volkmann, H.-E. and W. Schwengler (eds) (1985), *Die Europäische Verteidigungsgemeinschaft. Stand und Probleme der Forschung*, Boppard am Rhein: Boldt

Wall, I.M. (1991), *The United States and the Making of Postwar France 1945–1954*, Cambridge: Cambridge University Press

Waltz, K.N. (1954), *Man, the State, and War. A Theoretical Analysis* (1959), New

York: Columbia University Press

Waltz, K.N. (1979), *Theory of International Politics*, Reading (Mass.): Addison-Wesley

Wedgwood, C.V. (1967), *William the Silent*, London: Cape

Weilemann, P. (1983), *Die Anfänge der Europäischen Atomgemeinschaft. Zur Gründungsgeschichte von EURATOM 1955–1957*, Baden-Baden: Nomos

Wielenga, F. (1989), *West-Duitsland: Partner uit Noodzaak. Nederland en de Bondsrepubliek 1949–1955*, Utrecht: Het Spectrum

Willis, F. R. (1965), *France, Germany, and the New Europe, 1945–1967* (1968), London: Oxford University Press

Yergin, D. (1977), *Shattered Peace. The Origins of the Cold War and the National Security State*, Boston: Houghton Mifflin

Young, J.W. (1984), *Britain, France and the Unity of Europe 1945–1951*, Leicester: Leicester University Press

Ziebura, G. (1970), *Die deutsch-französischen Beziehungen seit 1945. Mythen und Realitäten* (1997), Stuttgart: Verlag Günther Neske

Zijlstra, J. (1992), *Per Slot van Rekening. Memoires*, Amsterdam and Antwerpen: Contact

Index